MY WHITE
BEST FRIEND
– NORTH

BASED ON THE ORIGINAL CONCEPT BY
RACHEL DE-LAHAY

co-curated by Frank Peschier, Nathan Powell, Suzanne Bell,
Kenneth Olumuyiwa Tharp, Adam Lowe and Lekan Lawal

methuen | drama

LONDON • NEW YORK • OXFORD • NEW DELHI • SYDNEY

METHUEN DRAMA
Bloomsbury Publishing Plc
50 Bedford Square, London, WC1B 3DP, UK
1385 Broadway, New York, NY 10018, USA
29 Earlsfort Terrace, Dublin 2, Ireland

BLOOMSBURY, METHUEN DRAMA and the Methuen Drama logo are trademarks of
Bloomsbury Publishing Plc

First published in Great Britain 2023

A catalogue record for this book is available from the British Library.

A catalog record for this book is available from the Library of Congress.

ISBN: PB: 978-1-3503-5203-2
ePDF: 978-1-3503-5204-9
eBook: 978-1-3503-5205-6

Series: Methuen Drama Play Collection

Typeset by RefineCatch Limited, Bungay, Suffolk
Printed and bound in Great Britain

To find out more about our authors and books visit www.bloomsbury.com
and sign up for our newsletters.

CONTENTS

MY WHITE BEST FRIEND – NORTH

Theatre in this country can be so London centric. I'm so proud to see this project be taken up North. I cannot wait to hear these brilliant writers dare say things they have, up until now, kept quiet.

Rachel De-Lahay (2021)

In autumn 2021, twenty writers of colour from across the North of England sat down to write personal letters, saying something they never got to say, to someone who needed to hear it. These letters were then sealed, and read out, unseen, by actors on stages in Liverpool, Manchester and Leeds as part of a coordinated theatre piece. None of this would have been possible without the ground-breaking *My White Best Friend (And Other Letters Left Unsaid)* by Rachel De-Lahay, first performed at The Bunker (2019) and the Royal Court in London to critical acclaim, and the support and guidance of Rachel herself. Rachel's original provocation and letter are the inspiration and the catalyst for the incredible, intimate and rich writings from these Northern writers. These letters explore the personal and political impact of things left unsaid, and those that we don't dare say.

My White Best Friend – North was a collaboration between the Eclipse Theatre, Liverpool Everyman and Playhouse theatres, and Manchester Royal Exchange Theatre.

My White Best Friend – North was originally performed at:

Liverpool Everyman and Playhouse theatres

The Everyman/15 and 16 October 2021
Writers: Dominique Walker, Kiara Mohamed Amin, Brodie Arthur, Levi Tafari, Yasmin Ali, Keith Saha and Chantelle Lunt.

Eclipse Theatre

The Holbeck/22 October 2021
The Riley Theatre/2 November 2021
Left Bank/9 November 2021

1

Writers: Nick Ahad, Marcia Layne, Jamal Gerald, Malika Booker, Khadijah Ibrahiim, Chanje Kunda and Naomi Sumner Chan.

Manchester Royal Exchange
The Royal Exchange/23 and 30 October 2021
Writers: 'mandla' rae, Yusra Warsama, David Judge, Samuel Rossiter, Cheryl Martin and Nikhil Parmar.

There is a makeup pouch on the table. Please put this on and then continue reading the letter.

To my dear friend, Fiona.

For months i have mulled over whether or not to write this letter, for a number of reasons. We met in bittersweet conditions.

Circumstance, work and systemic racism connected us. But our souls are what truly connected.

You are such a sweet and caring person and your aura shines through. I can't get that image of you out of my head rushing round with your little makeup bag packed full of everything someone like me was looking for.

I want to thank you for the support and solidarity you showed me. On day one you shared with me your experience of working for big, known brands on film sets. You felt the lack of diversity was an issue and decided to go freelance as a way of regaining control. That really struck a chord with me.

Your 'change the game one set at a time, one job at a time and one person at a time' attitude is incredible. I hope you and your boys are well.

At the beginning of 2020 i was so looking forward to filming for a new movie you were working on. A major blockbuster, my first time on a real movie set, meeting real big celebrities and rubbing shoulders with a world i'd always dreamed of.

Another day at the office for someone with such a colourful history in the industry like you, haha.

As an aspiring actress growing up, i'd built all of these pictures in my mind of how amazing it would be. After a brief success in theatre i was ready for the next chapter of my acting career. This was set to be the perfect opportunity to network.

It's one month before filming and i take a trip down to Milton Keynes for a costume fitting in Pinewood Studios. The Pinewood Studios. The UK's answer to Hollywood and i was going there.

I'm sure you're familiar with it, being the hotshot stylist that you are, but wow. I could not contain myself.

Although my part was a tiny piece of a huge production it felt massive all the same. I kept thinking back to when i was little. I was obsessed with a series called *Tiena*. It was about a young girl who wanted to be a star and she would daydream all day about it.

It was as if my dreams were becoming reality. Picture it, i'm sat on this minibus with people i don't know. Some familiar with this world and somewhat content, others who, like me, couldn't stay still for excitement.

We were going to be in a big movie!! We all get chatting and it comes out that one of the cast is 'Camilla' and, omg, we were ecstatic. As if we're going to be filming with not only a superstar cast but a superstar singer as well. Someone pinch me because this can't be real.

However, my excitement was soon met with disappointment. Getting fitted for the costume was to be a short but insightful glimpse into what was to come.

Some of the staff were so rude and arrogant. Making statements such as, 'oh what do they wear where you come from? I'm no good with ethnic prints'. Hmmmmm me either queen i'm from Liverpool; i usually just wear jeans and t-shirts to be honest, with belter shoes.

You can tell a lot about a person by the shoes they wear so mine are always cool as anything.

The best 'laugh' was chatting to a young woman who described herself as 'Aryan' and said her boyfriend referred to her as 'Hitler's wet dream'. I think i told you about that as soon as i sat in your chair to be honest. So, yeah, that was interesting.

She even had the audacity to ask me, 'do Black people with red hair exist?'! How i contained myself from filling her mouth with something more fitting like my fist is still an absolute mystery to me.

When the dressers gave us our costumes they had roles attached to them. Paupers, lower class, upper class, princess and queens. Naturally princess Adolf was hoping for the princess ensemble and that's exactly what she got.

When my number was up and it was time to be robed, me being the queen that i am, it was only right for me to assume my natural role in the pecking order. Queen it was. ☺ she was sick when i told her i was a queen. The princesses had already formed a little clique and they were all of a sudden acting like royalty. It made me howl. I still giggle at it now.

Although the conversation was choice, overall i was happy with how the day had gone. Really happy actually. I was one step closer to what i believed was going to be an amazing opportunity for me.

The four weeks in between fly right past and it was time to head down to Blackpool to start my first week of filming. I was going to stay in a local b'n'b for the week so i could be on top form.

I was up and out by 6 am for a 6.30 call. I was so tired i couldn't even see straight but my mind was focused on one thing. All-star cast!

So i skipped to Blackpool Tower in about five minutes flat. Do you remember your first day on a big set? Was it overwhelming? Were you a mess like i was?

Upon arrival i could see trailers, camera vans and big giant tents for hair and makeup and i was to report to Costume first. After much deliberation on the day of the fitting, my costume ended up being a somewhat random selection.

I looked like a huge Quality Street. A mixture of the big purple one and the green triangle.

I wasn't buzzing with it but it would do. Anyway i report to the ad managing costume and i'm dressed and back out in a mere twenty minutes.

Good considering the tent was packed with hundreds of people all waiting to be seen. I am told to head to Hair and Makeup and i'll be called.

I sat and sat. I sat for what felt like forever and the tent began to get emptier and emptier. Until the only people left are the crew and supporting artists who were either Black or another minority background.

Makeup artist after makeup artist coming out holding our cards in their hands and not calling us. Wow.

In my whole entire life i have never felt as Black as i did that day.

This is day one and i didn't even get on set. No superstars, no lights, camera and definitely no action!

This was the same the next day. My call time was pushed back, less money but that did mean less time sat in a costume that i couldn't move in. Every cloud.

So for two days me and the other supporting artists, all Black of course, sat getting to know one and other and sharing stories of the micro aggressions we'd experienced on this particular production.

This is all before we've gotten on set by the way. I have always been an outspoken person. You know i'm never afraid of speaking what is true to me, so i opened my mouth and, before you know it, i'm sat in a chair getting my hair done by the loveliest woman God bless her, Fiona, but she didn't have a clue.

I was to wear this extravagant wig with gold bars and box braids and all sorts on it. She mulled over whether or not to braid my hair but then she decided to just use granny pins to literally pin my hair as flat as she could, then pin the wig on a wig cap she placed over.

The weight of this masterpiece was unreal. Amplified by the fact that the pins are cutting me to bits.

So now i'm half ready, i only need someone to be brave and throw a bit of makeup on my face. But time's up.

The ad comes and says we must get on set whether we are finished or not; we won't be in focus anyway. I am furious at this point because i'm feeling enormously overlooked and, to be quite blunt, taken the absolute piss out of.

So all the Black supporting artists get dragged onto set looking like a rainbow just shat us out and we are naturally together as we have been for two days in a tent with no hair and makeup.

We're told to spread out amongst the other supporting actors. We had by now formed our own little clique so we didn't really want to mix. We were already feeling singled out.

We made the most out of the circumstances and now we have to separate.

Obviously all of these people are white and they all have their faces done perfect and some are really getting into their roles, yano, looking down their nose at us as we enter. But i mean why wouldn't they. They've been getting their face pampered at 6.30 am, they've been on set filming with A-Listers while we froze in makeshift tents on Blackpool Pier in the dead of winter.

So after five minutes on set it's time to break for food. But, oh no, not for us Black folk, we have to get straight back to Hair and Makeup so we can be finished in time for the next set up because us not being done was really holding back the schedule.

Ahhhhh poor them.

Back to Hair and Makeup we go.

Finally i see a little brown lady bobbing about the tent doing people's hair and makeup and i'm thrilled.

It's you.

I'm staring at you so hard in the hopes our eyes will connect and you will choose me next. You did.

You sat me in your chair and for some reason our traumas connected. I explained how much of an awful time we were having on set and getting through Hair and Makeup and you explained that it was no better for you behind the scenes.

You were feeling very alone and quite isolated. No wonder we connected: we were riding the same wave.

From that day on you were the highlight of my days. The only thing i looked forward to was sitting in your chair and listening to your lived experiences and allowing it to teach me how to be patient. You also allowed me to teach you to be bold and be brave.

A few days into filming we were directed to film the scene where the prince enters and all the princesses line up wanting to be picked. Their parents behind anxiously waiting.

I was excited, this was going to be my first proper scene where i might actually be seen. Please explain to me why 'Hitler's wet dream' wants to come and ruin my moment by telling me my wig is a bit stupid. There are literally people bopping past with full-on bird cages with swings in them. Make it make sense, babe.

I thought that would be the end of the discrimination but it turns out it was only the beginning.

We were finally able to go and get lunch instead of starving in the hair and makeup tent.

I'd complained for two days about being hungry, watching Camilla pick from an array of fresh food and smoothies. I think everyone got sick of me, but you can't manage a whole day's filming on one cup of Haribo's being passed around the set with strict orders to only have one; i was ready to actually be fed.

So, finally, i'm queueing for the grand dinner, and an ad thinks it's funny to say to me, 'oh you'll be happy, there is chicken there'. I couldn't actually believe what i was hearing. This same guy later showed me a lost phone with a home screen of a young woman who looked nothing like me, saying, 'what? That's you isn't it?'

The only resemblance was the fact that she and i were both Black.

When i said are you being serious, he says, 'oh come on don't start all this'. All what exactly?

So after this we return to the set and a lady called Lisa who me and the other supporting artists had gotten close to over the days was on set looking somewhat upset?

I'm not sure if you met Lisa but she was the most amazing Canadian lady of Chinese heritage.

Me being me, i approach her to find out what's wrong. I find out that two members of the cast have been sniggering about her heritage. Coronavirus was mentioned and then when they seen her looking they said, 'be quiet, slanty eyes is listening'.

She explained that this was reported to the ads on set and they expected Lisa to remain on set until the take had been done correctly.

You'd mentioned to me previously about some of the ways that the casting crew can fail the supporting artists and this definitely felt like a huge fail.

Safeguarding the welfare of all artists should be paramount surely?

Clearly they had been there all week and, for reasons of consistency, they had to stay in the frame for this scene.

No that wasn't going to work for me because from personal experience i know how damaging this is.

So i began to kick up a fuss. I proceeded to approach those who had said it and explain to them that the working day finishes soon and when we're not working i would love to hear all they had to say about it.

This may or may not have escalated.

Words were exchanged and all of a sudden the director wants to know what's going on and why the reset isn't happening.

She is made aware and still these women are sat on set laughing and joking. I was furious.

After my second kick-off something was done and i do believe the ladies were released from filming. However, after this the set up on set was a continually hostile environment.

For a whole week i cried my eyes out in the hotel that i had paid for to ensure i gave you the best of me.

I could have commuted and come in tired and not in the mood but i wanted to make the best impression. Instead i find that no matter how much of me i would give i would always be irrelevant.

I was under no assumptions that i would be treated like a star as i know how disposable supporting roles are but i at least expected to be treated as a human.

Just as you had treated Myself and other Black artists, that's why you were so important Fiona. I know you said it's not always like this and it's getting better but as a first experience i'm alarmed if this is it after progress.

You're like an angel sent by a higher power to save those ready to quit. Those who haven't the strength to pull through such vile circumstances.

On day five i was asked to step inside a machine fitted with hundreds of cameras that took a full 3-D image of me in costume and hair and makeup.

This is so they can add you into scenes where necessary but there was no way i was giving them the privilege of having my image, so chances are you won't see a whiff of me in the movie, you know, for consistency reasons.

I hope this is the case. I wouldn't want to be seen in such a hypocritical production.

It had the most diverse cast i've seen and still basic things were overlooked in regards to our needs. And yet, they were over the radio telling the ads to split us up as, 'there's too much colour in that corner'. The corner only had Black people in it. I'm pretty certain they didn't mean the colours on our costume. It was made clear that our feelings were just as disposable as we were.

Since the production, we have kept in touch over social media. I follow your career as i'm aware you do mine.

'Nice to see you doing more period styles on Black hair. Looks like you've been working on *Bridgerton*. How exciting!!'

I will always think of you when our Whitney Houston comes on the radio. I'm extremely grateful to have met you. As well as meeting you i also met an amazing group of creative people whom i have also kept in touch with.

Throughout our horrible experience we connected and made lifelong memories together.

And i'm also grateful to Sony Pictures, for this experience, for unlocking a fire in me that i hadn't felt before. For allowing me to shine in a way that made others feel comfortable to do the same. For unlocking the true activist inside me.

And i will continue to turn my traumas into pay cheques. Including this one.

I have waffled on over multiple pages and i hope the message lands. You are an original angel!

All i have ever wanted was to act. One week on a job that does not even count as acting and i was ready to throw the towel in.

It made me feel as though no matter what i do going forward these are the brick walls i'm always going to be in front of.

I wasn't sure if i had the strength to continue. But you gave me my power back.

Together in those moments, in that beauty chair i felt powerful. You and i put the world to rights sharing stories, experiences, pain and even tears. We got nostalgic over old Whitney songs and shared stories about our powerhouse mothers. Praising their strength and resilience and all the while not even realizing that those same women made it possible for us to be sat where we were, together and united.

Such a powerful experience and your presence is one i will never forget.

Hopefully our creative paths will lead us back together on set somewhere beautiful.

I can't wait to hear about all the amazing things you have been doing to make this a better industry for us.

I'm so proud of you, i hope you're proud of me too.

Take care, Fiona.

Your Whitney-loving friend,
brodie

Brodie Arthur is a creative from Liverpool who uses her lived experience and knowledge to drive change in and around the city. She creates and facilitates work to empower and educate, working with partners to advise and implement tools and strategies to help diversify the work they create and who they work with.

In lockdown 2020 she co-created and starred in a piece of innovative doorstep theatre, *Knocking On (20 Stories High)*, which went on to win the Achates philanthropy prize. Her latest work *Family Healing*, co-written with Leah Watson Lee, will be performed at the Unity (Liverpool) in 2022 as part of their Up Next Weekender.

Brodie is passionate about making work that is accessible and speaks to the audiences and participants on multiple levels. Young people are at the heart of her work as she understands the importance of art and creativity, in particular for young Black people in Liverpool. Brodie feels strongly that the arts weren't always made accessible for her, and people who looked like her growing up, and throughout her career she has actively fought to make sure that the children coming from similar backgrounds and facing the same barriers as her are given equal opportunities.

To Phoebe '10 Women' Pallotti,

What would I have done? I want to look at the conditional pluperfect tense. What would I be? Where would I be? Who would I be without you? You've got my son. You've got my son.

You know I was just listening to Roberta Flack song 'The First Time Ever I Saw Your Face'. It goes, 'I felt the earth move in my hand, like the trembling heart of a captive bird.' That's how I felt when Nyah was born and I saw him for the first time. Nyah was born and you know that's my heart right there.

I just don't know how it happened with Nyah, you know. You were living with me when I was pregnant with him. I was pregnant with my little munchkin, who is now nineteen years old! Fucking hell, Phoebe; we are getting old.

Nyah is older now than we were when we first met. We were twelve. How the fuck did that happen? I only feel eighteen years old myself, but with more of a belly, more cellulite, and more difficulty getting to the top of the fucking stairs and shit. But apart from that, I still feel eighteen.

Now, Nyah. It's obvs been lockdown and Nyah had gotten out of control. Like turned into a hermit. Or like those Japanese gaming addicted adults in their parents' house. I know Nyah was only eighteen and couldn't go anywhere because of lockdown and only lived with me. So speaking with his friends via headset and gaming was the only thing he had to do. And me, all I had was bloody wine! One or two glasses in the afternoon or evening turned into full-on holiday drinking. Like people on an all-inclusive holiday and it's Sangria for breakfast. Me fucking 24/7 drinking. Nyah teetotal and gaming all night 'til 7 am and then sleeping 'til 3 pm and getting up at 4 in the afternoon.

Me shouting at him for being lazy and not lifting a finger. Him having a go at me for drinking all the time. It came to a head and you came to the rescue. You came in your car, took Nyah to Sheffield to give me a break. You banned him from bringing his PlayStation and agreed to have him live in Sheffield to study in a new city.

He started volunteering for young children and enrolled in college for September, and met some new friends in Sheffield. The you came back to Manchester after a few months, after lockdown was over. That's why I give you props, Phoebe.

I've stopped drinking. Nyah has stopped gaming. Nyah has moved to a different city and started making friends, going to parties, kissing girls in raves. Everything a nineteen-year-old hero boy loves doing. I don't mind having a heterosexual son, really. A lot of people are these days. I love Nyah.

How many people, who have a teenager causing havoc with a sick mum, would adopt him? You always co-parented him anyway. And at age eighteen he moved to Sheffield in the middle of winter, in the middle of a pandemic.

And now it's 2021, you've given me a taste of my life back too. I pulled a twenty-six-year-old firefighter in a gay bar because of you. It was a miracle. I'd been such a boring bitch. I'd not been going out or anything. Not been on the pull. And now I'm coming out of the closet myself at the age of forty-two. How the fuck did that happen, Phoebe? It's all down to you.

We did have sex with each other when we were teenagers, but I thought everyone experimented sexually at that age. I didn't think much of it. But I haven't been married, and I've been having relationships with men and casual sex with women on the DL. You were the only woman I'd been with, for a while, but there have been a few more in between.

Lesbians seem not to like bisexual women because we like sex with men. Just because you are a meat eater, doesn't mean you don't also like seafood. I can't be bothered. I prefer bisexuals like you, anyway.

I think you were my favourite. Sex with you is soft as cloud, as candy floss, as pillows, as satin; as slippery as silk; as sumptuous as drapes flexing folds of paradise. Sex as soft and circular as a wet dream. Sex with you is being cocooned in your lushness, your garden. Not building to a climax, but meandering like a river along contours of mountains and valleys. It's like an odyssey, a prayer, a sanctuary. I feel like a bee in an orchid.

There is no banging. It's erotic stories for women. Our story is written. And you are not mine. I let you fly back to your man. And I fall from the sky back to the laps of men . . . until the future. Until other women come to life in my bed.

You give me freedom because I am not yours and you are not mine; we are both free.

I don't know how you are so confident but it rubbed off on me that night. Obvs we went into a gay bar because we are queer. And then there was this white guy with bulging muscles in a tight-as-fuck white T-shirt looking the quintessential gay pin-up. The kind of front-cover-of-*Attitude*, or *Gay Times*, or a fucking Jean Paul Gaultier eau de homme model. I don't even like white guys, but you can't argue against an Adonis incarnate.

Anyway, a quintessential gay man in a gay bar. He was by himself, and you randomly asked him to join us. It was a bold move. It turned out he was an off-duty fireman. You couldn't make this shit up. Call fucking 999, my fanny was on fire and needed hosing down!

Anyway, I was fine with the fact that he's gay. We are in a gay bar, I thought. We are all about the gays.

I wasn't drinking alcohol because I was about to go out like Amy Winehouse if I wasn't fucking careful. Lockdown, as I said. So, I was fucking drinking Virgin Sex on the Beach, of all things. Meanwhile you, Phoebe, were getting slowly wankered.

How, I don't know, but it turned out this firefighter called Steve was one of us. Your bi-radar was on fire. He was bisexual. He was twenty-six years old. You whispered in my ear, 'You better fucking take this guy home, or you are fucking cancelled for being dead from the waist down. When was the last time you even got laid?'

I wasn't looking for a man. Especially in a gay bar. Especially after lockdown. But this guy was Scottish as well, to top it all off. With the Scottish accent of a fucking brave heart. Shit!! I was without a defence.

I started laughing, remember. And he said, 'What are you laughing at?'

I told him that you said I should take him home. Then this big grin spread across his face and I thought, Oh shit, man; I'm finished. I'm done.

I wasn't even wearing any knickers. I was trying to be sensible, and then this Scottish stallion needed breaking in? How had I wound up here?

You said, 'Why don't we have a threesome?'

I was like, 'For one, I'm stone-cold sober and my heart can't manage. And two, if I am going to do it, I ain't sharing. Soz. You know us bisexuals are so-called "greedy".'

And you're poly, and a relationship anarchist; you've got a boyfriend now. And you're dating a woman already. You are the one who's greedy, not little bisexual me.

But I have been living a monastic and celibate life for the past year or so because of lockdown. So even when things opened up again, I remained closed. But you came from Sheffield to Manchester, and took me to the Gay Village. Fucking met a Scottish stallion with a rainbow dick. A prism for my heart. Anyway, I'm not up for sleeping with strangers. I'm not into white guys. Yet here I was, completely defenceless against this twenty-six-year-old Scottish stallion. I said to him, 'I'm forty-two years old.'

And he said, 'You're gorgeous.'

I told him I was bisexual as well. But even though I am feminine, I like other feminine women too. And sometimes I like to play the boy part. He said he wanted to play the boy part on me. He was definitely fanning the flames.

'I am sure that could be arranged,' I told him.

Against my better judgement, I took him back to our gaff via the Spar, as you know. He was disappointed they didn't sell extra-large condoms. Well, you will have to do what you can with the sizes they have available. Girls like condoms. Girls insist on condoms. Wear a condom and go hard, or go home.

That night cheered me up. You always know how you get me to smile again. I love you 'cause you are fun. And you are a bad influence. From my experience, Black straight female friends don't actively encourage you to sleep with a stranger for the joy of sex, for freedom, for liberation, for hedonism, for rebellion, for choice, for fun.

Actually, tell a lie: my younger sister, she is also a bad influence when it comes to snogging randoms. She's not inhibited at all. Incidentally, she doesn't have any white friends. She says I always have them. Well, I always have you. But I think I prefer my way. When Lwimbo was younger and going out, they only drank alcohol. And the only drug they took was weed, which technically is not a drug; it's herb. In the 90s, in the rave scene! Lwimbo said that drugs were what white people did, and she didn't have any white friends!

I was different. I had the time of my life when we were at college together. I absolutely loved it. Going out to Megadog or a phat jungle night, dancing in a warehouse. Coming up off an E just as the bassline dropped and everyone was shouting rewind! Rewind and come again. And the DJ brought it back. Fire! That's when you really get down.

The days we took acid or mushrooms. You know, they're only just doing research now on the use of MDMA as part of the treatment for PTSD. We could've told them that for free. And considering our traumatic childhoods, the therapeutic value of getting wild and dancing saved our souls. LSD and psychedelics – trippy magical, Alice in Wonderland times we had – and the times we were speeding through the night and dancing 'til dawn.

Up all night, bright as day in the streets. Not been home or to bed. And there were all the bongs and chilems. We thought we were Cheech and Chong. None of that smoking spliff nonsense. If we were going to get some weed, we would have to fill a whole glass chamber the size of a fucking fire extinguisher.

It was amazing. Sometimes we'd use buckets, or fashion makeshift bongs out of two-litre Coke bottles.

I love you 'cause you're totally left wing. Chain yourself to a tree to stop it being chopped down, anti-establishmentarian, socialist, feminist, sexual liberationist, warrior woman. I liked the sort of freedom we had to get off our faces and dance around the clock. It honestly saved me. But university kind of killed that one off. Somehow you got into Cambridge!

Can't believe you went to Cambridge fucking University. You went into care at fourteen and I was homeless at age sixteen. In sixth form we were the only ones who didn't live with their parents. We both managed to get our own bedsits. Mine was on Wood Road. How apt.

That's what brought us even closer together. How the fuck you managed to get into Cambridge, I don't know. I only managed to scrape into Huddersfield University through clearing. It's 'cause you are so clever. And 'cause some teachers believed in you. But mostly because you were gifted with self-belief and never had a poverty of ambition. Even though you didn't have any food in the house when you lived with your mum. Waitressing at thirteen years old, just to eat.

Big up your status, Phoebe. You got ninety-nine problems but being Black in a white country ain't one. But I can't take your props off you, 'cause most people who go into care, white or not, don't end up at Cambridge Uni at eighteen years of age.

Maybe the teachers encouraged you and believed in you, coupled with the fact that you are a fucking genius. In England Black people don't get coupled in that way. But you deserved it.

I love you so much not because you are a fucking boss. Not because you are insanely intelligent; you have a PhD in medical anthropology and are a professor in women's health! Not because your life's mission is reducing global maternal deaths and making the birthing experience as empowering as possible for women, and championing refugee women's maternal health care. What I value the most about you is your kindness. You are the kindest person I've ever met. You've been the kindest, to me.

I'm not quite sure how that happened. You grew up without your father and with an alcoholic mother who, from when you were about ten years old, left the cupboards bare. And at age thirteen put you into care. I was all alone in the world at sixteen years old and so were you. But we had each other, and now we're forty-two and you have my baby. My baby is nineteen years old now and you have him with you in Sheffield.

That's why I give you props. Phoebe, you honestly, saved my life and Nyah's life. We had both pressed the 'fuck it' button. Fuck it, I don't care anymore. Fuck it, I'm going all-in on my crutch. That was our attitude. Whether it was gaming or drinking, respectively. And neither of us are doing that anymore. We are both thriving. I've not had a drink or any mind-altering substances. I'm trying to have a monastic way of being.

Fucking middle-aged hippy stuff. Meditation and mindfulness and going for walks and fucking gardening. I love that shit. I have used up my lifetime quota of getting fucked up off booze or substances. I'm finally done. Done, done, done. Not once a month, nor every now and then. I'm done for good.

I'm not chasing something that gives me a comedown ever again. What's the point? I can't be bothered at all. I love transcendental meditation now. Fuck me, I'm a fucking hippy. I can't even blame having a white friend for that. You don't do that shit.

The other reason I give you props is for your sexual confidence too. Honestly, I'm so obsessed with my body size and shape. And plus, I never pursue people I fancy or chat people up because I used to get called a slag at sixth form. I cared too much about being looked down on. That made me behave and got me sexually fucking constipated.

You had a great sex life in your eleven-year marriage and since you split up, you've been living your best bisexual, polyamorous life. Amazing.

I've never been married or lived my best bisexual life. But I've been, fuck knows . . . in the sexual fucking wilderness. I've had flings and short-term relationships, or long-distance, long-term relationships with men. And sexual encounters with women. I'm a rolling stone. I will settle down one day. Probably. Maybe.

But on the plus side, I'm not married to a man, and I'm not childless. I'm free, and I'm a mother.

I don't have to wonder what my life would've been like if I hadn't got married. I know.

I don't have to think, what would my life have been like if I'd had children. I know what it is like to be pregnant, and to give birth and to be a mother.

But I also know what it's like to be a full-time career woman and have sex with another woman. And I know what it's like to love a man and love a woman. So, all in all, it's been perfect.

Though I do think I'm ready for monogamy now. I'm getting a bit too old for pulling. Well, I still can, but do I want to carry on pulling randoms perpetually? Not really. But it was soooooooo much fun up 'til now. I'm a Black woman with a joyous story. We need to hear more about Black joy, because it's fucking exhausting only hearing about our trauma all the time.

One of the best times I ever had, was you going to Amsterdam with me for my thirty-first birthday. That was epic. On the Eurostar, drinking prosecco from King's Cross to Brussels and from Brussels to Amsterdam. You smuggled a knife because how else would you cut the quiche you brought to eat on the way? Fucking white privilege. You explained to security that you needed it for your quiche and they let you smuggle it on an intercontinental journey. Love you bitch. Love you bad.

I can't vouch for all white people. But you're alright. You are queer and fabulous.

Love you,
Chanje xxxx

'I accepted the commission for MWBF because I thought it was divine providence that I got asked.'

Chanje Kunda is a poet, playwright and performance artist. Her work explores twenty-first-century life, and aims to use art as a tool to transform lives, shift consciousness and also bring joy to an otherwise serious and stressful modern existence. She predominately works as a solo artist in performance, across the literary, theatrical and live art sectors.

UK performance highlights include features at the Royal Albert Hall, the Southbank and the Royal Exchange, in addition to touring arts centres and festivals throughout the country. Internationally she has performed at the Calabash Literature Festival, Jamaica. As an artist-in-residence in the Netherlands, she has performed in Amsterdam, Rotterdam, Eindhoven and Groningen. She has also toured work to Zimbabwe and South Africa. Other international representation includes selection by the British Council for IETM conferences in Romania and Croatia.

In addition to her live performance work, Chanje has produced audio visual performance for digital media. During lockdown in 2020, Chanje had creative commissions from DadaFest International Festival, Manchester International Festival and the Imperial War Museum.

NOTE: Any stage directions are written in italics. Please do not read these aloud, just do them.

Chantelle's *chants play to an empty stage.*

Chantelle   No Justice, no peace!

Mia *takes a step forward from the wings.*

Chantelle   No Justice, no peace!

Mia *steps forward again.*

Chantelle   No Justice, no peace!

Mia *takes another step forward, towards centre stage.*

Chantelle   No Racist Police!

Mia *takes a final step centre stage and pulls on a high vis Police Jacket.*

Chantelle (*voice faltering*)   No racist police.

Chantelle (*whispers*)   No racist police, no racist police . . .

Mia *picks up the letter and reads.*

Mia   How easy it was to utter those words when Officer MAGA stood before me at a protest. Almost three years later, I was no longer the broken shell of an officer she and her friends had chiselled away at back at The Academy. My voice did not shake and my lips did not tremble. The words tore from my body with a growl that reverberated from the surrounding buildings. The flames behind my eyes had held her in place, paralysed in the knowledge that the predator had finally become the prey. Some of the people gathered there said they'd never seen me looking so angry, they called it inspiring. Who'd have thought, the angry Black woman, inspiring. I could have exposed Officer MAGA right there and then, she knew it, so did I. That was enough for me.

Yet, it wasn't Officer MAGA who plagued my thoughts after the protest, it was you. Officer Hops, as you were affectionately known by our classmates, on account of your doe eyes, button nose and the striking similarities between you and the naive bunny cop from that Disney film – For the benefit of the tape: I will not be referring to Mia by her nickname, as I don't have the money to fight Disney if they come after my broke arse. You were both pretty too, is it weird to call a bunny pretty? A cartoon bunny at that? I suppose Jessica Rabbit fans would, although, she wasn't actually a rabbit . . .

I digress, you were a pretty human and, unlike many pretty humans, you didn't like to rub it in people's faces. You were easy to talk to and down to earth for your age, which is probably why we got on so well from our first day at The Academy. Police Academy, I can't say I never imagined I'd end up there. Truth be told I could easily have gone the other way but, even back then, I was never the type to give up on a challenge. So, there we were, Cohort 7 (of God knows how many others at The Academy) huddled nervously around the canteen tables for what felt like our first day of school.

While some of the louder characters held court from the centre tables, the quieter recruits had nervous conversations from the side-lines. I'm usually what many people consider a colourful character, loud even by Scouse standards and quick witted, but the me that rocked up for the first day of police academy was one who still wasn't sure if the extrovert in her had died completely. I think you sensed that loss and we passed the first nervous hour together talking about our recruitment processes and pre-police lives. I learned that you should have joined up on a previous cohort, but you'd struggled with the fitness tests, it had taken a few tries before you passed and they'd let you in. You told me that this was your first 'proper job' out of uni and you had worked weekends at xxx while you studied. PC Spray Tan had loudly interjected at this point, to inform me that xxx only employs models and to give me a pointed stare.

I told you about my years with the council and showed you pictures of my boys. You squealed appreciatively and made those cooing sounds that are standard procedure when presented with unsolicited baby pics. I returned some 'aww' sounds of my own when you showed me a picture of your fluffy white dog, your best friend since childhood. I sensed that you were an only child even before you told me, you too sensed that childhood was not a topic that I wished to discuss. That day felt like the beginning of something special, a great friendship between two budding officers.

I liked you from the second I met you, Mia. I thought you saw me, like really saw me, every broken bit of me. Now I'm not sure. So, I do what any detective worth their salt would do. I dig out the old case file and pore over the evidence.

Mia (*in a stuffy tone*)   Exhibit A: One Gift from Mia, presented to Chantelle on their last day at The Academy.

Mia (*in a sweet voice*)

'**Chantelle,**

It's been a pleasure working with you. You always gave me reassurance and support when I needed it and your positive energy always made me feel happy.

I admire you doing this job when you have two little people to think about at home as well.

Keep doing XXX and XXX proud.

Keep in touch.
Love always
Officer Hops.'

This one was bittersweet, Mia. The first part is true of course, I had helped you through some tough times. I'd stayed behind to help you build up your fitness levels, running laps and practising circuits with you in the weeks before our fitness tests. Despite being the fastest long-distance runner in our cohort, I dropped back the second I saw you struggling on a long-distance run around St Helens. I remember seeing you slowing down and recognizing the look of someone who was about to hit the dreaded runner's wall. So, I kept pace with you and whispered, 'just focus on your breathing Mia, in through your nose, out through your mouth, one foot in front of the other'. I repeated those words for the duration of the final mile, until you reached the end of the run. I was so proud of you that day, even if we did have to sit down on the cold ground until your legs stopped shaking. I would have helped you in any way I could, Mia. I shared my revision notes with you and helped you memorize the five sticky fingers of theft rhyme ahead of our exams. Remember when we used to pair up together for all of the Personal Safety Training activities? We nearly handcuffed ourselves together a few times, but we had such a laugh that week. It was hard to keep a straight face when they had us grappling around on the floor like wrestlers. At lunch we would go down to the padded training room to practise our restraints, just in case any nerves hit when they tested us in front of the class. You were always so unsure of yourself, but I knew you had it in you and it was great to see your confidence grow over time. It was me who told those divvies in the other class to leave you alone when they said you weren't strong enough to be a Police Officer. Those meatheads conflated their gym-acquired strength with the strength of character it took to be a good Bobby. I was quick to remind them of the difference and to tell them to leave you the hell alone. So yeah, I suppose I did reassure and support you, a lot.

I do have a few points to contest though, Mia. In your note you said my positive energy always made you feel happy, but my energy wasn't always positive, we both know that. What about that day, you remember the one? It was the morning after our introduction to diversity and inclusion when our trainer, PC Gammon, had encouraged speculation that the force was only recruiting Black officers for the next intake. PC Spray Tan said the force was just letting Black officers in 'though the back door', regardless of our scores at the Assessment Centre. I could see you watching me, eyes full of sympathy, as the conversation gained momentum and more and more people piped up in disgust at the idea that 'too many' Black officers were coming into the force. A delighted PC Gammon was spoon-feeding them fake news and they weren't even stopping to think. My resolve broke when he declared, 'they have a Black Police Association, why can't we have a White Police Association? Personally, I don't see colour though, I'm just saying, it doesn't seem fair'. He looked around innocently, as nobody disagreed, but my hand had shot in the air at his last remark. In my best non-confrontational Black woman voice I informed PC Gammon that Black officers had to pass the same exams as white officers and there was no magic back door, or single race recruitment for Black officers. Likewise, I reminded him that the Black Police Association existed because Black officers were so underrepresented and powerless within a force, which was essentially one great white police association already. The silence that followed was telling, as were the glares that came my way. You weren't glaring Mia, but I couldn't quite catch your eye because you were studying your cuticles. Afterwards, you told me how brave I was for standing up to PC Gammon. The next day when PC Powerlifter threw a ball at my face, the classroom went silent again. 'What the hell! Why did you do that?' I yelled, taking care not to come across as angry, as my eye throbbed and watered uncontrollably. 'Sorry, accident.' PC Powerlifter had shrugged nonchalantly and continued this newly established game of catch.

It wasn't always easy to tell if we were still cool after that, Mia. Especially after the locker room incident. I hadn't told anyone about my mum but, as Mother's Day approached, I confided my recent loss to you. You were so kind and comforting, listening with a sympathetic ear as I described pulling back the curtain on that fateful day. I could see Officer Mean Girl leaning in our direction and trying to look as if she wasn't listening. Do you know she used to be a drama teacher? Like a true professional, she performed best in front of an audience. We were getting ready in the girls' locker room when she struck. 'It's Mother's Day soon, what are you doing for it, girls?' The question was innocent enough but she glanced at her wing women who chuckled obediently as I hastened to yank on my patrol boots and lace up so I could get out of there. 'I don't know what I'd do without my mum, like, not having her here. Could you imagine not having your mum?' she asked loudly, staring at me. It was enough to set me off and I ran from the locker room and sobbed in the toilets like a proper high school saddo. The weird thing was, you didn't mention what she had said, not once. Even when I returned to the classroom, red eyed and hiccoughing silently. You just asked me if I was okay. Me, okay! What about them, Mia? You saw the whole thing play out and said nothing. I was starting to see things too though. I could see that you didn't sit next to me at lunchtime anymore and I felt the awkwardness when our conversations moved from the corridor to the classroom and (*emphasise the word 'they'*) *they* could see you talking to me. Since the ball incident, they had gone out of their way to humiliate me and get one over on me. My grades and fitness levels were too high for the 'Black one they let in through the back door' narrative to stick but they kept taking aim. Funny how those balls only ever seemed to hit me, first PC Powerlifter, then Officer MAGA: (*Adopt a sarcastic girly voice*) 'It was an accident, obvs. No need to be like that about it, Chantelle, we weren't aiming for you.'

The Academy did manage to strike a few blows though, Mia. Do you remember the interview training we did with PC Gammon and his sidekick, Constable Karen? How awkward was it when I had to tell PC Lurch that he couldn't say half caste anymore and that mixed race was more PC, excuse the pun. Did you see him shrug like he wasn't bothered? I'm not sure you saw that bit but I know you saw what happened next. Constable Karen told us that it was okay for witnesses to use the N and P word, to describe people of colour, and warned us against reprimanding them because it could jeopardise a case. I felt like I'd entered a parallel universe when the other officers agreed that it made sense to do this. Once again, it was up to me to set the record straight (*raise hand and adopt a neutral tone*): 'I think, as Police Officers, we should make people aware of the law, in all situations, and if someone uses a racial slur in front of us we should remind them of the law and request them not to do this again or we will take action.' I thought this was a reasonable, measured response. I wasn't speaking as a Black Officer but a Police Officer, an impartial upholder of the law of the land. Imagine my surprise when my classmates argued that I was putting my own values and standards above my duty as an evidence gatherer, while PC Gammon and Constable Karen remained resolute that this was the College of Policing way. I wasn't having this one though, I did not join the police just to let racists off the hook and I wasn't about to be okay with casual racism. I asked to speak to Sergeant Sleazeball and, a few minutes later, he puffed his way into the classroom to tell us that the information was correct. According to them, it was okay for witnesses to use racist language in front of an officer, and we were not obliged to reprimand them. No one else spoke up or objected but I saw the smirks, the nods of approval and the satisfied smiles at these backward rules. Your eyes were on your cuticles again in the classroom, but you caught up with me in the corridor afterwards. 'I can't believe that!' you fumed. 'That's awful what they said in there, well done for speaking up Chantelle. I just want you to know that I agree with every word you said!' You smiled and squeezed my hands and I felt grateful to have an ally. I understood that not everyone had the confidence to speak out like me, not everyone was brave. Sometimes I wish it wasn't just me though, that I didn't have to be that person, you know the awkward one who has to question things and disagree with everyone else. I wish the burden didn't always land on my shoulders. People might see things differently if it wasn't always us Black people harping on about racism like the fun police. It sounds different when it comes from white folk, probably less angry.

Anyway, I'm not sure what came next, if it was the Islamophobic meme PC Lurch showed me, or Constable Cadette changing his profile picture to one with blackface when he messaged me. I don't know if it was the Tommy Robinson post that went unchallenged in our group chat, the time they made jokes about Grenfell victims or Officer Mean Girl making fun of my afro hair in the girls' locker room. Eventually, my voice died and I stopped calling them out. Your messages had stopped too. Sure, you still caught me up with all the gossip from the nights out they forgot to invite me to. You told me you were shocked that Officer Mean Girl and Officer Posh were flirting so hard when Posh was about to be engaged. Your anger at PC Lurch, for pulling out his warrant card and harassing a homeless guy, almost made me believe that you might stand up to someone but, alas, it wasn't to be. When I told you how shocked I was at PC Lurch and you hopefully replied, 'Someone should really say something', that told me all I needed to know. It was always going to be me; I was always that someone. I was the defiant one calling people out, while you were the one that people liked. I don't blame you though, Mia, like as I said, Police Academy was like school, and it was far easier to roll with the cool kids than risk their wrath by disagreeing with them. I'd not heeded this most basic of rules and you'd watched as they'd excluded, mocked and bullied me into submission.

Mia (*in a stuffy tone*)   Exhibit B: One WhatsApp message from Mia dated 21 April XXX:

Mia (in a sweet voice)

'Ignore the people that were discouraging you. . . I heard that, and I won't stand for it! We are a team, and we all help each other through not pull each other down. . . I will back you 100% girly and we will smash it <3 <3 XXXXXXX.'

These messages meant so much to me at the time, Mia. Now that I think back though, Exhibit B doesn't comfort me the way it used to. I mean, when your classmates have teased your friend, again, to the point of tears and laughed as she ran to the bathroom crying, they might ask what you did:

Mia (*in an official tone*)   Did you follow your friend?

Mia   No.

Mia (*in an official voice*)   Did you check on her wellbeing before she left?

Mia   No.

Mia (*in an official voice*)   Did you say anything to the officers who were picking on your friend?

Mia   No.

Mia (*in an official voice*)   What did you do, Mia?

Mia   Well, I messaged her once I was home. Chantelle can always rely on me to back her up with a DM.

Mia (*in a stuffy tone*)   Exhibit C: An e-mail to PC Gammon, nominating Cohort 7's classmate of the year:

> **'Dear Gammon Face,**
> **I would like to nominate Mia for the classmate of the year award. Throughout my time at the academy, she has been caring kind and thoughtful. She checks in on me when I've had bad days and Mia is someone who you can always rely on to say the right thing. I have no doubt that Mia will be an exemplary Officer.'**

I was so pleased when you won that award, Mia. I knew you needed the lift after another trainer had said you weren't strong enough to be a police officer. People shouldn't mistake your kindness for weakness. Sure, it frustrated me that you stayed on the fence during classroom 'debates' and activities. Like the train track one where you couldn't decide if you'd let the train stay on course and hit the group of kids on the active line or divert it to hit the little boy playing on the inactive line. Ridiculous scenario, like how come we can't shout ourselves hoarse in any of those options? I sure as hell would have used my foghorn to move all of those kids off the tracks. As usual, I was in the minority with my argument that the one kid on the inactive track might have known the track wasn't on and that's why he was playing there in the first place. Therefore, by diverting the train to him we'd have been killing someone who might not have died otherwise. I was forced to continue arguing my points when the debate spilled over into the canteen. Most of the others wanted to divert the train to the lone boy because the activity was clearly about saving the most lives (*adopts a posh arrogant tone*) 'and who cares if some stupid little Einstein knew the tracks were off. What do you think, Mia?' Do you remember what you said?

Mia (*laughs nervously*)

Mia   'Ooh, don't get me involved in this, I'll just go with the majority.' That was you all over though, Mia, confrontation made you nervous. I knew you wished you were braver, so I couldn't really be mad at you. I smiled because I knew you needed it, you smiled back, glad that we were still friends. Of course we were, it wasn't fair of me to expect so much of you. Not everyone could speak up like me, I knew that. Yeah, the selfish part of me did wish that, just once, you were as brave in front of our classmates as you were in our messages, but I couldn't ask that of you. Even if you knew you could always expect it from me. It was never your fault though, Mia, you are who you are, and I am who I am. I understood how hard it was to take a stand on things like this.

You weren't to know that the worst culprits from our cohort would follow me to my first posting. You couldn't have foreseen that they would join up with some of the more seasoned officers at my new station, or that those officers would make the tactics at The Academy look like child's play. You didn't see the happy demeanour, which had inspired you so, crumble and falter beneath the attacks that I was subjected to at my first Station. You weren't there, Mia; it was just me and them, them and me.

I'm not sure if you heard that I'd gone off sick or the rumours that I'd tried to kill myself. I thought I'd hear from you while I was off but maybe they were keeping the whole thing under wraps, the bullying, the racism, the report. The famous report, do you know they crimed it? Yep, it was logged as a hate crime against me. To be fair, they probably spent all of five whole minutes deliberating before they NFA'd it – that's No Further Action for the uninitiated. You'd have been proud of that report though, Mia, I was as brave as you remember. I named names, places, locations, incident log numbers, the lot. I didn't let anyone off the hook for what they'd done to me. It wasn't all gloom though, credit where it's due, I mentioned you in the report and said how good you'd been at checking up on me and making sure I was okay after they'd targeted me. I made sure the bosses knew that you were one of the good eggs.

When I returned, I was moved to a new station where the other officers took pictures of me sitting in the corner of the office desperately trying not to have a panic attack. Most refused to work with me, which was a relief, at least that meant they'd leave me alone. Eventually, the bosses took pity and sent me to your team. It felt so good to see your smiling face as soon as I walked through the door for my first shift. You drew me in for a warm hug and I knew it was going to be okay there. We didn't talk about everything that had happened; I knew you were just trying to make things easier for me at my new station by not mentioning it. Just like that, it was like the early days at The Academy, even better because it was just the two of us, from Cohort 7 on the team. We ate lunch together, whenever we were both at the station on the night shift. We laughed about some of the ridiculous jobs we'd been called out to and commiserated one another on the trickier jobs. You told me all about the body that had washed up on the beach and how your boots kept sinking into the sand when you tried to lift it. Making it impossible to heave the body back to shore without falling down, a few dozen times, with a corpse pinned on top of you. I told you about the dude who had pulled a knife on me and the state of his house when we got inside. There was dog poo everywhere and I didn't know which was worse, the knife attack or having to search his stinking house afterwards! It was great to hear you laughing at my stories and so good to have you back in my life after everything I'd been through. Thanks to you the other officers warmed to me, and I was soon part of the team. The bosses sent us all for personality tests while I was stationed with you, they were mandatory for every officer. They ranked us by colour: Reds were the leaders, Blues more methodical, Greens were caring while Yellows were creative. I remember how proud you were when you told me that you'd scored 99 per cent green on the test.

Mia (*in a sweet tone*)   'The examiner said he'd never seen such a high-scoring Green before!'

Mia   You left your posting first. We ate cake together and I joined the rest of the team in wishing you well on your next assignment – after you'd returned to the Assessment Centre for a week of admin. I bet you didn't expect me to follow you there! It had already been agreed that I wouldn't go back to Cohort 7 but some jobsworth thought it'd be a good idea for me to go in and speak to my classmates about everything that had happened – eighteen of them, one of me. It was okay though; I knew there was guaranteed to be one friendly face waiting for me in the classroom.

I remember the familiar floating feeling that preceded a panic attack, I'd only started getting them since joining the force. It washed over me as I stepped into the classroom and saw their hardened faces and crossed arms waiting for me. Some of them had made my life hell for nine months, yet they sat there looking at me like I was the problem. I poured out my soul and told them what they'd put me through for almost a year. How they'd acted to punish and exclude me just for being me and, worse, how they'd carried it on after The Academy and recruited other officers to join in. I spelt it out to them with a video about white privilege and finished by saying the thing that we've been taught never to say as Black people, that elusive card that only brings us trouble. I told them: 'I think you did this to me because I'm a Black woman.' I'm not sure what the bosses thought would happen, but I expected what came next, the screaming, the head shakes and furious cries of 'we're not racist. She CAN'T say that!' I found our white South African colleagues' assurances that (*adopt a serious voice*) 'this absolutely is not racism' mildly amusing, Mia. Like, come on lad, you're hardly the authority on racism there. We'd all heard you saying how great it was growing up in South Africa in the 80s.

What I did not expect, Mia, as I battled with one furious rebuttal after the next, was for you to finally speak up.

Mia *starts to cry.*

Mia   'But – you – could – have – come – to – me, why didn't you come to meee!'

Mia   Everyone stopped in their tracks then, the whole conversations stopped. Instinctively, I embraced you, told you everything would be okay and that I hadn't wanted to burden you with it all. Ironically, Officer Mean Girl sat on the other side with an arm around you too. She spoke to you in a soothing voice and told me, in her usual sarcastic voice, that she hoped we could work together in the future. Then she guided you upstairs with the rest of the class and that was that. It was over. Do you know I couldn't stop thinking about you that night? I wanted to text to check up on you, make sure you were okay after you'd got upset. Then it clicked, Mia, you didn't fucking text me! Not a quick 'hey how are you' nor a 'do you want to talk about it' not a call, not an email, not a smoke signal, not a damn thing. Nothing! That was the last I ever heard from you, and I've always wondered what I'd say to you if I saw you again. Would I be able to roar as I had when I saw Officer MAGA or would my voice falter and fail as yours had, so many times before when I needed you. Well, here it is, Mia, here's what I'd say if I ever saw you again:

I thought that we were friends, I thought that you had my back the way that I had yours. Whenever someone was unkind, or you needed a hand, I was there, but you could never return the favour. I was someone who made you feel good about yourself, always on hand to stroke your ego and reinforce the narrative that you were a caring person. I mean, sure you cared but the thing you cared most about was what other people thought of you. So, you toed the line, Mia, you didn't upset anyone or go against the majority. Which is why you never said a word when I was defending my identity in front of the class. It was much easier to keep your mouth shut, look the other way for some of the trickier parts and keep me onside when no one else was looking. Your white tears were effective in halting the best chance I'd ever have of holding those horrors to account and you knew it. In that moment you chose which side of the tracks you were on, pulling your lever and sacrificing the mean Black girl who made Mia cry so that your group of friends on the other track could run off without a scratch on them. We never did finish that conversation about why I didn't come to you, but we both know that wasn't the point of your performance.

Thank you for teaching me that it's not always my enemies that I have to watch out for. Sometimes, it's the ones that call themselves friends who cause the most harm. Do you know when I think back on the hurt that my time in the police caused me, it's you who I think about the most. I remember in my performance review, PC Gammon told me how we both had such caring natures. He couldn't understand the other officers' behaviour or why they would treat your blonde arse so differently to mine when we were so similar. But, then again, he never could see colour.

Mia *lowers the letter and looks out into the audience with a shocked expression.*

Chantelle Lunt is a writer, presenter, educator, activist and entrepreneur. She is a national BLM campaigner and the Chair of Merseyside Alliance for Racial Equality, a non-profit organization committed to promoting racial equality, across Merseyside, through grassroots community-led education and engagement work. Chantelle supports local and national organizations in decolonizing work, community and education spaces, promoting racial literacy and expanding knowledge of Black history. Chantelle presents a morning radio show and the *Why I'm No Longer Talking to Institutionally Racist Police* podcast. She writes about the contemporary civil rights movement and UK policing for national grassroots campaigns and independent media platforms. Chantelle was one of the writers selected for the BBC Writersroom 'Write Across Liverpool' screenwriters development programme and is currently developing television and theatre scripts.

Hi. I know it's been a long time. But I was thinking of you today, and I thought, I really should write. Old-school, you know? A proper letter.

I've been thinking of when we met. Even before that. When I got the interview. I know you were used to meeting big important people, but I wasn't. I was truly green. Like the first April leaf on a cherry tree.

For me, it was exciting – imagine, if you can remember what it was like to be that green – you've got a big interview, at a big theatre. You've just recovered from the worst clinical depressive episode of your life – so bad you almost died, without even overdosing. I know. You didn't know that. Nobody did. I'm a performer, too. I act normal.

But imagine, all that is over, and you're back. You're thin, everybody thinks you're fifteen years younger than you are – somebody the other day thought I was thirty years younger than I am, and I love it, every single time.

I'm just trying to get you to see, how it all was for me. When we first met. Just imagine, yeah? Imagine that now you have the chance to direct someplace where you're guaranteed to get reviewed. Unheard of for a Black woman. What more could you possibly want? That was me. I thought, this is it, this is my chance.

I did notice that the boss was hideously hungover at the interview. But I decided to ignore it. And ignore it when he said having a Black appointment was his predecessor's idea. Maybe because I wanted it so much, I didn't think the interview went well. Then I didn't hear back for weeks. And I knew a good friend with a much more impressive CV had gone for it too. So I shrugged, and smiled like it didn't matter when people kept asking about it, and thought maybe next time.

When I heard I got it – I don't remember much of anything from the second I heard. The future that opened up – everybody was so happy for me, and I was so happy for myself, and I jumped on a train and got a brilliant big old flat around the corner from a Waitrose and I just knew, I just knew.

Even though the boss would sometimes say a few 'off' things – like telling me he couldn't give me anything to direct right away, even though I'd won awards, because

'I haven't seen your work myself, darling.' Or, 'I don't see the point of "Black" theatre. It's not really necessary, is it?' Or, 'We can't do more Black work, there aren't enough good Black actors.' The kind of bullshit I heard thirty years ago in Manchester, but nobody is stupid enough to say out loud anymore. I'm sure you've heard worse.

And I put up with people saying to my face that I'm 'exotic'. Yeah, that's right, to my face. Or, when I finally did get to direct, and got nominated for a couple of awards right off the bat, people telling me, 'I don't think of you as Black.' Because to them, Black people don't get nominated for awards, especially when it's not a Black play.

And the idiocy about my hair – what is wrong with these crazy people, they want to touch my hair? Do I look like a fucking cat to them, that they can pet me?

When a critic said, in front of the boss, that he couldn't have done a better job directing one piece than I had, I saw the look on his face. It wasn't a happy look.   ·

Anyway. I ignored all that, because I had an ally. Who backed me up when I brought in an unknown white working-class writer – it was his play that got nominated for the awards. Who took me out for drinks, and gave me the ins and outs of the local theatre ecology. Who was always friendly, always smiling, always there to help. Who told me which actors were really good. How to give effective feedback to a brand-new writer. You know – things a director making her mark needed to know.

There was a writer who had a famous first play, and good plays after, but nothing that surpassed the first. It happens. When I told him I thought his new play was funny, he said, 'Yeah, but.' Expecting me to say something undermining. Unkind. I said, 'I enjoyed it.' He looked confused, and my ally said, 'She's not like that. Not our girl. She means it.' And he looked relieved. Grateful, poor man. And I was touched. My ally. You. Sticking up for me.

When a project I was in charge of – and directed on, with others – won a big award, you had the grace not to look surprised. You were my biggest cheerleader.

Until. Time came to extend my contract. The original funding was only for nine months, and I had stretched it to a year already. The boss agreed I should stay for another six months. You – my ally – you were responsible for putting in the grant application. So you saw how much I would be paid for that six months. It was the going rate then for an associate director. But it was the same for six months as you got paid for an entire year.

So you tried to convince me that I was wrong to go for that much money. But one thing I always know is what the proper pay is for my job. I'd already been working below the rate, and I had no intention of getting paid less than I should. It was fair pay for that role.

So you – my erstwhile ally – you tried to say I was insulting another good friend of mine, who was getting paid even less than you were. But my friend had a very big bank of mum and dad. I don't have that bank – Black, single, female, lesbian, independent theatre artist.

If you had asked for my help to get better pay – for you and for everybody – I'd have helped. But you didn't. You don't think that way.

When the emotional blackmail failed, you sat on the application and didn't put it through. Sat on it and sat on it and sat on it until I ran out of money. And the boss didn't lift a finger to make you put the application in.

So I ran out of money. I mean totally out of money. I had the estate agents for my lovely flat banging on the door the last month I was there, asking for the rent. I told them to take the deposit. Through the locked door.

I moved to another town. I had to try to go on benefits for the first time in my life. I didn't know anything about it, didn't understand the system. Didn't get any in time. I think I never got a penny. Ended up homeless.

By then I was already deep into another depression. But I got a few directing jobs that got me enough money to hightail it back to Manchester.

But I'm grateful to you. My ally. You taught me a lot.

Until then I still believed that if you did outstanding work, you would always be rewarded for it. As a Black female ageing lesbian, that was unforgivably stupid. Thanks, ally!

I crashed and burned every summer for five years after getting back to Manchester. The terror of being penniless in a strange town – forget the rent – I didn't have enough money to buy food. I couldn't catch a bus. I learned that all the Baccarat crystal and the silly designer watches were worthless at the pawn shop, when I took them there 'cause I wanted to eat. The only things I could pawn were the gold and emeralds my mother and sister would send for my birthday. My birthstone. And I'd pawn them over and over and scrape to get the money to get them back again, because my mother and sister sent them and I couldn't lose them. I couldn't.

I remember meeting a colleague – Black, of course – at a Cash Converters, and we gave each other that smile. The one that says 'I know'. And the terror of going back to that, of being destitute and homeless and humiliated, that terror rules me, so that I work and work and work. During the pandemic I've lived on that computer, never away from that keyboard.

And it's not just Black artists, I know that. A woman I worked with this past month, older like me, white, who makes such beautiful things – I've hardly ever seen such simple, simply beautiful things – she said she has to say yes to everything, every gig offered, and she'll have to keep saying yes to everything till the day she dies.

I knew as soon as she said it, she's just like me, with this terror of being penniless – thank you, ally. Thanks to you, I'll stay hungry. I'll never stop hustling. I'll never be the same green thoughtless – I hate remembering pawn shops and Cash Converters and walking for an hour because I didn't have bus fare to sell a ticket to a friend because I couldn't afford to go to town to see the show and get home again. Yeah. It changed the work I do. So, yes. Thank you, ally.

No. I never told anybody any of this. What's the point? So a so-called white ally fucked me over. People get fucked over every day. Worse. Much, much worse. And I learned. So much. Thanks, ally!

When the crashing and burning didn't stop, I realized that I would die of my depressions without ever cutting or taking pills or anything – as I was getting older, my body couldn't take the strain. So my wonderful Newton Heath GP, Dr Mansoor, saved my life by getting the Crisis Team out every summer, and then getting me onto Borderline Personality specialist treatment. I knew I had to stop those huge crashes or die. He helped me.

My true friends gave me a beautiful house at mates' rates so I could live. They helped me get a PIP. I wouldn't have had a chance to see how much my real friends loved me, if you hadn't fucked me over so thoroughly. Thanks, ally!

When my career began to take off again, it was in a totally different direction. Working with refugees and asylum seekers. Performing solo shows about the truth of my own mental health. Creating a new Black festival. Coming back to the publishers who got my career started thirty years ago. Working on things that are important to me, that have meaning for me. Feeling free. And still winning awards. Thanks, ally!

Now I want to be clear. I know you're only one white person, not all white people. Two of my best, closest friends for over thirty-two years are a white lesbian couple who took me to their house and fed me and watched over me when I collapsed in that huge clinical depression fifteen years ago, because there are never any psychiatric beds available in Manchester. They found my latest new flat for me – beautiful, bijou, affordable. They came for me after I'd been shielding for fifteen months for a glorious trip to a country house garden for my last birthday.

Another white friend went and picked up my prescriptions for me while I was shielding, going way out of his way to do it.

These people love me and I love them.

And not every white person is stupid enough to try to touch my hair. Or callous enough to strand someone in a strange town and never check in to see what happened to them. And after all, wasn't it my fault that I was too feckless to save money, on my freelance theatre salary? I do wonder, though, if you were so affronted and upset because I was a Black woman who was going to be earning twice as much as you did.

Anyway, Manchester is my home. Atlas was a Greek Titan who had to be in physical contact with his mother, Earth, to stay strong. But of course you know that, you're so well read. I have to stay in touch with Manchester, and I almost forgot that. Thanks, ally!

Before I met you, I didn't believe anyone could be so . . . petty. So casually destructive. Now I know better. Thanks to you. My ally.

Cheryl Martin is Artistic Director of Manchester's Black-led Arts Council National Portfolio literature organization Commonword and Co-Artistic Director of Global Majority LGBTQ+ Black Gold Arts Festival. She has worked as a poet, playwright and director, and was a former Associate Director, New Writing/New Work at Contact Theatre. She was part of the 2019–20 British Council Australia INTERSECT programme, and was Guest Curator for Homotopia 2018. A Manchester Evening News Theatre Award winner as both writer (musical *Heart and Soul*, Oldham Coliseum Theatre) and director (*Iron* by Rona Munro, Contact), Cheryl's solo stage show

Alaska featured in 2016's A Nation's Theatre and 2019's Summerhall Edinburgh Fringe & Wellcome Festival of Minds and Bodies in London. Her first solo poetry collection, *Alaska*, was longlisted for the 2015 Polari Prize. Her film *One Woman*, an Unlimited Wellcome Collection Partnership Award, toured festivals including the Unlimited Festival at the Southbank Centre, Barcelona's L'Altre Festival, and Edinburgh's 2021 Summerhall Digital Fringe. She directed: *The Walk: A Sleeping Child* for 2021's Manchester International Festival, which launched the journey of the giant puppet Little Amal; *The Gift* for Graeae's Crips Without Constraints online; *Made of Gold* outdoor performance for Black Gold Arts & DaDaFest 2022; and taught for Manchester Metropolitan University's Manchester School of Theatre drama school in 2021 and 2022. Cheryl recently directed *Dominoes and Dahlias (+ Oware!)* for the Royal Exchange Theatre's Dream Project of Caribbean Elders, which toured the North West in summer/autumn 2022, and 2023.

NOTE: To the reader –

Stage directions in italics are instructions for you – please don't read aloud.

Please characterize all emphasis in speech – with subtlety please.

Do not read staccato as the layout may suggest – please trust the structure of the words to support the rhythm.

Play the spaces in the text – take a breath – or something similar.

Now please open Letter 1 – thanks.

LETTER 1

So
Okay
I think

Yeah

Please read the rest of this letter whilst trying to perform a trembling squat.

Okay
So
I want to do so some
Audience stuff
Here
At the start

33

The top
Some sort of
Interaction
Participation
They did it a lot in the last one so
I know
I don't have to
It's not the rules
Wasn't in the commission
Contract
Agreement
But
I want to
To do a sort of
homage
hom*age*
To the last ones
The first generation of
Letters

Okay?

So
Using sitting to standing as a scale
Sitting being
Never
Standing being
Always
Please rise out of your seat as much as you think you
Are
Or
Have been
Racist
Not
A racist
Just
Racist

Allow the audience to commit to this.

Now
If I'm right
And if you're honest
Really deep down digging honest
Then we should all
At least
Be in some sort of
Trembling squat

And the more we hold it
The more it hurts
And the more it hurts
The more we want to sit
To be a none racist
Or to stand
And be a full racist
Now
I doubt anybody here will want to stand
(To boo a knee or to get too familiar with a monkey emoji)
But
You can't deny that it will hurt less if you do
And
If I'm right
And
If you're honest
Like
Really deep down digging
Then
We're all a bit racist
Aren't we?
All a bit trembling in a secret racially biased squat
All thinking we can ease the pain by
Sitting down
But that's too easy
Too polite
Too

It's just as easy as standing up

So
Okay
You can take a seat now
Thanks

You can also relax now – thanks.

Did you feel the burn?
Hurts yeah?
The pain is real
The realest pain
Imagine how much it hurts receiving racism for as long as you can remember

The pain is real
The realist pain

Okay
So
Suppose I better start

Go to open Letter 2 – but don't – not yet.

No
Wait a sec
Time for one more
Erm
Is there an usher close by?
Excuse me
Can you do me a favour please?
Can you go and ask the security guard if they've ever worked in Marks and Sparks Chiswick
And if they say yes
Tell them I said they're a
Raasclaart Pagan Warlord!

What accent did you read this in and why? Now tell the audience – gather someone's opinion – now try it again – thanks.

Ha!
Right
Stop now
So
My
White
Best
Friend
Yes
So
Okay

Go to open Letter 2 – but don't – not yet.

No
Right
One more
Last one
Honest
Deep down digging
Okay
So

Can you please raise your hand if you've ever been asked for cash upfront for a cab?
Before Uber
Obvs

Please count the hands raised and make a note of race and class – share your findings with the audience – thanks.

Thanks
Yep

Make of that what you will
Great

So
Okay
My white best friend
My WBF
Yes
Okay
So

Please now open Letter 2 – thanks.

LETTER 2

Dear
My white best friend
I'm sorry we don't socialize
Play footy anymore
Drink together

I'm sorry you don't smoke with me
Sort of

I wish I cared about others
For others
Like you do
Proper man
Rod Stewart
Car
And a white van
Man
Take you where I can once I've took them there
Man

I hope I grow up to be like you
One day
Sooner
Rather than later
Man

You tell me to settle
Slow down
Start a family of
My own
I've told you I'll adopt
Like
Unofficially
You did me
But you're always like

It's not the same as having your own
You should have one of your own
Nothing like it
Your own

But how would you know?
Don't mean to be cruel but
You have none of your own that I know of
So
You see
The magic is
This blindness of love
That makes you
Think I'm
Yours
Your own
But I'm not
And
Yeah
I suppose I'm writing this to spell out the truth
That when it comes down to it
I'm not from you

Okay

Okay
So
When your sister
My aunty
Got cancer
And then her daughter
Your niece
My cousin
And then all of you
All of the Judges
You all checked in with each other
Then checked in with the doctor
You all took cancer to court

Proper
To track, trace and chase the hereditary cancerous gene away
But you never checked in with me
I wasn't a Judge that day
So

Okay
Look

I don't mean to be
Insensitive
To the devastation caused by cancer
And I'm trying really hard not to be
Hypersensitive
When I tell you
That I'm jealous of a gene
And all the Judge's cancer court committees
Because that's what silently highlighted the separation
The difference
The fact that
I
Am not one of
You
Even though I'm corner-stoning my face off
And by that I don't mean I'm in a corner
Smoking my face off
Dad
I just

I try so fucking hard to
To
To be

Okay
So

You should have your own
Nothing like it
Your own

So
Okay
Dave
Dad
I know you're not racist
A racist
But
Come on
You do see my colour

You do know there's a difference between us
Biologically
Don't be polite
You don't have to be
I understand talking ain't that easy
When you're a dad
Dave
When you're a man

Okay

So

Here we go
You and yours traced the gene
The cancerous catastrophe
Back to
Your dad
My
'Grandad'
A gene that we all know I would never have
Inherited
And
I know
I understand
I expect nothing less than for you to be too
Scared
Distracted
Vulnerable
Too silent and filled up with toxic
To speak up and point me in the direction of my other
Dad
The Black one
The one I could have wanted to find
But never
The one who could have come and claimed me
But never
The one I could track and trace
If ever

I'll adopt
Like you did me
I'm not yours
But still we –

> **What are you talking about?**
> **You are mine**
> **You're my little Day**

No
Don't sit down Dad
We can handle the tremble
Together
We need to
Tremble
Together
Tremble
The pain is real
Tremble
The realest pain
Tremble
The pain is
Tremble
And
The realest
Tremble
And
If I was yours there is no way you wouldn't speak to me about where I came from and
how I got here and the need for me to know my medical history now more than ever –
And I know you just fell in love with a pregnant young woman and promised to care
for my mum and me and I know I was never planned or prepped for or read up about
– And I know it's different times now and forward thinking parents who officially adopt
have all these angles covered and have read up all about theirs and prepped for them –
And I know you love me as if I was one of your own but you found something that I've
not got and you went to Ireland to see where you came from to see where your cancer
carrying gene came from and you never asked me to go and I've never been to Jamaica
I'd never even thought about it but I did when you all went to Ireland – And then I
thought about him and the thought that maybe I should find him – You know – Because
you're definitely not going to tell me to – And I understand that I understand your fear
of the unknown but I'm your son and I'm your only child and I believe you believe I'm
yours but

You should have your own
Nothing like it
Your own

Which is mental
Total bonkers
You have diddly squat biologically
So how can you know what it is you keep telling me?!
Tremble
Dad
Dave
Mate
Look
If I was

Yours
You would have found out
Figured out if I had
Or am in danger of having
It
And
If I was
You
The man I want to be
One day
Sooner
That's what I would have done
Straight away
Because you're you
My dad
My bestest white superhero friend
And I'm supposed to be
Yours
Your son
But
Tremble
And
Tremble
And

We
Need
To
Train
This
Trembling
Muscle
Because
It's
The
Only
Way
We
Can
Fight
This
Together
Trembling
Together
It can't all be on
Me

Us
We can't be the only ones hurting
Tremble

And a couple of weeks ago we went on your

Stag! Stag! Stag!

To Newcastle
Was beautiful until we arrived
With all the

Lads! Lads! Lads!

And two of us were of colour
Me and my mate
And the rest looked like you do
They all looked the same
And on one of the days we went
Clay pigeon shooting
In the countryside
A dear taxi ride away
And the instructor
Unapologetically
Told jokes
Roy Chubby
Shouldn't really go there anymore
Brown style
And everyone laughed
And no one could not laugh because it would ruin things
And then the day would be shit
And then he said
The repeatedly offensive instructor said

If you shoot gun wrong
Or if you don't follow instructions correctly
Then you'll end up wi' two black eyes

And then he said to my mate
My mate of colour

But you've already got two of them haven't you

And everyone laughed
And me and my mate looked down
And no one got offended
And me and my mate looked down
And we couldn't ruin the day
Your stag
The fun

And we couldn't kick off over a little joke
And
Tremble
And
Tremble
And
Well

You could of
All of you

Please point to a few white people in the audience – thanks.

The white ones
You could have took offence
Told him to
Watch it
Told him not to
Talk
Think
Speak
Look
Joke
Mutter another word to your son or his mate
But you all just

Please take a look around – take your phone out of your pocket – put it back – thanks.

You all
Wait
Pretending not to notice
Or maybe not noticing at all
Sat
Sitting
Waiting
Whilst I
Me and my mate
Tremble
We trembled
We've been trembling for years
Decades
Centuries
And you
All
Wait

So

Okay

You're my dad
My father
And I owe it to you
My bestest white superhero friend
To give you
A little
Nudge
A little
Push

Okay
So

One more
Sorry
I know I promised but this just
Popped in
Just now
So

Okay

Please open Letter 3.

LETTER 3

Ainsley
Ainsley Sherwood
I think
His mum
My nana
Is called
Brenda
She lives
Lived
I don't
You know
Was over twenty years ago when I met her
She told me I have a

Brother and sister
My own
Anyway
If anyone knows anything about anyone called
Ainsley Sherwood
Can you speak to me after the show please?
To someone
It's important

Nudge

Is there an usher there?
Excuse me
Can you do me a favour please?
Can you speak to the security guard and ask them if they know anyone by the
name of
Ainsley
Ainsley Sherwood
It's important

Nudge

It's

Push

He's my son's
Dad
His
Black
One
Biological
You know

Push

He needs
We need
Nothing really
Just
To know how Brenda's doing
And
To find out what genes my son is wearing

That's all

Thanks

Okay

So

David Judge is a playwright, performance poet and actor. David's latest play *Chatback*, for the National Theatre Connections programme, was first performed at the National in June 2022. His previous play *Sparkplug*, which David wrote and performed, toured the UK and was shown on Sky Arts in May 2021. In TV, David has worked with Sky on a development project, and he wrote his first episode of *Coronation Street* which was broadcast in June 2021. David's other plays include *Skipping Rope*, which was shortlisted for the Alfred Fagan Award, and *Panlid* was commissioned by Talawa and the Royal Exchange. As an actor, David played Tybalt in the National Theatre/Sky Arts feature film of *Romeo and Juliet* and he is currently playing Don John in Simon Godwin's *Much Ado About Nothing* at the National.

NOTE: This excerpt needs to be read by a Black woman, aged 20–40 years, with a regional accent. This piece is a read for all white people. I have many white friends and some of them are best friends. This is to encourage them all, all our white best friends, to do better.

My name is Michelle;

I am Robin's best friend. Tonight, I will read you a letter she wrote about her friend Dominique. This is about their relationship.

I am reading this for Robin, who is all of Dominique's white best friends over the years. Robin stated, as her other Black best friend, that my voice was necessary to read aloud her letter to you all.

So here goes. . .

Hello, my name is Robin. I am a combination of all Dominique's white friends. Dominique is an anti-racist and works for the people, she's a mum of two, a lecturer, runs one charity and is co-founder of a social enterprise and a PhD student; but here she is grouping us all together, like all her collective experiences with us are an indication of the future treatment she will receive. Maybe this is why she was hesitant to write this for Francesca and Nathan, wary even, but she still loves me, us, wholeheartedly. She has dared to love White people, dared to do it. . . when it is justified in a multitude of ways to never. . . Daring to love is something we must recognize, we must see love as a transformative practice that will free us all.

Her most recent man is white; if that is not an indication of who Dom is, or the contradictions and conflicts that Dom represents, then I don't know what is. Maybe she didn't even consider his whiteness and what it means to others in the face of all the community work she does. Or did she NOT give it enough thought like, when she joined the police. . . Maybe she met him, and they got on, they laughed and love one another. Or this is evidence of the Black activist to white partner pipeline. . . Dom used to joke with me about these activists with their white partners. Dom says Race is always consciously or unconsciously a factor, so she defo thought about it, and what it meant.

I've learnt a lot from Dom. I learnt some stuff for myself too, but I can't pretend that most of what I know hasn't come from Dom. Racism is always a melody of denials and refusals to accept empirical truths. Black and white people often have two conversations that never meet. Our thoughts as white people will be abstract, distant: discussing policies, practice, procedures when it comes to inclusion or anti-racism; whilst we often agree about the need for unity and equality of the races, it is from a protracted stance, fantasy, a distanced gaze, whereas Black peoples locate their experiences in reality. It's upfront, in their faces; Black people don't always believe in policy, practice, because they have experienced the interlocking systems of racism – the cultural, institutions, individual and societal racisms. The injustices, the inequalities – They feel this, and They tell us, and yet, they are not believed. Black people are not trusted in their retellings, their emotions, their lived experiences. Do you see why I asked Michelle to read this instead of me now? Am I being a performative ally by asking Michelle, am I running from the difficult conversation?

Public discourse on race and gender has always created new ways of thinking and knowing but bell hooks (2013) assured us that 'talking about class and the various ways class difference separate groups has been much harder'. The notion of us discussing race, class, gender and all the identities within Dominique is necessary, because we rarely understand the ways that class differences disrupt racial unity. Class is something white people love to mention; it is true we love it, because we have all experienced its disrupting, separating, discriminatory nature. Or maybe it is because there is a belief, that in some way we could have suffered more. The notions of integration and a multicultural stance mean that Blackness is different for most Black people. So, the notion of unity through the racial lens alone, or through a shared racial identity, means there is no shared Black identity.

Class, race, gender, feminist perspectives were brought to the forefront to create unity, and at times it has worked, but in 2021, it often puts us in different spaces. Blackness was often seen through commonalities in religion, music, food, cultures, and there are experiences which only Black people know, feel and have experienced. Blackness is a journey – it is worth the exploration, but at times bonding between Black people, especially when there are class differences, can prove difficult, think Kemi Bad-Enoch Powell.

For whiteness. I would argue that the unified white racial identity, and notions of white supremacy don't have some of the same separations, there are obvious diversities of thought, but there are common agreements which take place within whiteness based on nationhood, imperialism, and collective agreed histories; therefore, white supremacy is so persuasive, hidden, hard to detect and disrupt. It takes precedence over all other forms of identity. It was designed this way and serves its purpose. Understanding race and racism through discussions of white supremacy is something no one wants to talk about, but how do we move beyond race, if we cannot fathom how whiteness and its shared meanings, values and purposes are often in our everyday interactions?

It is this that causes the blushing. . . we must challenge white supremacy.

I mentioned Dominique's conflicts and contradictions, these are our discussions. I try to do the best I can, support her thoughts and our discussions, and I would love her to understand that I know more, that I'm still learning, still processing; but willing. A lot of people are not. Whilst not a race scholar, she would never use the word; I am reminded of the time we had dinner with Mark and Michael.

We were all sat around the table, Malbec was flowing; it's our staple; the lamb she made with the gravy with the mushrooms was beautiful. Michael stated that 'the centring of white people's thoughts, feelings, during Black Lives Matter protests and the eventual social media black squares, the rush to buy all the race books, was causing undue harm and trauma to Black people who were already exhausted, and we were all now having to carry these so-called new followers to the movement, a movement centuries old'.

Dom replied that she agreed, and that it was the destructive nature of white supremacy.

Then replied, 'white supremacy, a gallery, a wall of whiteness . . .'

I was shocked, 'how did we go from black squares to white supremacy?'. . .

Dom explained, 'rather than focus on Black lives, Black trauma and pain, listening to Black people . . . the media felt it more fitting to focus on mostly white middle-class experiences of dealing with Black Lives Matter protests, and its outpouring across the world; we still centre white people in this . . . Dom continued, 'this was never about you, I know you did not want to see us, or address how you feel about racism, about BLM, about George; but this was about Black people, our declaration that we didn't want to die, because racism kills'.

I felt silenced, this isn't 'white talk' – I am not divorcing my role in perpetuating racism.

This was a subtle drag I felt, as the only white woman in the room.

I went to the protests, I marched, I'm an ally, I did TGPs Ally 101, and I understand my privileges and status associated with just being white, but I wasn't always aware, in tune, of how bad, I didn't think our responses to BLM would affect Black people in ways we didn't even fathom . . . or think about.

Or how everyday racism and its effects continue to harm the body and mind.

I just didn't know.

Do we centre whiteness when we focus on individual white people's experiences when talking about race?
Is it privileging white people when we just want to learn?
We, I want to do better . . .
She would disagree, this is the very foundation of white supremacy.
But I just want to be heard as well.

Mark is white also, he agreed. Dom looked at me as she went to get another Malbec; I knew that look . . .

Our conversations take me to our youth, I have known Dominique most of her life.

I had seen the news, I watched in pain, and anguish, my breath taken away.
How could they kill him?

He was there every Sunday, playing basketball.

We had seen (blank) a month ago.

We pulled into the petrol station, he walked over to us.

He had just got out of prison.

If only we knew what was to come . . . we all went to the same primary and secondary; how could we foresee what was to come.

We talked on our school days, and Dom told him that he needed to keep his nose clean and stay out, he laughed and said he would try.

I picked her up at her mum's, cars everywhere, parking was a nightmare, cars on both sides of the street, and I noticed the press at the top of the street. She got in and stared forward, the pain was etched across her face; we drove in silence towards our familiar childhood haunts. We pulled up outside the sun bed shop.

Dom began to talk, she expressed what happened . . .

He was walking with his girl, and his cousin home, they got to the pub and a lad came out and greeted them with a barrage of racial abuse, calling them the N word and 'microphone head'. Them not wanting to further an argument, walked on,

CCTV later showed they tried to get on the bus, which drove past them.

They walked into the park, a short cut, a cut through to the village.

Moments later, they did not realize that they were being hunted. They violently ambushed Anthony in the park, he fought back, they put an axe through his head, an axe . . . who knew racists had ice axes . . .

This was a racist murder, her brother had been killed in a racist attack, a racist murder, a few streets away from my house. How could she sit with me and tell me this, whilst still reassuring me that they would get the killers. They had not arrested them yet, but she was sure. I saw, through her tears, the determination.

Things blurred in her memory of her retelling, she cried at times, and stared straight forward at other times.

I wanted to minimize the space I took up in the conversation, I was careful not to rationalize or remark with good intentions or thoughts. I just listened, she didn't want my advice.

I was centring her,

It was her pain at that moment.

I drove her home, we joked about meeting up after the press and everything had gone away; we didn't speak again until after the funeral.

We didn't meet again until at least a year later, and she was different. I welcomed it.

I reflect and think to other incidents, other times which caused more visceral responses.

Dom kicked a white lad who called her 'hot chocolate';

how when we were on the bus and another white lad made a comment about the size of her lips, and was smiling and gesturing in her face; just hers not any of the rest of us, and yes, we were all white; so, she kicked him in the face, and we had to drag her off the bus.

or the time when some unknown Black lad from Halewood came to our area and one of the friends of the lad I was dating, called him a 'jig a boo',

I didn't know what one was . . .

but Dominique told Jon he was being racist.
He said, well 'not you, him . . .'
We were all silent and she went home early.
or when you would tell me about running through certain council estates, racist abuse and often violently defending herself; violence seems to be the language the racists understood.

Or we could discuss more recent incidents such as reasons she didn't get promoted, the routine white man discussing 'the Black woman who got away' story, or 'the Black women I slept with' . . . so we're okay. . .;
And another incident whereby a guest speaker on gender equality used the N word during a work conference.

In all these incidents, just like the ones when we were kids, white people stayed silent. We ignored the things that make us turn red in the cheeks. Saying nothing, doing nothing, leaves marks, scars, they cause harm . . . Empathy demands more. And I'm not being all woe is me or anything, but to be truly empathetic is difficult, but it's important. Not just to put yourself in one's shoes, but to remove yourself and focus on another, focus on the difference in its wholeness.
Focus on Blackness.
Focus on the Black person in front of you.
A human.

So, after our conversation, and reflecting on our dinner.
I knew better, I knew better than to think of me in these moments, I had done the work, and was still learning. But I still needed to do better.
Maybe this is what caused her to stare at me, she saw me in that moment, and she realized I had forgotten.
I had disregarded her pain, her trauma.

Does time ever heal the scars of Racism for Black People?
Racism kills, it harms the mind and body; to normalize what we have seen in 2020, and over the years and to rationalize and hide behind our own racisms, pleasantries, good manners, Malbec, food, black squares and for centuries causes pain.
Dr Guilaine Kinouani (2021) reminds us that this is 'a professional racism, we may say'. This centring of ourselves in 2020 and 2021, white people complaining about ally fatigue, signing up for anti-racist courses, buying all the anti-racism books on Amazon, and then forgetting a month, a year, later.
On reflection, we think we are learning, we think we are listening; but are we really. . . who do these performative acts serve? Did we become anti-racist?

Black people have continued to survive,
Dominique has thrived, she has developed, she's the chair of a charity in his name; we believe because of Black people's dignity, because of Black people's commitments to social justice, and transformation though love and anti-racism.
We believe because we have civil laws, the Equality Act 2010, an optics-based government which continues their institutional performances; we think because Black people just get on with it, that they continue to contribute to society through the everyday,

music, culture, we believe because they can retell their stories that there is nothing distressing to experiences of racism and the everyday experiences of racism, when it is proven it affects one's health and complete wellbeing; it's a threat to public health.

And the reality is this: if you are Black and those you seek support from are unwilling to look at racism and the trauma it inflicts, these individuals or systems are simply unwilling to look you in the eye (Kinouani, 2021).

Still, Black people rise, they stand, dignified, existing to resist.
But it is white people who are afraid to look them in the eye; we fear their pain, we become distressed by their trauma, we invalidate their experiences, so we don't have to deal with them. We expect them to shrink themselves, to be silent, we do everything in the hope we will forget and invalidate their experiences into none-existence. . .

But no longer, I will do better.

White people must do better, listening, centring others, denying racism, minimizing our differences is the danger.
There are many ways to be anti-racist, to resist, starting with dialogue is one way,

a way of daring to love, daring to recognize that love, communion, listening, self-respect, empathy, compassion and not thinking of yourself, is needed.

It is step one, I am still learning, this is step one. . .

Kind regards,

Robin,

P. S. Thank you Michelle for reading this on behalf of me, Robin, it means so much, this is about you, Dominique, weaponizing incompetence is something we all need to work on.

Dominique Walker is a lecturer at Liverpool John Moores University within the School for Justice, teaching across policing studies, criminology, criminal justice and sociology. Dominique's research interests include Black feminist thought and theory, intersectionality, hate crime policing, race and racism. For ten years, Dominique was a trainee detective constable within Merseyside Police Protecting Vulnerable People Sigma Hate Crime Investigations Unit. Dominique has also worked to challenge hate crime and promote equity and fairness in her community, and with her family created The Anthony Walker Foundation (AWF), a charity set up after the untimely death of her brother Anthony in July 2005 – Dominique is the Chair of AWF. AWF works to promote racial harmony through education, music and sport.

In 2014, Dominique was awarded an Honorary Fellowship by Liverpool John Moores University for her commitment to celebrating diversity, community development and cohesion. Dominique is currently studying for her PhD in sociology, criminology and social policy at University of Liverpool and is co-founder of the Goddess Projects (TGP), a social enterprise designed to help Black women and women of colour to achieve in all aspects of their lives. Dominique is also mother to two young girls, aged nine and eighteen years old.

Dear Chief,

I've been wanting to write this
letter for some time now.
I couldn't find the words to
articulate what I wanted to say.
I want to share some memories with you.

I want you to take a moment to relax
and brace yourself.
I promise I'll be gentle,
I'll warm you up and start slowly.

Do you remember the first time we met?
I was in my early twenties, in my second year of
art practice after graduating.

You were in your early forties,
in charge. White, obvz,
about 6 ft, brown hair and stubble,
with a tint of silver.
A posh accent yet you claimed to have common parents.
Slender lips. Appeared to be a good boy,
but I could see right through the act.

I was happy to meet you because
I got invited to join an artist development
programme for 'BAME' artists. (Eww.
I would never do such a thing now.)
You said to me, 'I've met you before.'
And I said, 'Really? Was I drunk?'
Because I would remember meeting
someone in your position.

There would be events in your building
where the whole theatre and dance sectors were invited.

I couldn't believe I was in a space
with so many great artists.

You were about to make a speech and
I remember feeling quite in awe of you.
Inspired by your boss energy.

I felt out of place.
I entered, feeling shook;
my spirit was haunted.
I couldn't put my finger on it.
I knew there was something wrong.

A fellow Black artist asked me,
'Why are we in a space filled
with so much colonial history?'
Then I knew why I felt so off.
The ancestors were pissed.

There was an after-party,
and I loved partying with well-known artists.
Although a lot of them were bitching
about you and your institution.
It be like that sometimes.
You told me, 'Everyone is so mean to me,
but you're always so nice.'

I said, 'Get used to it, babe; you have power.
People will always have an issue with you.'
What I really meant to say was,
'With your power and privilege, I don't give a fuck.'
We pecked each other and said cheers.

A month later, you were drinking one night,
it was 10.45 pm,
and you messaged me on Facebook.
I already knew you fancied me;
I didn't think you would make a move.
We got to be professional, after all.

Rebelling can be fun.
Over time, it led to us talking more,
exchanging images
and chuckling together – until 3 am.

We ended up seeing each other at a local play.
You offered to give me a lift home, so I accepted.
We stopped at Tesco first
because you needed to pick up
lunch for your kids.

You invited me to join you;
I decided to wait in the car.

After, you dropped me outside my house,
and it felt like you didn't want me to leave.
I said, 'Thank you for the ride.'
And you kept talking, talking and talking.
I must admit, you are a charmer.
And I'm sure it's that charm that helped you
become an artistic director of a big institution.

I imagined what
would've happened if I'd stayed in your car that night.
If I'd said to you, 'Park up around the corner;
I want to suck you off.'

Would you have said no?
I don't think so. I once said to you,
'We'll never sleep with each other.'
And you said, 'Aww, don't say that!'
I was not surprised by your response.

Sometime later, I was in residence in your building
and we bumped into each other.
I had a hole in my trousers; you noticed.
Yes, of course, you would look at my bum!

So I asked if you were kinky.
You said, 'Well, it depends on the occasion.'
Most people wouldn't dare say something
like that to someone like you, but I did.

I told a white friend about your flirtatious ways,
and she didn't seem to believe me.
Probably because she's worked with you,
and knows you are married with kids.

As a queer man,
I get messages from married and taken
'straight men' all the time.
I'm used to this.

Sarcastic:

I mean, there's no way a white man
with power would ever abuse it!

I love this friend who didn't believe me,
but she tends to gaslight me.
And I can't be bothered having this conversation with her.
Although, I know I should.

I told her I was going to do my
one-to-one performance that focuses on privilege
with a guy for our first date.
And she said, 'You have to understand
that talking about race
makes white people uncomfortable.
It's much easier for Black people to discuss it.'
The ancestors were pissed.

As I said, she's worked with you.
She contracted some venom
from your building, and it
seems to be still living inside her.
She's a white woman,
with some power of her own,
who slept with an emerging
Black male artist.
I guess you both have that in common, too.
But that's not my story to tell,
or my letter to write.

She did mention that concerning #MeToo,
it's mostly heterosexual men
that have been criticized,
but she pointed out there are also queer men in power.

She's right. I don't think she's
ever considered her behaviour, though.
I do remember her being tipsy and horny
and telling me to get with her. I didn't.
But why did she assume she had the right
to ask that of me?

If I put out a statement as a Black queer man,
would anyone pay me any mind?
I acknowledge that my male privilege will help
in a lot of instances, but is my Blackness or
maleness the first thing that comes to mind?
Society rarely listens to Black women.
Would anyone listen to me?
Or would they pick me apart too?

I'm hypersexual. I make work
that often explores sexuality and people might think
I was asking for it. They might say
I should never have replied to your drunk messages.
They'll say the danger of it all excited me.
And they'd be right on that part.
It would make a good TV drama for Channel 4.

We both love to party, don't we?
At a Live Art festival after-party,
I felt your tender touch when we spoke.
I get an electric shock when I'm reminded
of the first time, you grabbed my crotch.

I reacted by grabbing yours in return.
It became like a greeting.
We were both comfortable.
Is it bad that I didn't mind
being touched inappropriately?
Without consent?
I guess everyone's relationship
to their bodies is different.
But is it healthy?

An older white guy also
grabbed my crotch on a queer night out.
The night was meant to be a safe space.

The same night, a white woman seized
my afro like she was about to fall off a cliff.
She and other white women have
used my queerness as an excuse to access
my Blackness. As if, being women, they
had the right to touch my queer body.

Then they would say things like,
'I would love to have hair like yours.'
The ancestors were pissed.

To be fair, when I was younger,
I did something similar.
I was one of those queer men
who thought it was okay to touch women
and to comment on their body parts.
The older I get, the more I see how
much rape culture is normalized.
We all are guilty.

Another time, this white guy and I were flirting at your venue.
It was Halloween, and he annoyed me with the way
he sexualized me and my body.
In frustration, I grabbed his privates,
as a way to say fuck off.

I didn't think anything more of it,
until later, when he expressed he was upset.
I was apologetic, I never intended to hurt his feelings.
He questioned my politics,

because I talked about
white supremacy in my work,
and taking up space.

He asked,
'Why did you feel like you
could take up my space?'
He thought I was aggressive.
But I told him, 'You created this version of me.
Why are you unhappy, when I gave you exactly
what you expect from me?'

You and he created a space where people
would touch each other and it would be okay.
You and he created a space where my Black body
was an object to be touched and watched.
I've learned the hard way that none of that was okay.

Since high school,
I've been used to people of all genders
touching me without consent.
That's no excuse.

I remember being twelve, when two Black girls,
who were friends of mine, fondled me.
I remember when I was fourteen, and a seventeen-year-old Black guy
gave me head in Potternewton Park.
At the time, I thought I didn't mind these encounters.
But that's a problem,
I should have said something.
I was too afraid to make it a big deal.

I still can't say the words
'I've been sexually assaulted' out loud.
I haven't learnt how to build boundaries
when it comes to my body,
except for my hair.

I've internalized all the sexual assaults
I've experienced, not realizing
or feeling like I've been assaulted.
The older I get the more I see how
much rape culture is normalized.

I have some questions:
Do you want a break from needing
to have answers for everything?
From leading everyone in the right direction?
Is that why you want to submit and be dominated?

Who wrote the statement on behalf of your institution
in response to the murder of George Floyd?
Was it you? Why wasn't Breonna Taylor mentioned?
When you said my dick looked 'juicy',
did you think of your wife and kids?
Did you imagine their faces?

Are you as passionate about
Black lives as you are about Black dick?

Beat.

How you doing, Chief?
Is this too much? Do you want me to calm down?
Do you want me to stop?
Don't worry, I'm almost there.
I know you can handle it.

At a social gathering,
I asked you, 'Do you like chocolate?'
And you looked at me, paused and said yes.
I wasn't asking if you liked Black men,
but I saw you lick your lips.

I told you that you have nice eyes,
and you said I have a nice face.
And then you asked if I was going to pass the spliff.
You later pinned me up against the wall,
you were starting to come up from the MD.
During our first kiss,
I said we shouldn't be doing this,
and you said, 'Why not?'

You pulled out my dick started to stroke –
like you've been
waiting for that moment.
As if you had it all planned out in your head.
You were always so descriptive
about what you would do to me on Facebook.

If I said no, what would your response have been?
I'm reminded of the times when I've rejected men,
but they kept coming back.
I just wasn't interested,
and then I eventually gave in.
I ended up having sex that I didn't want to have.
To be left alone,
as the harassment was too much to bear.
I'm learning to be firmer,
to be more direct when I say no,

and to not change my mind.

How do you think the audience is feeling?
Do you think they are listening?
Are they shuffling in discomfort?
How do you think your colleagues would feel?
What about your white friends?
Would there be any deep sighs when race was brought up?
Will they reflect on my words tomorrow morning?
Think about if they ever touched someone without permission?
Do you think anyone that you're reading this to would ever admit that
they sexually assaulted someone?
That they were part of the problem?

I'm conflicted,
as I always had a fantasy to fuck my boss.
You're technically not my boss,
you're close enough, though.
I question if I even find you attractive.
Or do I find your 'power' attractive?

I'm a powerwhore because I know
I could do more good with your power
than you ever could.

Will you commission me to make something
that has nothing to do with race?
I know! A show about my love for Haribo.
Something that didn't have to
be about making a change.
Or does hearing about my trauma make you hard?
Make your colonizer dick dribble?

There have been a few times
where white men with power similar
to yours asked me what my type is.
And I said I prefer Black men.
They were shocked.

They were shocked because
they're used to Black men
telling them that they prefer white men.

I replied that ain't me because I don't hate myself.
However, they keep creeping into my DMs,
asking for the BBC. (That means Big Black Cock.)

If I preferred white men,
I most likely would be married
and have a house by now.

This is not an exaggeration.
I met a millionaire the other day,
and he said that he could marry me.
And I didn't even give him the goods at that point.

I've always wanted a sugar daddy,
but I don't think I could commit to the role of sugar baby.
I would get bored, or angry, or both.

A friend said I need to learn how to finesse.
But then the millionaire asked me

if I wanted to have a threesome.
I asked, 'With who?'
He sent me a picture of another young Black guy.
It was clear to me, he had a fetish,
and I didn't want to make his dreams come true.

Another friend said a rich white man
with two Black boys is giving 'slave master'.
I can never win.

Do you think he is passionate about Black lives
as he is about Black dick?

Beat.

You posted pics of your food on Instagram and
I asked if you could cook for me sometime.
You said, 'If you fuck my pussy up.'

I've never understood why cis men
call their assholes pussies.
Does it stem from their attitude to women?

You waited for me, bent over your kitchen counter,
with only a T-shirt on, when your partner was at work.

I was anxious but intrigued,
even though the day before,
we video-called so I could watch you
ejaculate five minutes before your board meeting.

This time you kept saying, 'It's okay.'
But I was terrified of getting caught.

I also wanted your partner to find out
the truth about you.

You don't talk to me much now.
It's all good because I still see you at Zoom meetings.
Even the ones that I'm not invited to.

There was one where Black Lives Matter
and 'change' was being discussed,
hardly any Black artists were present.

I sent you a text saying:
'Hey Chief, I hope you're good.
I'm currently on the Zoom call,
and I'm curious as to why there
isn't much Black representation?

I find it quite odd that "change" is being discussed.
But there hasn't been much change made,
even though your venue has
a network of Black artists.
I would love to speak to you about this
further whenever you get the chance.'

Your response was wack.
You didn't know why I wasn't invited to the Zoom,
and you were going to find out.

You also mentioned hiring Black people
to help with the racism in your institution.
Ha! You're adorable. I know you're trying,
but I need you to work a little harder,
if you're really about making that change.

Are you still passionate about Black lives
as you are about Black dick?

Beat.

Eurgh. I'm exhausted.
And frankly, bored of talking about white people.
Unpacking the assaults.
Accepting them as assaults.
Yes, I wanted to write to you, yet
I was hesitant. I didn't realize it,
but I had some healing and taking accountability to do.
And I need to continue to do this.

Despite being numb.
I'm going to start saying no,
as I should've said no before.
And I'm going to keep my hands to myself.
The ancestors are proud.

Here you are, Chief, handsome and flawed.
Just one example of the many white male artistic directors,
who have flirted with me, groped me,
and made their fantasy a reality.

The ones that are queer,
the straight ones,
the married and the curious.

The ones that want to be seduced,
the secretly naughty ones
who want to be punished,
and the ones who want to escape,
because they're bored of their power.

After all I've written in this letter,
and with all the power that you have,
what are you going to do with it now?

Will you ever care as much about Black lives
as you do about Black dick?

Yours unfaithfully,
Jamal

'I accepted the invitation because I came up with an idea that could potentially shake the table. I do love to cause trouble, and this opportunity has given me another chance to do it. I believe the concept of My White Best Friend (And Other Letters Left Unsaid) *intends to be provocative, and that's something I love to be.'*

Jamal Gerald is an artist based in Leeds. His work is conversational, unapologetic and provocative with a social message. He makes work that he wants to see, intending to take up space as a Black queer person.

He has made work for poetry slams, films, parties, cafes and theatres. In 2018, he was awarded Arts Council England's Artists' International Development Fund to do research in Trinidad and Tobago. He was commissioned by Transform and Theatre in the Mill to make *Idol*, which premiered at Transform 19.

His writing has been published by Dog Horn Publishing, Oberon and Live Art Development Agency.

Jamal's work has also been shown at Kampnagel (Hamburg), SPILL Festival of Performance, Leeds Playhouse, Battersea Arts Centre and the Barbican.

Jamal was a Recipient of a Jerwood Arts' Live Work Fund Award in 2021.

NOTE: Where the directions are set centrally, in italics, please don't read them aloud, just do them.

An actor walks on stage to the music of Asian Dub Foundation – 'Real Great Britain'.
The auditorium is half lit, so the actor can see the audience.
They open a folder.
Music fades.
There is a red jacket on the chair. Please put it on.

Okay, here we go.

Deep breath.

Dear Everyman Theatre – my *ex*-white best friend from many moons ago . . .

How you doing?

This is all a bit 'meta' isn't it?

What have we got here?

A boss actor on stage personifying *you*.

An embodiment of this beautiful, important, historic institution.

Everything you have been

Everything you are now . . .
and everything you hope to be.

I did think about asking to strap some neon lights to the actor's fod

but I think that might have been a bit overkill.

So, we settled for something a bit more subtle.
a nice bit of red and a touch of crushed velvet . . .

And an old bit of garlic bread in your back pocket from Paddy's Bistro for good luck.

So, what is this letter all about?

Why have I asked you on stage tonight?

To talk about our *love affair*?

Or our *breakup*?

To air our dirty laundry in public?

Don't worry, Ev.

Think of this is more of a *conflict resolution*.

A kind of intervention.

All part of the journey of our *Truth and Reconciliation process*.

And not just for me, but also for the other people of colour in the room, and hopefully soon outside of this space.

And just in case you feel worried or nervous, about what is to come up . . .

I want to reassure you that my objective of this letter is to explore my truth with

No Blame and No Shame.

I learnt recently, that when people are shamed, they can become defensive. Clam up.

Making no room for movement.

There will be no more fighting, campaigning, and lobbying from me . . .

No more wailing, gnashing of teeth, or sitting in that well of despair . . .

I'm done.

To be honest with you, I'm exhausted by it.

The most important thing in this exchange is my wellbeing and the wellbeing of the people of colour in this space.

And . . . yes, white fragility is a tough concept for some.

But if this is to work, we need to have open ears and open hearts from *everyone* in the room tonight . . .

> *Take a moment to make eye contact with as many audience members and staff as you can.*

Okay. So here we go,

Is everybody ready?

> *Click fingers.*
>
> *Lights will dim.*

Dear Ev,

Our love affair began thirty-three years ago, back in 1988 when I joined your *Youth Theatre*.

This was a proper life-changing moment for me.

Because, before I found you, I was always watching my back.

Growing up as a British Asian kid in predominantly white spaces was intense.

From Birkenhead to Rainhill, St Helens.

All places I still have a love/hate relationship with.

Love the pies . . .

. . . not so much the rugby.

Beat.

Or being spat at on a bus when I was eight.

Being told to grow a thick skin by teachers for the daily taunts of being a smelly Paki.

As a teenager, being tied to the gates of a railway station on a Sunday afternoon, and whipped by a gang of lads . . .

while people walked by with their heads down.

They were the hardest lads in the year, who I desperately wanted to be mates with for some sort of status.

And of course, I kept going back for more . . .

My armour increasing with each beating or act of humiliation in the hope that one day they would accept me.

Beat.

Fuck me! That got heavy quickly, didn't it?

Just to let you know, Ev, this isn't onstage therapy for me.

I've been there, done that and got the mouse mat.

All this is *context*, an important part of *our* story.

Because *you* saved me.

When I arrived *here*, on *this* stage at the age of fifteen

you became my *first safe space.*

Of course, back then, we didn't even have that language.

We didn't know what a *safe space* was,

I just knew . . .

That I belonged *here*.

In the Youth Theatre there were other Brown and Black faces, not loads but enough.

And in terms of the white kids, they were all welcoming

1988, just before the dawn of the second Summer of Love.

A beautiful mash up of baggy Jeans, Acid House and Smiths Quiffs

(But let's not talk about Morrissey tonight, cos he's another one!)

Finally, I could be who I wanted to be.

I relaxed; I grew taller (*well not that tall, I'm still a short arse*)

You equipped me with the armour and confidence I needed to go back into those other white spaces.

And over time, I didn't feel the need to be a whipping boy anymore,

And so, because of you . . .

theatre became my white best friend.

You gave me the courage to develop my acting skills and by the age of twenty-two

I waved goodbye to Liverpool and the Everyman, moved to London and became a jobbing actor.

Living in Brixton and then Hackney, I became part of a Black and Brown majority

And I relaxed completely . . .

I hadn't realized how much fear and tension I had been carrying with me all those years.

And then something unexpected happened.

I began to see some of my white friends back in Liverpool through a different lens

And that, Dear Ev, included you.

You seemed somehow *different*.

And please don't take this the wrong way, I still loved you.

But you see, most of my *new* theatre friends were now Black and Brown.

Theatre Royal Stratford East, Cardboard Citizens, Graeae, Tara Arts, Tamasha,

Black Mime, The Roundhouse, Oval House,

And, not just in London but everywhere else I worked

Leicester Haymarket, Red Ladder, Peshkar, Breaking Cycles

And then eventually I found my new proper bezzie Contact Theatre.

Now don't get jealous, cos I know you've always had a bit of an inferiority complex when it comes to the Mancs. But they nurtured and developed me from being an actor into becoming a writer and director with a Black and Asian directors' course back in 2003.

And by then I *really* began to see you in a different light.

And I'm not saying you didn't care; cos I know you did in your own funny sort of way.

Just maybe not enough.

Because as I was soaking up all these other spaces, I suddenly became aware of your . . .

. . . other side

The other side, that didn't look like the beautiful-culturally-diverse-Benetton-Coca-Cola-advert of your 1980s Youth Theatre

The other side being the *professional work* on your main stage.

Look around the space.

Soak it up.

As a young person, I had never seen a Black or Brown face in a show here.

But what really hurts the most is that at the time, that just felt *normal*.

And that's a heavy blow.

Did it feel as normal for you as it did for me, I wonder?

I remember coming into your foyer.

Huge black and white photos of all those amazing actors I'd seen on the telly

Matthew Kelly from *Stars in Your Eyes*!

WHO KNEW HE WAS A PROPER DEAD GOOD ACTOR!!!? RSC and everything!!

Willy 'Chips and Egg' Russell.

Bill Nighy

Yozza

Yozza Fucking Hughes!!!!

And of course, who could forget national treasure . . .

Roger *McCough-Sweet.*

And in amongst all the *boss white fellas*, you even managed to squeeze in some amazing women aswell!

Julie Walters and Alison Steadman. Proper Legends!!!

They were all there. . . the famous class of '74 and many more.

And don't get me wrong, we loved them all dearly. . . it was inspiring.

This was Liverpool. Proper working-class, legendary, socialist theatre.

But when I looked back, I realized that none of them represented me or my mates in the Youth Theatre or indeed the multi-cultural population of Liverpool – African, Caribbean, Chinese, Arab, South Asian, the list goes on.

And of course, there were exceptions . . . I found out about Cathy Tyson many years later, but she was nowhere to be seen when I was there.

So, by the early 90s

I started to distance myself from you and we drifted apart, just like some of my school mates who used to talk about Nig-Nogs and Paki shops,

and of course, the Union Jack wielding, Bengali-baiting *Morrissey*.

And I never put you in the same category as them, but I could feel it in my gut that something felt really *fucking off*.

This was *Liverpool* . . .

Home to Britain's oldest Black community dating back centuries.

And when I heard that Specials song at a mate's house that really struck a chord . . .

> *Please walk over to the boombox on the table and press the play button.*
>
> *An extract of 'Racist Friend' by the Specials will play.*
>
> *Listen to the music and the words.*
>
> *When it starts to fade come back to the letter.*

Over the next ten years, every time I came back to visit family in Liverpool

I used to anxiously walk past you, like an ex-lover's house.

I witnessed from afar your slow demise to a grinding halt.

I can't imagine what that must have felt like for you, I know for me and the people of Liverpool it was devastating.

But when you opened up again a few years later with your old *frenemy* from down the Road . . . the Playhouse.

It felt like a new dawn.

I like many, was hopeful. One of your opening shows was a revival of *Yellowman* directed by Indhu Rubasingham and an amazing Black cast.

But after that it was hard to see what was being offered up in terms of cultural diversity.

Okay . . . so, the next bit is a tricky bit.

What happened with us after that I will censor to spare you or I any blushes or pain on stage.

And because so much has happened in the past fifteen years. I'll read the landmark moments as a list.

1. I moved back to Liverpool and set up a theatre company with my partner to try and redress the balance of cultural diversity and theatre in the city, partly because your programme and youth theatre was now so painfully white and middle class. It broke my heart, but it also spurred me into action.

2. I made a show with Contact and Birmingham Rep which landed on your stage with a majority Black cast, you sat up and took notice. We began a dialogue again.

3. Shortly after, I tentatively asked why your famous Rock 'n' Roll panto had an all-white cast even when you had Black cartoon characters on your posters. I was then asked to join your board. I went from being a lobbyist to a *critical friend*.

4. I spent five years on the board gently asking the tough questions. Where was the diversity in the youth theatre? Your main stage? Your Staff? Your audiences? Some changes were made on stage, but it was like pulling teeth.

(Don't worry. I've checked with the lawyers, it's fine to use the phrase *pulling teeth* as a non-libellous remark!)

5. During this time, you gave me an opportunity to make a show on the Playhouse Main Stage: it was a success!!! Well received by audiences and critics, but most importantly it's who was in the audience and what they looked like.

6. Things became tricky for us. As the only person of colour on the board it was exhausting. I noticed a conflict of interest in terms of the work I wanted to make with you and my governance. At the end of the day, we just didn't share the same core values.

And so, we parted again, but this time for some reason it felt *more painful*.

Then last year after the murder of George Floyd, the Black Lives Matter movement changed the agenda for every individual, every organization within every sector globally.

The challenges we had spent decades fighting for were now finally being heard and starting to make cracks.

And the oppressions we may have kept to ourselves or only shared with close friends and allies were now finally being talked about in the public domain.

Speaking truth to power with solidarity.

Unabashed.

Confident in our narratives.

Within the theatre sector, these are some of the common experiences that have come out of the past year.

Some of these *may or may not* apply to you.

You make a judgment, Ev.

Images of people of colour being pushed to front of brochures and buildings to satisfy diversity when it doesn't reflect the true story.

(Window dressing, they call it apparently.)

People of colour being checked by security whilst white counterparts walked on by.

People of colour being mistaken by staff as cleaners.

White casting directors only connected to white clients.

Diversity population statistics being skewed to justify low diversity numbers.

People of colour being asked to lead on diversity agendas regardless of their role and responsibility within the organization.

Artists of colour being asked to play non culturally specific parts because of the colour of their skin.

People of colour being assistants and being lined managed by white counterparts with the same amount of experience.

White artists feeling threatened by people of colour coming in, because they can't see the talent and only see them as satisfying diversity quotas.

Take a minute.

Does any of this make any sense to you?

Does it resonate?

Where in your body are you feeling this the most?

Your head? Your heart? Your stomach?

I hope you know why I'm telling you this.

I hope you know why I'm asking you here to share this publicly.

And let me be clear this *is* messy.

I've wrestled with the many levels of this. When is it personal? When is it political?

When am I doing this for me, when am I doing this for others?

But at the end of the day, just so you know, this isn't about me or my ego or a clash of personalities or a grudge.

This is about *you*!

There is always a danger of an artist of colour being a 'critical Friend' to an arts venue. I've seen it happen a lot.

There is a power dynamic going on and a conflict of interest.

And just like the boys at the railway station, sometimes we subconsciously take a whipping in order to feel accepted or to take a place at the table. In the hope one day that it might be worth it.

Or it's about the fear of speaking out.

People become afraid that they won't be employed again or even worse lose their current job.

And so about six years ago, I went back to my old Black and Brown theatre mates.

It was less tiring.

We kept our distance, and every now and then I would get incensed and write you an email about how white you were becoming again . . .

Sometimes it was about the board, but usually about the panto.

Did you ever think about the irony of a Rock'n'Roll panto being all white?

Rock'n'Roll originally being Black music?

I think that might have got lost on you.

And you know what? There *was* some progress in terms of cultural diversity on stage, but to be honest, a lot of it felt like box ticking.

Or the Arts Council being the headteacher telling you to finish your diversity assignment.

Yes, you did bring people of colour into your building as artists, practitioners, directors, producers.

But most of them felt isolated and it was an open secret that they found their time with you *'Tricky'*.

And it wasn't just the people you invited in that found it 'tricky' but also people on the outside.

Audiences, community leaders, and politicians also found you 'tricky'.

Many had given up on you a long time ago, possibly as far back as the class of '74.

Now, for those of you listening in Black and White, I've written 'Tricky' in inverted commas

Because for all these years, Dear Ev, many of us were using 'Tricky' as a euphemism for what we now see as *Institutional Racism*.

Beat.

How many arses in the room clenched then? Why don't you take a moment to check in.

Make eye contact with audience.

Breathe in.

Soak up the energy.

Institutional racism

This is the definition of Institutional racism as told by the McPherson Report.

'The collective failure of an organization to provide an appropriate and professional service

to people because of their colour, culture, or ethnic origin.

It can be seen or detected in, processes, attitudes and behaviour that amount to

discrimination through prejudice, ignorance, thoughtlessness, and racist stereotyping which disadvantage minority ethnic people.'

Wow. That's a lot to take in.

How are you feeling? Is it sinking in yet?

And no-one is saying, Ev, that *you* are a racist.

So please don't feel defensive or attacked.

Please don't be *that* dinosaur, please don't be LAMDA (and the rest!).

Like many, you have found yourself in the heart of a culture war.

No-one is saying that the people who run or work in your buildings are *flag waving-Paki bashing thugs*.

Or bigots who wants to *send back the migrants*.

This is about *you* as a beloved institution who is largely funded on public money that has a responsibility to represent and serve.

Right let's go back a second. Break it down.

'It can be seen or detected in processes, attitudes and behaviour that amount to discrimination through prejudice, ignorance, and thoughtlessness.'

Ignorance

and

thoughtlessness.

Prejudice

Ignorance

and

thoughtlessness.

Prejudice? sometimes. . . . but not overtly I think.

Ignorance? 100 per cent!

Thoughtlessness? most definitely.

This is what institutional racism is.

I recently discovered there have only been two new plays produced on your stages by local writers of colour since 2003: one was by me and the other by Maurice Bessman.

This is what institutional racism is.

Last year we did get the chance to talk this through a bit with some of your people and many ex-members of staff who are of colour to talk about what it felt like.

It was behind closed doors on a Zoom; we spoke our truth and began the path of reconciliation.

No blame no shame, and the stories poured out of us, and we felt listened to.

And over the past year things have been slooowly progressing.

But we all know these are baby steps.

I can see that you are begging to open up, almost falling over yourself to get us all in.

But sometimes I wonder if there, is there anything you're afraid to say out loud?

I have heard other theatres say it.

'What really? Every show has to have a person of colour in it

What about the quality?'

'Where are we going to find them?

Aren't they all in the Lion King *again?'*

An observation might be that if you and others had invested in diverse communities and artists many years ago, then you wouldn't have found it so *tricky* to find the people now

And when you have more people of colour in your building and heart you won't be asking about *them*.

How are we going to get *them* in?

It won't be an *us and them*.

It will be an *us and us*.

Because now is your long overdue *Doctor Who* regeneration moment.

I don't know what your audience and staff will look like tonight when you read this letter.

Is this the audience and staff you can see in the future? Is it starting to happen?

Why don't we take a look?

>*Please click your fingers, the lights will come up.*

Now for some audience participation.

>*Ask everyone in the audience to take a good look around them.*

In terms of the cultural diversity of audience and staff does this looks and feel right?

On my count of three.

People give a thumbs up for yes (*demonstrate action*).

Flat wavy hand for maybe (*demonstrate action*).

Thumbs down for no (*demonstrate action*).

1 – 2 – 3

Keep your hands up.

Now, Ev, make a judgement on what you think is the consensus.

Take your time.

And mirror the gesture back at the audience.

Everyone in the room soak it up for a moment.

How does it feel?

Right, everybody, hands down.

Okay we're nearly there.

I want to leave you with one last thought if I may.

If this is the next chapter of our truth and reconciliation.

But we know many more artists, staff, audience members of colour who haven't had a chance to tell you their story

Please make that space for other hundreds or possibly thousands that might have had similar experiences over the past fifty-seven years.

Not in six months or a year.

But now.

Royal Court in London have named their institutional racism and are inviting people in to start a healing process.

Hundreds of ex-employees from the Barbican in London have published a book about their experiences of institutional racism. They have said . . .

'We invite other organisations to make visible the cultures of discrimination that are perpetuated in their community. It is by bringing these concealed realities to the public sphere, that we can confront and dismantle systems of power together.'

And if you are a beacon and leader, Ev, then maybe it will resonate city-wide, nationally and internationally?

We know there is a lot to do post-pandemic, but can you make this one of your priorities?

And if you think McPherson's definition of institutional racism feels a bit strong.

And people might react to the word racism in a way that is 'tricky'

Then maybe, Ev, could it be part of your responsibility to help educate?

And what I've learnt is that the journey from the violent racism to the institutional racism isn't that far.

I remember sitting in the gallery at the Stephen Lawrence enquiry at Elephant and Castle back in 1997.

Hoping with every fibre of my being that change would come.

But as many of us know, things have gotten worse.

Post-Brexit, racism has got worse in all its guises.

Racial violence is on the increase.

I have, as an adult, still experienced racial violence, and profiling from the police.

We have a government with racist policies that would make Thatcher blush.

Housing, healthcare, education, welfare, criminal justice,

And of course the Arts.

And that's where you come in, Ev.

Cos while all this shit is happening to us outside of your four walls.

We need you more than ever.

As a space to breathe,

A space to be welcomed . . .

A place where we see ourselves reflected on and off stage.

A space that is safe.

For us to share the things we have in common, and the things that separate us.

a space where we can be activists

A space not only to tell our stories of oppression but also our other stories

and a space where we can just chill the fuck out . . .

or just dance   our   worries   away.

Now go and open your doors wide open

Visit people in their communities

Bring them back here into your space

Into your heart

And give them the same hug that you gave me thirty-three years ago.

No Blame

No Shame

Just

Hope.

Namaste.

Asian Dub Foundation – 'Real Great Britain' plays out.

Keith Saha found his love for theatre at Liverpool's Everyman Youth Theatre in the 1980s before going on to be an actor, a composer, and musical director until he eventually became a playwright and director.

In 2006 he co-founded 20 Stories High, a company which collaborates with young, working-class, culturally diverse participants, emerging artists and world-class professionals. With the manifesto 'Everybody's got a story to tell and their own way of telling it', his plays often draw on his own experience of being in the care system.

As well as developing new writing, he also is interested in pushing new art forms – his plays often include elements of Hip-Hop theatre, rap, dance, visual art and live music as well as puppetry and mask.

For television he has recently shot a pilot for his own series, *Looked After* with Twelve Town and SKY, based on his own and others' experience of being in care.

Awards include: Offie/Offcom award for *Touchy* (2022); Stage 100 Award for *Knocking On* (2021); Achates Philanthropy Prize *Knocking On* (2021); On the Edge Festival Young People's Choice award for *Broke 'N' Beat Collective* (2016); Brian Way Award and Liverpool Echo award for *Ghost Boy* (2011).

Published plays include *Melody Loses Her Mojo* and *Broke 'N' Beat Collective* with Bloomsbury and *Black/She's Leaving Home* with Methuen.

In his spare time, he has an unhealthy interest in vintage video games and his favourite food is Nasi Lemak.

MY WHITE BEST FRIEND – THE SILENCE OF THINGS [IN JOURNALS]

Hi

Hey

Hello

I'm not sure how to greet you at this time or how to write to you. There is so much I would like to share with you. There is so much to be said that is not easily spoken in a conversation. So, I thought I'd share my journal notes instead, until I find the words that could be the start of a truly heartfelt letter.

JOURNAL NOTE 1

At the crossroads, I meet myself questioning the way you navigate our working relationship. Do you recall when you thought it was important to tell me that you accept all people for who they are, especially Black women? And yet I've watched you reject them at the drop of a hat if they do not follow through on your ideas.

I've questioned your behaviour towards me, the reality of your attitude, patterned in kind gestures with the intention to gain something for yourself. I question how easy you transform a smile into unkindness. How the emotional impact of your anger has affected many.

I'm not sure why you think you have a licence to be rude. I often wonder who will address your actions without suffering the repercussions of your harsh words. Your conduct doesn't go unnoticed but most people have a tendency to overlook it.

JOURNAL NOTE 2

I've watched how you work privilege and fragility in spaces; how it bends and turns to suit your situation. It's quite sad, how you've entered into a community, work it, and claim rights over its narrative and the richness of its people. How you try to ostracize individuals and create rivalry.

Your actions remind me there are people who believe Black folk have few rights, have little ownership of our culture or lack the importance to produce work. There are many people who think we do not feel pain, and this is why are often treated as objects rather than as beings. It's a long history, lacking thought, from those who assume positions of power. It is fuelled with disorders of space and belonging.

Without wisdom and tolerance, it is filtered through a Eurocentric lens, and revolves around personal gain. A cycle of abuse, it is minor in the eyes of those who practice divide and conquer.

Where unity is never considered a means of communication. Where we can never take an equal seat at the table.

I remember when I tried to speak to you about some of the things Black women go through. How marginalized and neglected they are by wider society.

Your abrupt response was, 'Black women are supposed to be strong.'

I wanted to say to you, 'Who the hell told you that Black women must always be strong?' It's true we have a strength, steeped in resilience, to survive the hate dished out to us, but we have feelings too, which are not always attended to. And often undermined.

The truth is, I'm so tired of calling out yet another injustice, another stereotype, that I said nothing to you. You were reluctant to find out more or enter into a dialogue. You said I read too much into things. I stayed silent. I knew the conversation had shifted; it would become heightened, the charting of a narrative that would you find difficult to accept.

You are so outspoken on what you believe. You are stubborn and unwilling to listen. You are so quick to say racism is not real or is a thing of the past.

That day I saw through you and I chose not to be an activist. I chose not to call out a wrong. Instead, I wrapped my hair with these stories to keep them safe in the space that is unsafe.

When things are weak at the seams or when they fall apart, the source of the problem should be addressed, otherwise we hide them inside our bodies.

The truth is, I just want to be an artist and let my art speak. I want to write my art. I want to be me, free to express through doing the work I love. Never standing in your shadow. In the shadow of a colonized society.

It's common knowledge that a white artist is just an artist, given so many opportunities to create, whereas a Black artist is always a Black artist, never an artist who makes work for all regardless of heritage. The lack of representation is nothing new – the one-in and one-out an unspoken act, a policed practice. A practice that defines our future.

There are so many tags attached to us: tags we never asked for; tags that others put on us; tags we don't want; tags that don't define us; tags that scream aggression; tags that marginalize; careless tags; abusive tags; tags upon tags upon tags . . .

There are moments when I want to release the things I've held inside – the things that bubble up inside me at night. The things that make me restless. There are times I want to curse out the shit – especially on those nights when my thoughts take over my sleep – and when I wake up, the lies are still there. The lies I tell myself that one day things will change.

I often think you might change your ways. It may happen at the change of the moon, the new moon, orange, pink, red, blue moon, any old bright or dark moon will do. If change is a thing.

JOURNAL NOTE 3

I read yet another story of an attack on a Black body. The media said very little out loud about the attack on the Black woman shopping for a handbag. She was accused of looking suspicious, so the shop security tried to remove her by throwing her to the ground. And of course, this injustice didn't make the national news. It circled the internet for a day or so and disappeared. The task is to acknowledge, to remember, to exercise rights. The problem is, it's normal; doors are very rarely opened to tell these stories. So many doors are closed, doors not opened to welcome folk like me. There are doors on doors. So what's the point, I ask myself? The time we live in is now and yet I find self trying to unearth blues, make sense of the ills with a crazy desire to reclaim self to meet self in the mirror – asking the same questions.

You may ask what the attack of the woman has to do with you. Any attack is an attack, and your verbal abuse alongside so many other things, reminds me of the things around me. Things from my past come back. The question of rights, identity and belonging.

THE TEST BED: WHICH ONE DO YOU TICK?

What does it mean to be. . .?

Black and British

African Caribbean

African

What are these boxes? Which one do you tick in reality?

The flashback

At Intake High School, where the kids called me names like Nig-Nog, Black Sambo, Golliwog – so boastful in their dislike for my Black skin.

THE TEST BED: WHEN DID THE COLOUR OF YOUR SKIN GET YOU IN TROUBLE?

Those same kids at Intake cheered and laughed when the Geography teacher, who refused to call me by my name when reading the register, preferred to refer to me as Jungle Bunny. He would shout, 'Get out of my class!' and throw his chalk at me. His breath stank of coffee and cigarettes, his teeth were stained and his tweed jacket carried the weight of dandruff.

THE TEST BED: YOU CAN'T CHOOSE YOUR OPPRESSOR

Flashback: the dinner lady is upset with two white boys who called her little Hitler. For some reason she thinks me and my friend Jenny are laughing at her. In fact, it's cold and there is snow on the ground, and we are tickling each other. We laugh as we chase each other around the school yard. Jenny and I hug each other to keep warm. We are the only two Black girls in the school. We don't have many friends, the kids are always calling us names, like Kizzy from *Roots*; they imitate whip sounds, make monkey noises.

THE TEST BED: CHOOSE YOUR PUNISHMENT

The racist kids in a racist school. Could you imagine being friends with them? We never laughed at their pitiful jokes. And yet we were accused of partaking in the unruly behaviour of the two white boys.

I tried to defend myself against the accusation. I tried to stand up for myself, whereas my friend said nothing. I was sent to the Head's office. I was not only accused of laughing but also swearing at her. I stood and watched the lie grow like a sick tree from her mouth. She said here is where I would learn to obey.

The Head said I should choose my punishment. The cane or expulsion.

I chose neither.

She left me for two days to stand outside her office, until she made a decision to send me back to class.

Imagine: each day is a task – an act of survival – that requires preparation – to untie the silence, the mistreatment, the microaggressions.

The act of challenging the aggression – the sparseness of spaces, unsafe spaces – white spaces – frames me ugly, frames me aggressive, devalues me, underestimates my worth.

I am all of the hurt – those women like me want to speak on it, write on it. I am all the discomfort you feel about me, the shades white folk like to hide away; it's all the colours folk bury to cover the shame. It is hair, it is skin, it is the footnote in history. It's a lot to say, too much to hear, so much to carry in the body. Imagine the weight of it.

JOURNAL NOTE 4: AFFIRMATION

If you can find laughter, you can find the will to smile.

Let out the pain and speak your truth.

My body holds memory, so I compose my thoughts so I can write them out. One day, I will share them like the day you had a bloody outburst.

Apparently, I'm getting in the way – because I questioned you. The way you sat in a meeting talking shit about a Black artist in a room full of white funders. You thought you had the right to discredit the artist's knowledge – opened with 'as a woman of colour'. Of course, this makes those in the room feel better to engage in the lie. Your side-line jokes were not funny, and even though none of them laughed openly with you, no one stopped it or addressed it. The subtleness of it all. The wider spaces you fit into, and here you are.

I've never felt comfortable, and cannot pander to your expectation to be in charge of what is my heritage. Somehow, somewhere, at some point, you were led to believe you are the voice, the leader, to reap the richness of art from marginalized artists.

JOURNAL NOTE 5: EDITING

I want to send you a letter. I've held back. In fact what has transpired is the slow rhythm of daily editing, the process of reworking the words.

I asked for an intervention to deal with your lateness and random outbursts whenever you felt you were not in charge – in charge of me and another artist. I asked for intervention from a white colleague because there were no Black workers in this organization. I asked for an intervention so I do not offend you, the offender – because the last time I tried, I had to deal with the so-called act of white women's tears.

Tears are a thing that set up sympathy for the person crying, detract from their own behaviour, and exclude the emotion of the other person – who then feels emotionally put out to dry.

You are really good at the tears in public spaces. Imagine how that excludes my story when there is no consideration of your actions. The rage of liquid aggression manifesting into anger.

That amplifies the trauma buried in Black bodies – the resilience and tension in the body – always returning to resilience because of the possibilities or the potential of change.

JOURNAL ENTRY: NOTES TO SELF

There are people who will claim your friendship but don't really see you – an interrogation for change.

I don't have many white friends, because most white people don't mix too much with other communities. They often only ever have the one Black friend. That Black friend is the yard stick to measure their unconscious bias. They never stop to realize that their one friend is always in a constant state of defending their self from the jokes, which are not really jokes, like:

The sun is out, it'll soon be as dark as you, or

I don't see colour, or

You're different from the rest, or

The abusive act of touching your hair, or

You're a cheeky little monkey, or

The awkward silence when someone calls you out for your name, or when they never truly stand up for you in public.

It's all too awkward, too uncomfortable, for them to understand it or to call it out.

JOURNAL NOTE 6

I recall when you described yourself as a woman of colour; you said it works for you. You said the kids at school used to call you names because of your brown curly hair; you told me your dad is Spanish and mum Scottish.

I guess I found some kind of sympathy with you because of the common ground of being teased at school for being different.

I even overlooked some of your behaviour, the way you question artists about their work, sometimes criticizing them, claiming you have more skills, more knowledge about their cultural heritage. I've watched the way you work privilege when it suits you.

Your circle of artist friends are mainly white women. You said you feel comfortable around Black culture and artists, but I never see you promoting either, unless you have produced or co-signed it.

I do question some of what you do, but never openly, since people seem to like you because you speak on race and racism. I notice you often call out white people to Black people but never in public. I've caught you laughing at their jokes. But behind closed doors you whisper how stupid white folk can be.

NOTES ON EDITING AN ARTIST

Remember when you said I should be more like Debbie? I wonder if you meant like her in looks or opinions.

You knowing Debbie is of mixed heritage, raised by her white mother. She is very open about not really knowing her dad, who she describes as 'that Jamaican loser'. Was I supposed to be like Debbie, who acts all awkward when the topic of race is discussed, so stays far from any conversation? Debbie who once said she wishes her skin and hair were more like her mother's? The same Debbie who once said I act too Black, my work is too Black, and that's why people find it difficult to work with me – and suggested I tone it down, so I appear less cultural?

And you agreed with her, then said you would put a good word in for me, to theatres, because you had a lot of pull in the art world.

The thing is, I don't want your help; that's not the kind of help I require if it means I can't be myself.

Pause, take a breath and think about . . .

Me, an African Caribbean woman, artist, writer, always waiting for the next opportunity to create and show off the work that is close to my heart. The opportunities are far and few. Art organizations, arts spaces, theatres, they still haven't made the changes to become fully inclusive.

JOURNAL NOTE 7

I remember when I got a job at an arts space. You were shocked to see me working in the same place as you, in a leadership role. A little bird told me you were pissed off because I got the director's role. I heard you tried to push Debbie to get the job. It's just like you to do that; just like you discredited and took away work from the artist you spoke shit about in that meeting.

I'd like to say you are good at what you do. But you are better at being late.

You are always running late. A few times, you failed to turn up for your sessions. And I covered for you, so many times. But that day when the company CEO started questioning me about your commitment to the job. . .? That day when there was a meeting, and everyone waited for you, and guess what: you turned up late and turned on the tears and created a narrative to put the blame on me.

You came in with a tale that you felt isolated from the project and were never given a chance to shine. You said you felt bullied and lost your confidence, when in fact you were double-booked; you were dishonest, and never took the time to explain to the organization you had no time to work on the programme.

You said you needed the extra cash – tried to keep it a secret, in the hope that no one would call you to account. You said that since I was Black, I should understand the struggle of a freelancer; I should have your back and cover the lie at my own expense.

As soon as you were questioned about your poor attendance, though, you deemed me the bully, believed I exposed you. You knew you could – that they wouldn't need any evidence to back up your lie.

Black women are bullies. Black women are too loud. Black women are too forward; they are difficult; they are all the shit and lies folk want them to be.

JOURNAL ENTRY: DRAFT LETTER 1

Dear Sarah,

I am writing this letter – from my desk, from my front room, from my bedroom, from spaces I love. I'm writing in spaces where I create; where I read; where I write, smile, laugh and cry.

Today I read bell hooks' *Sisters of the Yam*. I wrote morning pages to open my spirit, then I read back on my morning journal – it's filled with affirmations and accountability of self, love, self-care, – it's a ritual to start my day, to start writing. I move from one notebook to another. I love notebooks; some pages are filled with mood charts and notes of the day – who did what, and how I'm feeling. Some notebooks are filled with things I wish I could say, things I might say.

I often procrastinate; it helps me to feel out my real thoughts. Today I should be working on a commission – 'The cultural trauma of death and dead rites' – addressing the way African bodies release the sadness. But for some reason, reading hooks and going through my journal made me stop and count the number of times you have disrespected me, how the undertone of your words weighed down on my corn toe – and what came to mind is something my mother would say – unkind behaviour is like rotting mango on the roadside – it looks sweet but it's better to leave it right there on the roadside for the dogs. I don't think of you as a dog – far from it.

But there is a sense of knowing.

When there is space to think out

what white society does to divide us.

Most of the time our true thoughts

are unspoken.

The mind holds so much, it releases

what feels right for itself. Not always

what is right for self.

Because it is unsaid,

it doesn't mean it is not heard.

When all is spoken in the body

and then it is lived out.

We know the shift of emotions,

how it unravels in the body.

It's not a colour, or a shade

of nothingness.

It is of substance

and breath;

it is feelings,

an announcement

that we exist.

On some level, I'm filled with ancestral rage. You're not to blame for all of it; that would be unfair, as I jot notes on the page to write this letter to you. It's late; there is silence. The quietness outside reminds me of the silencing of voices that should be given space to speak, to breathe, to express freely without backlash. The problem is, white folk can hear but refuse to listen, or acknowledge the presence of the person's pain. It's too hard for them.

I can hear the pulse of my heart sounding out as I try to untie my tongue, as I write this letter to you. These words don't come so easy. They are not easily spoken outside – where safety is an issue. Safety for wellbeing, safety from what is not said, in circles I am not invited into.

There are things that should be said in the moment – when things happen, in those moments when unkindness unfolds. When words flood out into conversations that are no longer conversations but accusations, asserting things called the lie, this is when the emotions of friendship slip and tremble and become difficult.

The thing you claim – when it suits, when the social environment is white – becomes true. The problem is the space is always white; it has Black borders. Black is always a guest in waiting, never part of the whole story.

I imagine speaking these words to you, and maybe I could, maybe I would, edit self as white folk edit me. The way you edit me; the way you use Blackness to champion your needs, to make yourself the authority, while dehumanizing my Black body. I've held my tongue to keep peace, but in truth, I write this letter to you, to question you, address your ways – to untie my tongue, the same way as the dead spirit ties the navel string of the living. I want to break the silence, not bread to make peace, so my can body speak freely.

You once told me your Spanish father has descendants from India, after I shared my great grandfather was East Indian. I guess it was your way of explaining why you were 'a person of colour'.

My note paper speaks
I read Ntozake Shange 'nappy edges'
she writes,
'I am equal to whatever lil white girls got
from whoever they got it from'
Hello

I am here rewinding the conversation we had, when you claimed I was speaking about you to another artist who was very annoyed at you. I wasn't sure what had taken place before I entered the theatre. I was working, and you claim you were listening at the door. You claim you overheard a conversation. The fact is nothing was said. You were angry that there were three Black women in a room. You had offended one who said nothing. Your way to deal with the situation was to curse us all out.

I wish you didn't befriend and then in the same breath treat Black woman so bad.

I watched how you enjoyed the company of Joy, Veronica, Paula, Sheila.

I watched you curse them out because they challenged you. It was the same way you did me bad. You never acknowledged you were wrong; your words led people to think

I was an angry Black woman, a bully. In that moment, your selfish emotion cracked through my skin and your tears became a weapon to break me down.

I am forced to write this. Writing is the way to express it – everything – the madness, the sinking belly feeling. It's all performance playing out on the page. It doesn't take much imagination to know what it's all about.

But what happens when this journal becomes the letter. The things unsaid.

JOURNAL ENTRY DRAFT LETTER 2

Dear

I trust you are well

Hello

Hey Girl,

How are you doing?

(ah wha de rass. . .)
oh, hell to the no, no, no,
dis vexes me, I wants to bruk-out and fling words like I'm that fourteen-year-old girl at school.

I learnt how to cuss bad words from Denise to protect self from the racist kid at school. Her mouth was hot like pepper; she could fire words really quick and I liked her style. I recall when some of those bad words saved me and got me in trouble at the same time.

As an adult I've realized that editing self is quite an affair and often not spoken about publicly – although there are women brave enough to speak out about almost every injustice they have been subjected to. I think that's why I like Angela Davis. I met her once, heard her speak on 'affiliations among women moving across the intersections of culture, race and class'.

JOURNAL NOTES: ADVICE TO SELF

The truth is, I need to write this rass thing to you. I've slept on it for weeks, months. A whole year passed into a next year and I'm still tip-toeing with a vexing spirit that visit, triggers my sleep as if duppy ah haunt me with heavy stones. The same rock stones you flung, to burse me, to drop in me in the cold ground. You left my belly turning restlessness.

Debbie heard it all. She saw it playout but stayed silent.

The truth is, the day you worked whiteness to save yourself, and those days after when my own breath locked off, knotted up in my throat like a noose around my neck. I wanted to talk openly. I was silence. 'Who did I think I was?' Black folk can't skip out of work, but you were able to not turn up and still get paid. You lied over and over, while every eye watched me – never saw how you forced me into a situation to cover your work, and still do my own – forced to over-perform. Your white girl moves just did whatever, whenever. I've never had the pleasure or the privilege to move in such a way. Instead, you cursed me out, screamed and then cried, and received hugs.

I found myself thinking about the kind of friendship you create, especially when your aggression presses down on my heart

you, late for work,

you, not performing your task,

you, blagging, bragging, your skills

but not doing shit . . .

shit smells really bad

(you, going on like your shit don't smell)

you, absent – dismissive

you, were missing

you were called out

so . . .

you, spat up flames, set me alight,

catch a fire with white girl lies, antics and tears.

and . . . it still stinks, after so long

I really wanted to tell you about yourself. I wanted to dip into the rawness of Jamaican rass clart while banging my heart. I wanted to lift up my skirt front. It's a sign of the loss of dignity, but I knew deep down, I lost nothing of my true self. Even when you came to test me, to shut me down, to white-silence me.

The real me wished I was thirteen when I didn't care or understand the repercussions of telling the truth. I would tell the racist white kids at school to f' off but I soon realized, the white world will eat you up, and then gatekeep your body. The hostile environment my parents arrived in is still active, and will take you out or leave you at the door of no entry.

I soon learned that my home language should be reserved for close friends of a similar background.

To release the hurt inside me, the pain caused by your action and the generation of folk like you is a task. The question is how do you let it go? How to keep it inside is what Black people are good at. But it always comes out. In mental health, in the sickness of the body.

When writing this letter, I saw my dead granny's pretty face, her voice resonating with words of politeness, dignity and Black Caribbean respect. Granny taught me to write my first letter, as a child. She told me to keep a journal of my emotions to release on page.

I wish you could see my teeth clenched, hands gripping pen, body shaking, as I open up this letter, with Granny's teaching . . .

I trust you are well; I hope when these few words reach you, they find you in good health.

Yes, my dear, the start of any letter of intent, so open it with good health and wellbeing.

BUT there are things unspoken in the body that are not filled with wellness or good health. They are stored in the back of the mind. We seek self-permission to offload, with fear of being deemed uncaring or complicit.

My body wrote these words to release the pressure rising slowly out of my older head of sense and sensibility. The soul never gives up. It's natural to swallow pride to find the goodness in a person. But to hold you as a friend means you control the relationship.

There would be limitations for growth and honesty.

There's a lot of shit Black folk can't always explain or say out loud. It's worse if you are Black and female; worse if you are dealing with a sensitive white person who struggles with the truth. The truth is, we have longed to see our efforts change the fabric of an unkind society. All the marching, all the protesting, all the debates, all the loss of life, and still here we are lacking recognition.

My question is: do you even see yourself; do you see how you let off steam, as a means of expression? With a half-hearted apology. It is more painful to watch this play out in the midst of your loudness, your anger, your willingness to shut down others by burying their voice.

You and so many others add to the collective trauma of Black bodies, Black girls' pain, girls who become women. There are women who carry the past, tangled inside their bodies. There are some more fortunate than others who have found the path to shake it like a rotten apple. They have reached self-actualization, to know it's not a chip they carry on their shoulder, or a disjointed failure to articulate what racism is. It's not hated for self-worth. We, Black women, understand our worth; we understand we live in the shadow of a colonized society, built on abuse and stolen wealth. We understand standing up to call it out takes courage. We understand change must come from where it began.

AFFIRMATION FOR THE DAY

Remember it is not the knock down,
rather how I get up

before leaving my home,
remember the road is long,

so, I walk with goodness of my upbringing,
I walk with the old ones,

I walk in all my power,
I walk with self-actualization
of my daily life

I anchor my feet to earth, lift
head to the sky

burn sage,
burn frankincense,

perfumed skin in lavender and rosemary,
oil my crown – from head to toes,

I say speak
queen,

I say the love of
Black womanhood

is magic,
it's ritual.

Recite affirmation of self-worth,
affirm self-worth,

anchor feet to earth, straighten back.

JOURNAL ENTRY REALITY SPEAKS

Prepare, prepare,

to be the only Black woman
round the meeting table,

gate keepers
of your voices.

Prepare to be the only Black woman
in the workplace.

Prepare for the name-calling.
Prepare for the Black jokes.
Prepare for your hair to be touched;

your body is a museum.
Prepare for your body to be touched.
Prepare for it to be brushed off.
Prepare for so-called harmless fun.

Prepare, prepare yourself girl.
Prepare yourself Black woman.

Prepare for the tokenistic gestures.
Prepare for white tears.

Prepare to not get certain jobs
because of your skin,
your hair.

Prepare not to get that job again
because of your skin,
your hair.

Prepare not to get that job again
because
you're too confident,
you look suspicious,
stopped and searched,
questioned
again, and again.

Go home,
don't get upset,
don't cry, don't get angry,
don't show your depression,
don't explain it,

don't show your depression,
don't explain it,
don't show your depression,
don't explain it,

anchor your feet to earth,
say a prayer,
God or some being will bless you
in the next world,

go to sleep,
get up,
prepare your invisible armour.

You see it's not the knock down,
you get it's how you get up!

JOURNAL NOTES

Today was like any other day – you're late for work again – unprepared. You laugh and say, 'You know how it goes. We can just pretend to do the work.'

Unfortunately, I can't pretend. I actually enjoy what I do and a repeat of your behaviour is part of what makes it difficult to achieve the quality of work I pride myself in.

If it is unsaid, it remains with me. But know that these words on the page do more for you than they do for me. If you can sit still for a moment, think beyond these words to be part of the change in culture.

These words educate you and traumatize me, since I've tried to leave you behind. I've spent hours writing and thinking of ways I can walk away from the story, to the point where I can say:

I've found ways to just switch off and turn up the sound of my consciousness – the joy of knowing Black is so beautiful.

It's forgiving, it's faith, it's spiritual, it's the blues, it's jazz. It's Marley's 'Exodus', 'movement of Jah people'. It's Dennis Brown's 'Promised Land', it's deep roots and culture, it's Jean 'Binta' Breeze, it's Nannie of the Maroons.

It's Rita Marley, it's Grace Jones. Black sings a better tune. It's a drum, it's steel pan, it sounds so sweet, it's ancestral.

I've got things to do.

Hi

Hey

Hello

I write this to you to let you know I occupy my own space. A space that celebrates me and my work, with no obstacles or conditions. I write this because I am in charge of my narrative, a narrative that speaks to me and is filled with optimizing. I write these words to you because I'm done with spitting feathers like stones, turning bad words in the pit of my belly; to stop my corn toe from burning me.

One thing for sure, writing to you wasn't easy. This letter may upset you, but when all is said and done, you will realize this letter is about hope for the future. This letter is about making a change through collective thought. This letter is about unearthing the real issues that trickles into the wider society.

I write this because I noticed that after your last verbal abuse, you took it upon yourself to evaluate me and edit my work ethic with two other white colleagues. You thought it was a good thing to deem me sensitive. Sensitive because I refuse to engage with your behaviour. Debbie saw it all. She kept saying to me 'I act too Black'.

Too Black! She's editing me again because society edits her; she thinks it's normal.

I asked her, if she thinks folk should be in charge of how a person should act, think and speak. A woman can't be free to be who she wants to be? That day I decided I was not answering another question.

I want to tell you that I'm done with stupid questions, with folk who think they have the right to gatekeep me.

Some don't get it or hear anything; some are like zombies, just like Fela Kuti said in his song: zombie turn left if you tell it to, just stuck in the shit of it.

My grandmother used to say, those who have ears to hear, let him hear; those who have a nose, let them smell. Smells like rain coming. And I've got stuff to do.

'When I was invited to contribute to the MWBF commission, I knew it would exercise and challenge [white] fragility – since it isn't an easy topic to approach. The creative process is culturally sensitive, thought provoking – at times [triggering] uncomfortable silence – to map out memories contained in the body. I thought of conversations I've not had – to safeguard my wellbeing from micro-aggression or the full-on

backlash that often follows. But here is a space to create [or rant on a page] a space to write out of the consciousness [filled with poems, emotion and intention] to say what Black artists often withhold.'

Khadijah Ibrahiim was born in Leeds, of Jamaican parentage. Educated at the University of Leeds, she is a theatre maker and published writer, who combines interdisciplinary art forms to re-imagine poetry as performance theatre. Hailed as one of Yorkshire's most prolific poets by the BBC, her work appears in university journals and poetry anthologies. Her collection *Another Crossing* was published in 2014. She's toured America, the Caribbean, Africa and Asia. In 2010, she was writer-in-residence at El Gouna, Egypt, and the British Council, South Africa. She was shortlisted for the Jerwood Compton Poetry Fellowship, 2017, 2019, and shortlisted for the 'Sue Ryder Yorkshire Woman of the Year' contribution to the arts.

Khadijah is the artistic director of Leeds Young Authors, the executive producer of the award-winning documentary *We Are Poets*. She was appointed Creative Associate in 2017 for the theatre production *Ode to Leeds* at Leeds Playhouse. She is the writer-in-residence at Leeds Art Gallery 2021.

Her recent work includes: *Dead and Wake*, Opera North 2020; *Resonance and Connecting Voices*, Leeds Playhouse with DJ NikNak; *The Promise of a Garden*, associate director with the Performance Ensemble; *Sorrel & Black Cake* writer and director with the Geraldine Connor Foundation. *Symphonic Dancers*, writer and poet for Phoenix Dance, and the recipient of Arts Council England Developing Your Creative Practice funding 2019.

KIARA MOHAMED AMIN

NOTE: Where the directions are in italic, please don't read them, do them.

LETTER 1

This is a series of letters an orphaned trans son wrote to his dead mother. A request from Kiara. Can all Black trans and gender non-conforming people feel free to move forward. Then white trans and queer people, everyone else, drop to the back. You may have an affirmation letter, handwritten and waxed sealed that was handed out when you came in, this is from Kiara to you. May the words hold you close and may they spark an emotion that you want to continue feeling in your everyday life.

To open this evening I'm going to perform Emotional Freedom Technique. I'm going to be tapping energy hot spots around my body and I will be saying phrases. They go from negative to positive, we're going to take Kiara's limited beliefs, maybe some of them are yours too, and reframe them. I will then ask you to perform them with me.

While tapping the pressure points, say the following statements at the same time. You will be tapping for however long it takes to say the limiting beliefs.

1 With four fingers on one hand, tap the karate chop point on your other hand. The karate chop point is on the outer edge of the hand, on the opposite side from the thumb.

Even though I feel worthless, I deeply and completely accept myself.

2 Use two fingers to tap the inner edges of the eyebrows, closest to the bridge of the nose.

Even though I feel dysphoric, I deeply and completely accept myself.

3 Use two fingers to tap the hard area between the eye and the temple. Feel out this area gently so you don't poke yourself in the eye.

Even though I feel talentless, I deeply and completely accept myself.

4 Use two fingers to tap the hard area under the eye that merges with the cheekbone.

Even though I feel unlovable, I deeply and completely accept myself.

5 Use two fingers to tap the point centred between the bottom of the nose and the upper lip. This is under the nose.

Even though I feel that I am not okay, I deeply and completely accept myself.

6 Use two fingers to tap the area centred between the bottom of the lower lip and the chin.

Even though I believe that I don't belong, I deeply and completely accept myself.

7 Tap just below the hard ridge of your collarbone with four fingers.

Even though I feel afraid, I am releasing this feeling, as I deeply and completely accept myself.

8 Use four fingers to tap on your side, about four inches beneath the armpit.

Even though I deny my truth to get my needs met, I deeply and completely accept myself.

9 With an open palm, tap the top of your head.

Even though I feel like a burden, I am choosing to let it go, as I deeply and completely accept myself.

Address the audience.

So everyone, please copy what I do and repeat the statements with me.

Please give pauses to allow the audience time as they repeat with you.

1 With four fingers on one hand, tap the karate chop point on your other hand. The karate chop point is on the outer edge of the hand, on the opposite side from the thumb.

Even though I feel worthless, I deeply and completely accept myself.

2 Use two fingers to tap the inner edges of the eyebrows, closest to the bridge of the nose.

Even though I feel dysphoric, I deeply and completely accept myself.

3 Use two fingers to tap the hard area between the eye and the temple. Feel out this area gently so you don't poke yourself in the eye.

Even though I feel talentless, I deeply and completely accept myself.

4 Use two fingers to tap the hard area under the eye that merges with the cheekbone.

Even though I feel unlovable, I deeply and completely accept myself.

5 Use two fingers to tap the point centred between the bottom of the nose and the upper lip. This is under the nose.

Even though I feel that I am not okay, I deeply and completely accept myself.

6 Use two fingers to tap the area centred between the bottom of the lower lip and the chin.

Even though I believe that I don't belong, I deeply and completely accept myself.

7 Tap just below the hard ridge of your collarbone with four fingers.

Even though I feel afraid, I am releasing this feeling, as I deeply and completely accept myself.

8 Use four fingers to tap on your side, about four inches beneath the armpit.

Even though I deny my truth to get my needs met, I deeply and completely accept myself.

9 With an open palm, tap the top of your head.

Even though I feel like a burden, I am choosing to let it go, as I deeply and completely accept myself.

Now that we have tapped out the limiting beliefs and core issues, we will now continue to tap and reframe them. We will be tapping for however long it takes to say the affirmations, just like before.

1 With four fingers on one hand, tap the Karate Chop point on your other hand. The Karate Chop point is on the outer edge of the hand, on the opposite side from the thumb.

I am worthy of love and I love myself.

2 Use two fingers to tap the inner edges of the eyebrows, closest to the bridge of the nose.

I will feel gender euphoria.

3 Use two fingers to tap the hard area between the eye and the temple.

I am talented.

4 Use two fingers to tap the hard area under the eye that merges with the cheekbone.

I am lovable.

5 Use two fingers to tap the point centred between the bottom of the nose and the upper lip.

I am doing the best that I can.

6 This point follows symmetrically with the previous one, and is centred between the bottom of the lower lip and the chin.

I belong with the ancestors and my chosen family.

7 Tap just below the hard ridge of your collarbone with four fingers.

I am brave.

8 Use four fingers to tap on your side, about four inches beneath the armpit.

I am not difficult to love and I end relationships that cannot be healthy.

9 With an open palm, tap the top of your head.

I am not a burden.

Allow the audience and yourself to bask in these affirmations for a few moments.

Please open the next letter, marked 2.

LETTER 2

14 February 2020

Dear hooyo,

I am dying.

Pause. Take a deep breath and breathe out slowly. Look into the audience.

I wonder, if you were here, what would you say about my life? Would you have been proud of me? The child you carried and gave birth to by the sea in Kismayo, the water being the first witness to my life. Grandmother told me that you were high when I was born and for a few seconds, no one realized I had entered the realm of the living. Well, no one but the ocean, the sea gulls and the stars.

Sigh.

I never really think of you. I never had to, you gave me up and all I knew was someone else. Today I was told that I'm dying and my first thought after my children was you. I wondered, what do I have of you that is me? They say I have your smile, the tooth gap to go with it too. The skin you helped drape over my bones. The hair you gave me as roots to my home. Who would I have been if I was loved by you, hooyo? And whose wild untamed camel spirit do I possess? Is it yours?

But that doesn't matter now. Growing up I was a pressed flower; completely flattened down, drained from nourishment, lost between thick pages of a book no one cared to read or remember. Sometimes I'd fancy that you knew the child you gendered a girl was actually in fact, a boy. And that perhaps you gave me away to protect me from my father. A man who was so violent, living with him was like living under Mount Vesuvius; never really knowing when you will all be consumed by the rain of molten fists.

The last time we spoke you left me with a prayer. From your lips to God's ears, and I really hoped She was not listening that day. You told me that you hoped that my life would fall apart. That I was not worthy of love and that I was as forgettable as a dried mango left in the sun. You were so angry that I chose myself over the family that refused to choose me. I paused to let you say all this and then I replied, 'this is not my fault'.

Please open the next letter, marked 3.

LETTER 3

17 April 2020

Hooyo macan,

Waxa idirtay ina duufaan ikoriso. Dibato badan aya soo maray. Habarkaga uu Shaqeeyay. Wali Maxa maqla adigo igu wacayo khanis oo idahayo waliga hoor maar magaridontid. Wax lagu qoslo Maxa eh hada majogtid sida igu caynlehed labeb-nimadeda. Zaaid Aa Ujeclan lehed taas. Nasib daro maxa eh awodeda weyn aa wax yaar umalese.

Please open the next letter, marked 4.

LETTER 4

26 May 2020

Dear hooyo,

I turned thirty yesterday and . . . it felt like it was the last birthday. Is this what you meant by you hoped my life would fall apart?

The doctor confirmed for the second time that I'm very unwell. I was told the cancer had spread throughout my spine. Yesterday I saw George pass away. We all did. I'm numb. I cried myself to sleep and I whispered a prayer;

Water and wind
Oceans and land
Fuelled by heat of the Sun
May the ancestors continue to protect all Black lives.

Pause. Take a deep breath, breathe out slowly. Look into the audience.

Who would I have been if I was loved by you?

Please open the next letter, marked 5.

LETTER 5

15 June 2020

Dear hooyo,

I feel like I'm wasting away. I'm unable to go to the bathroom without any help. I am in so much pain that I wish I was dead already. When I'm swimming between consciousness and unconsciousness, I try and remember what you look like. And I have questions. So many questions. That I had hoped to one day ask you. And yes I'm angry, how dare you die before I stood before you, as your son and not your daughter?

But my first question would've been: when you gave me up to be raised by a woman who made it her life's work to break me down, bit by bit. An artist really, dedicated to her craft. Did you ever feel guilty? Did you ever stay awake at night and wonder how I was? I think you knew but chose not to do anything about it. Of course you knew. You knew her, you knew what she was like. You and everybody else. Like a branded animal, even my dead name is hers. You knew what she was like and you still gave me to her.

I lay here drifting in and out of consciousness, the sun streaming in and warming one side of my face. I've been told for the second time that I was dying but nothing could be done because all the doctors have been dispatched to deal with the virus. I am just a fragment of myself. And EYE don't care anymore.

Who would I have been if I was loved by you, hooyo?

Please open the next letter, marked 6.

LETTER 6

23 August 2020

Dear hooyo,

Laugh out loud. Like you heard the funniest joke.

I am dying.

Continue to laugh until it fades away, your face dropping.

Pause. Take a deep breath. Look into the audience.

I've been told my liver is failing, I'm having cognitive issues and I feel like a rubber toy left out in the summer sun; limbs stringy, a fragile mollified sack of bones. Today I called my friends to ask them if they can continue to extend their friendship to my children when I'm gone. I sat the children's other dad down and spoke about how I wanted to be cremated and how I'd like our babies to be raised. It seems death is all around us, and of course it is a part of life but no one likes to talk about death. No one wants to talk about a life that you are not part of. It's uncomfortable, I get it. But I have so little control and talking about a life without me in it gives me a sense of control. And besides, Death and I know one another intimately, her and I go way back. We have tangoed many times and each time she stroked my cheek and said, 'not today, but I'll be back'. So I am not afraid of her.

And you, hooyo. During all of this, you are at the back of my mind. My therapist told me that compassion only happens when we feel safe and I have worked so hard to have the life that I do now. To have the luxury to feel safe in my own home. And so because of this, I have compassion for you. Begrudgingly. You're just another person stuck in the cyclical trauma, passed generations to another and you were so deeply entrenched that you could not see your own suffering.

In all the years I had left home because I refused to bow down to tradition, I spent a lot of time in my soul garden. My garden was neglected and infected with shame. I dug out the shame, carefully, so that it did not crumble and seep back into the soil. I cut away the bramble and dug deep in that garden. I found a little boy who was afraid. I recognized him, I had named him Kiara when I was fourteen years old. I held him and told him, just like the moon, pain had many faces but he was safe now. I planted seeds of love in that garden. It took seed and bloomed into my children. Children who know they are entitled to love, that they are special and their job is not to make me happy.

And even though I may be disowned from my family, I am not disowned from my ancestors. They are here, guiding me, giving me comfort and strength. I cannot be disowned from where I come from, despite anyone's best efforts. I see myself for who I truly am, a man who is whole, loving and kind.

Please open the next letter, marked 7.

LETTER 7

28 September 2020

Dear hooyo,

Guess what?! I'm getting better! I've gone through treatment, Alhamdulillah, I am getting better. I was dying – just not from the cancer! And I was so afraid. I really had picked out my funeral roses, I went to the florists to buy them myself! When a friend asked me what the flowers were for, I simply replied, 'for the funeral' and laughed. They didn't think it was funny. Best of all I can say to you, that you were wrong.

Talking to you during a time that I would have needed my mother the most made me realize that I actually didn't really need you. I became the parent I never had, like most queer Black children. I became the love I never had and gave that freely to my children and my chosen family. Someone I love told me that we enter this world through portals and our portals are our first wounds, the ones we endure in order to be here. And those wounds are just the starting point, it does not define us. And so we must create new portals, ones that help us grow and help us come back to ourselves. In our language the word to describe becoming is actually the same as returning. In order for us to become ourselves, we are undertaking the act of returning to ourselves. Wahan raba unnoqdo aniga nafteda.

Wahan raba unnoqdo aniga nafteda.

Wahan raba unnoqdo aniga nafteda.

Pause. Take a deep breath, let it out slowly.

I realized the greatest gift you gave me was giving me up. Letting go of me brought me closer to myself, I see that now.

I would often wish you were the alchemist I needed, to alchemize your heart in order to help your children grow into adults who knew they were loved, protected and wanted. But you didn't. I would go around in circles asking myself 'why?'

Why?

Pause.

Why?

Maybe in this long line of ancestral trauma I am the alchemist and my purpose in life is to alchemize my heart in order for my children and future generations not to have to contend with healing pain passed on. And give them the gift of focusing on their joy. What a luxury it must be to be focused on all the things that bring you joy as a child and then as an adult.

Who would I have been if I was loved by you? The answer is complex but I don't think I would have become myself or returned to myself. I would have been another chain link to the trauma, possibly passing it on. Where you meet yourself is as important as when you were born. I met myself fully during a time that I was preparing to die and learned that the biggest gift that I could give myself is the acceptance that I craved from others. I reflect the light that was not shone on me. I am worthy of love. I am worthy of love. I am worthy of love and I love myself.

Kiara Mohamed

Kiara Mohamed Amin (*b*. 1990) is a trans, Somali multidisciplinary artist based in Toxteth, Liverpool. His work focuses on identity, social issues and the role art plays in our lives in addressing these issues. He uses different mediums to explore inter-generational trauma and the community he lives in. His work has been screened at Tate Liverpool and the British Museum, with his most recent solo exhibition at FACT.

NOTE: Actions in italic are an invitation. Please do not read them aloud.

There is a pot of camomile tea on the table. Please feel free to have a seat and to help yourself to a cup before you start reading.

There is a jacket that you can put on if you wish.

There is also a small package on the table. Please do not open this yet.

Greetings Mr Sausman

I hope all is well with you and things are good. You may or may not remember I, but I was a student of yours in Arundel Comprehensive School in Liverpool, during the early to mid-1970s. I was in your history class. I remember you being quite strict, shouting at students, threatening to punish us for minor classroom misdemeanours, belittling us, all of which was common back then. I am sure it still happens today.

I remember in one of your lessons we were studying the Tudors. You gave us a whole heap of facts about the Tudors, then set us some work to do on the subject. Two minutes in and Ronald Lashley put his hand up and said 'Sir, me pen's ran out.' To which you replied, 'Well run after it, boy!' Next thing you know, Ronnie jumped up from his chair, rushed to the classroom door, opened it and ran down the corridor. You walked over to the open door, looked out left then right, walked back to your desk and said, 'That boy is in big trouble.' A few minutes later Ronnie returned to the room panting as if out of breath and said, 'I couldn't catch it, Sir. It got away.' Everyone in the class just bust out inna some big belly laughing. The laughter rang out around the room like a fire alarm. One youth even fell off his chair holding his belly. It was so funny, unforgettable, classic. You were not amused. In a rage you shouted, 'Get to Ms Cope's office. Now!' Ronnie still chuckling went to the Head's office. We were still in bulk, cracking up with laughter. You gave us a roasting and we continued with our work. At break time we were all buzzing about you and Ronnie. Wicked!!!

You're probably wondering who I am? Well I am Levi Tafari, a crucial, rhythmic, poetic, consciousness raiser and Urban Griot. A griot is a storyteller, musician, poet, historian, social commentator and a nomadic narrator from the African continent. I am an urban equivalent. I bet you didn't think anyone from Arundel could be so many things. To add to that list, I am also a qualified chef. I studied classical French cuisine at college and passed with a distinction, yes a distinction. Continue when your head stops spinning.

But you would not have known I as Levi Tafari at school, as that was a different time and a different life. I was captain of the school basketball team, I also played for Liverpool Boys Basketball Team. I was good at debating in class and very talkative. You would always tell I to stop talking and get on with my work. I was popular in class and would sometimes fool around which would irritate you. Also Ronny and I started a school disco at lunch time when the school was on a lunch time curfew after a serious incident with another school, concerning some of the girls from our school and the girls form St Cath's. You might remember our Posse of Ron Lashley, Allan Shang, Jackie Wilkie, Stephen Davies, Adrian Devers and Stephen Morgan.

If you remember the incident with Ronnie you will know which class I was in. Yes, Form 51, that's right. Like most of the other classes across the school the makeup of the classes were very diverse and multi-cultural. Youth with heritages from all around the globe. Youths from the Caribbean like Ronnie and I, born here in Britain with Caribbean parentage. Youths from West Africa, East African youths, the Middle East and North Africa, youths from India, Pakistan, Bangladesh, East Asia, Europe and Ireland. A few white British youths too.

You never revealed your heritage, although it was plain to see your heritage was East Asian, even your accent revealed that. Although when you spoke, you spoke with Received Pronunciation. I don't think you were ashamed of being East Asian. You always dressed very smartly in tweed jackets, dicky bows or ties and slacks as if you were a university lecturer. You tried to run jokes with us, but usually they weren't funny, not like other teachers in the school or the Ronnie incident.

The Black youths in our class were fed up of learning about the Tudors and the Second World War amongst other historic events, as those chapters of history did not appear relevant to I and I. We were never represented. There was never any mention of Black people making a contribution in any of these historical events. It's as if we were invisible, absent, non-existent. So we found the lessons boring, apart from when Henry VIII was beheading his wives.

Isn't it funny that I and I as Black youths were vilified and accused of being vicious and violent, and here's the king of England ordering the execution of two of his wives.

As a result of the white washing of history, a group of us Black youths decided that we wanted to cover Black history in your history class. Now between us, we knew a few things about Caribbean history, African American history and a bit about West Africa, but we were hungry for more as it would give us pride and empowerment, also to show our white peers that as Black people, we contributed to society making a major contribution to popular culture. We have had a huge impact on civilization and have major achievements to be proud of in this human story, we refer to as life. So one day when we were in your class, I raised my hand to get your attention. You asked I, if you could help me and I responded with, 'Can we do a lesson on Black History, Sir?' You looked bemused and calmly said:

'There is no such thing as Black history.'

Then you laughed.

I said 'There is, Sir. My parents are from Jamaica, and they talk about Marcus Garvey, Mary Seacole, Nanny of the Maroons, plus there is Bob Marley.' I remember you dismissing my whole reasoning.

I continued, mentioning Malcolm X, Dr Martin Luther King Jr, the Black Panthers, George Jackson, Angela Davis and the Civil Rights Movement. You then mentioned the Transatlantic Slave Trade. 'The Transatlantic Slave Trade is not Black History,' I said, 'It's White History that impacted on Black people.'

Again you dismissed my reasoning and accused I of insubordination and threatened I with a detention after school. The other Black youths in the class tried to back me up and some of the white youth in the class started jeering I and I. It caused a little tension in the class, which you quickly extinguished by shouting for order in the classroom. It was all over in a matter of minutes and the lesson resumed as if nothing had happened. Your response was cold and calculated.

I don't know whether or not you realize it, but at that moment you had further relegated I and I as Black youths in your class to nothing as if I and I didn't matter. To say there is no such thing as Black history is to suggest that I and I don't exist. Everyone on this planet has a history, a story to tell. Every culture, civilization and society on mother earth has a story to tell. So to suggest that Black people don't have a story to tell is damn right backward and ignorant. In fact it is contemptuous and outright scandalous.

Marcus Garvey, whom was a Jamaican political activist, publisher, journalist, entrepreneur orator and pan Africanist, created the U, N, I, A, which is the Universal Negro Improvement Association, which had over 11 million followers in the USA alone and members across the African and Caribbean diasporas in the early twentieth century. Garvey made Black people around the world feel empowered and gave us pride in ourselves. Malcolm X and Dr Martin Luther King Jr fathers were both Garveyites. They embraced his philosophies and opinions, that I and I as Black people should rise up and take our rightful place as the mothers and fathers of civilization and mothers and fathers of the human family. We now know life started in Africa, the cradle of life and civilization. Marcus Garvey said and pronounced many things, but one of the most important things Marcus said was as follows.

'A people without any knowledge of their past history, origins or culture is like a tree without roots.'

I'll quote him again so it sinks in.

'A people without the knowledge of their past history, origins or culture is like a tree without roots.'

Now I and I know that a tree without roots is dead or non-existent, caput!

So for you to inform us that there is no Black history is to say I and I is dead, a duppy, and even a duppy has a history, it was alive at one time. You couldn't even afford us a duppy history. You just dissed us in front of the whole class. Scandalous for real.

You didn't even try to humour us or engage us by saying, 'what would you like me to cover?' Or 'I will look into it and see what I can do.' Or 'I'll get back to you on that one.'

Now if I had asked you where do unicorns come from? and you said, There is no such thing as unicorns, I could overstand, that is understand to you with a Rastafari twist. You overs? Because you didn't overs when I asked about Black history.

You could of even said it isn't on the curriculum. Maybe you were unable to cover it as you didn't have any knowledge on the subject. I don't know. All I know is, you accused I and I of insubordination and threatened I and I with a detention. We could of even looked at Black history in Liverpool. Last year Liverpool's Black history group laid a flagstone for the first recorded African buried in Liverpool dated 1711 and no, that is not the time on a digital clock. The Irish community didn't arrive until 1848 during the potato famine, the Chinese community settled around 1895. As you can see, an African community has existed here at least a century and a half longer than the others that Liverpudlians always boast about, having the eldest.

We could have covered people like Charles Wotten, a Bermudian seafarer, whom was murdered by a 2,000-strong mob and thrown into the River Mersey during the 1919 race riots. There was an educational centre named in his honour that helped members of the Black community to go on to further education and then university.

Then there's James Clarke, a true hero. He was a legendary swimmer from Georgetown in what was then known as British Guyana, now known as Guyana.

James Clarke won many swimming competitions and saved the lives of many Scousers who would fall in the River Mersey after a good night on the ale.

He taught young people to swim and achieved many feats. There is a street named after James Clarke in Liverpool 8.

Also I have to give mention to John Archer, London's first Black mayor. He was born and raised in Liverpool. John Archer was a politician. He was a founding member of the Labour Party. He is most famous for becoming the first Black mayor of Battersea, London in 1913. His father was a Bajan ship's steward and his mother was Irish. Mr Archer was a pan-Africanist and founded the African Progress Union.

I could go on and on and on and on.

Even when we studied the Tudors, there was no mention of John Blanke, an African musician, whom was a royal trumpeter in Henry VIII court. He was present on the royal tapestry at the time. And when we covered the 'so called' great wars, it was painted all white. There were no mention of any Black soldiers fighting for Britain against the enemy. We know now that there were African, Caribbean and Asian soldiers whom played an active part in defeating the Nazis and Fascism.

I often wonder what your thoughts were when you had time to process the question of teaching Black history in school. As a teacher, did you not feel it was your duty to teach a comprehensive account of history in the classroom?

Arundel was a comprehensive school after all. You missed an opportunity, not only to cover Black history but local Black history.

I often wonder if, as an East Asian man living in Britain in the 1970s, if you had experienced racism, xenophobia or discrimination of any kind, from the staff and students at school or the wider British society?

You might not have had a drink for a while, take a moment to have a break and have a sip.

I know there was racism in school from some of the staff and students. It was a constant battle dealing with racist characters. Also to compound things I and I have had to deal with racism on the streets, where skinheads would attack I and I chanting racist songs and throwing stones.

I remember I earned a place to play in the Liverpool Boys Basketball Team.

I played three games for the team, we won all three games. We used to train in Anfield Comp at the time, and word must have got out that there was a Black youth training with the team. The following week, there was a group of skinheads waiting outside the school for me with Stanley knives and chains. I explained the situation to our team coach, whom dismissed my claims and informed I that practice was over and he was no longer responsible for my wellbeing. Luckily the school caretaker overheard our conversation and walked with I to the bus stop. I got the bus home to safety and never went back to practice again.

Who knows what might of been if I had continued playing basketball, for Liverpool Boys. It's crazy, here I am representing my city in a sport I love, and I had to give it up because of small-minded racist thugs.

There are two sides to every coin right! So on the other side of the coin, there were teachers, like Mr Thompson, Mr Rennard and Mr Casey whom were the complete opposite. Mr Thompson, Ibrahim Thompson, who organized a field trip for a group of us students to go and see the Great Bob Marley and the Wailers in concert in Manchester in 1976. The trip was organized at school, at we the students' request. For I personally the concert was a life-changing experience. At that point I embraced the Rastafari way of life and have never looked back. Rastafari has given I fulfilment in life, pride in self and a foundation on how to live my life. Give thanks to Ibrahim Thompson.

Please continue to read the rest of the letter standing up.

It was John Rennard, whom encouraged I to trial for the Liverpool Boys Basketball Team. John was cool, I and I could have a laugh with him. He would motivate I and I. He would tell I and I to believe in ourselves. He was on point. Give thanks to John Rennard.

Peter Casey was passionate about drama and he shared that passion with us, his students. He would always engage I and I in his lessons, so much so that he created a play for us to tour around schools in Liverpool and Manchester. The play was called the *Grimbarian*. The script was, a monster, the Grimbarian, who would terrorize a village every night, so the villagers recruited the help of three superheroes of which Kwaku Anansi the African trickster spider was one, along with St George and Davy Crockett. You see Peter Casey included some African folk tale into his play, so I and I felt represented. I played the wizard and storyteller in the play. The tour was a success and we were all riding on cloud nine. Give thanks to Peter Casey.

Do you get my drift?

By the way a 'Grimbarian' is someone from Grimsby. Isn't that crazy. No offence Grimsby!

It was those experiences with Ibrahim, John and Peter that inspired and influenced I, to become a writer and performer. Seeing Bob Marley and being empowered by his words and music, the storytelling of the African oral tradition. Along with my cultural experience at home, yard style living (that's Jamaican style to you). In the seventies my heroes were Mohammad Ali and Pele, the two greatest sports personalities ever. James Brown, soul brother number one, whom said, 'Say it loud, I'm Black and I'm proud.' I and I would sing that song all the time with raised fist, Black Panther style. Isn't it funny that we were told Black people didn't have a soul. It's funny because we created Soul music, we eat Soul food and we produced soul brothers and sisters.

The style of poetry that I perform is 'Dub Poetry'. It is poetry based on a reggae rhythm. Through dub poetry, I have become good friends with the great Linton Kwesi Johnson, Benjamin Zephaniah and the powerful sister Jean Binta Breeze, whom passed away recently in Jamaica.

You see, my poetry has enabled I to travel extensively around the world, soaking up cultures and histories from far flung places, that I never dreamed I would visit when I was in your class. I now have an eclectic taste for culture which is born out of my work and my travels. I always had a yearning for travel from an early age. That's why I studied to be a chef, so I could travel. People have to eat all over the world. Life is so funny, that it wasn't cooking that enabled I to travel, but my writing.

As a writer, I am now doing what you could of been doing when you were teaching at Arundel. As well as teaching poetry to students of all ages from primary school through to university I always include elements of Black history and culture. The students love it! Although there are some students whom question, 'Why do we have to study Black history?' My reply to them is this, 'You cannot study British history without Black history. There wouldn't be a Britain, Europe and America without African people. The Western world, kidnapped our people, enslaved them on huge plantations, stole our resources, exploited our labour. Used and abused I and I.'

Africans had great civilizations before Europeans arrived on I and I continent.

Great civilizations like the Kushite Empire, the many kingdoms of Kimet, which everyone knows now as Egypt. Then there is Nubia, the Ghanaian Empire, the Songhai Empire and the Empire of Mali. Which produced the richest man that has ever lived. That man was none other than the great Mansa Musa, the emperor of Mali, whom ruled over his empire from 1312 to 1337 CE. To this day he is still the richest man that has ever lived. And he was African.

He had that much gold that he would give it away like candy to the poor.

He also destabilized many economies across Africa. It would take years for many of them to recover. We could of covered some of these people and historical events in your class, it would've been comprehensive and edifying.

I hope you have learned something from this letter and it has made you think about your response to my question back in the day, those school days when we should of been soaking up as much information to make us whole and visible on the historical tapestry of life.

I will finish with a section of one of my poems that I use in schools to enlighten students concerning African history.

Please read the poem below in a rhythmic rap style. It's okay if it's a bit messy – just do what you can.

This is what the Africans did
Africans created the pyramids
we also built a giant sphinx
with skill and wisdom, it was no jinx
we discovered maths, yes geometry
and excelled in the craft of masonry
We had kings and queens to rule our lands
and armies to stop any invasion.

When the European thought that the earth was square
Black people, we didn't have no fear
we sailed across the seven seas
and left our culture in different countries
we built universities in our lands
we taught the Greek and the Romans
We taught them architecture and astronomy
we gave them medicine to keep them healthy
arts and craft plus literature
these things were part of our culture.

We played music, yes song and dance
in all things we were well advanced
agriculture was no problem
our forefathers had ploughs them help them
in religious matters we didn't lack
because, Christ, Buddha and Muhammad they were Black
we had fine garments to cover our backs
whilst Europeans wore furs and ran around in packs.
Now that is the truth and not just a fact
the first civilization was Black, did you know that?

When you have finished reading this letter, I want you to open the package that arrived with it. It is a copy of one of my books of poetry, Natural Black. *Which this poem is a part of. It is my gift to you, to show I don't harbour any grudges towards you, even though you dissed I in your history class. I hope you get some enlightenment from reading my book.*

'No such thing as Black History?'

I will leave you with this thought.

A month ago, I had the honour of unveiling a statue of Bob Marley on Jamaica Street in Liverpool, commissioned by 'Positive Vibration'. I performed a poem I wrote as a tribute to Bob Marley. Come and join I and I by the statue this weekend, you might learn something from me and I might learn something from you.

That's all for now, take care until next time

Your friendly neighbourhood poet/urban griot

One love, one heart, one destiny, PEACE!!!,

Levi

Please open the package. This is a gift for you to take with you as you leave the stage.

Levi Tafari is a crucial, rhythmic, poetic, consciousness raiser and 'Urban Griot', from Liverpool, England. As a writer and performer Levi has worked locally, nationally and internationally, from Africa to the Caribbean and Europe to America.

Levi has four collections of his poetry published: *Duboetry, Liverpool Experience, Rhyme Don't Pay* and *From the Page to the Stage*. Major recent projects include Poetry Quest, StoreAway, Our Liverpool, Great War to Race Riots, Superheroes and Black Poppies/Black Soldiers (Writing On The Wall). Recent commissions include poems for Sefton Canal and River Trust, The Clatterbridge Cancer Centre and writing and performing in a video for the English Premier League when Liverpool FC won the Premier League.

As a playwright, Levi's plays have been performed at the Unity, the Liverpool Everyman and Playhouse and the Blackheath Theatre in Stafford. He was writer-in-residence at Charles University in Prague and toured the Czech Republic. Levi has also toured Singapore, China, Jordan and has performed in New York and Poetry Expo in Kingston Jamaica. He has worked extensively in television including appearances in *Grange Hill, Blue Peter* and presenting a programme looking at Liverpool's involvement in the trans-atlantic Slave Trade, for CBBC. He also made *The Road to Zion*, a well-received film in Ethiopia about the Rastafari movement, for the BBC.

Levi also works in education, running creative writing workshops in schools, colleges, universities, youth centres, prisons and libraries, and undertaking residencies. He has collaborated extensively with the British Council on flagship education and arts projects BritLit and Inclusion and Diversity In Education (INDIE), which saw Levi working with fifty European schools delivering workshops to young people and sharing his vibrant poetry with the whole school community. He also has worked with the Windows Project for the past forty years delivering poetry and storytelling workshops across the UK, and is currently working with the LFC Foundation on their Mental Health Programme.

Levi Tafari's musical projects include working with Ghanaian drum and dance ensemble, Delado, the Liverpool Philharmonic Orchestra and his very own reggae fusion band, Ministry of Love. He has also played and toured with Urban Strawberry Lunch in the UK, Europe and the Far East. Levi has worked with jazz musician Dennis Rollins. Levi also works with Positive Vibration, Liverpool's Reggae Festival and Reggae Social Events.

Dear White Female Friend,

It is early morning, daylight filters into a canary yellow kitchen.
A white family is gathered around the blue dining-room table.
It is breakfast, the white father pours heaped teaspoons
of white sugar into his black coffee, and the sugar cubes
are yelling *father, father, it is me your daughter,*
stop please father. There is an empty chair between
two brothers and the sugar is screaming *father,*
stop, please, it is me your white daughter and I don't
want to be burnt. I don't want to melt into this black coffee.
I don't want to be Black.
And then my dead aunt is there in the empty chair
reading tea leaves, watching the screaming sugar
cubes, melt in their mugs and the family sipping
and drinking her.
What does it mean I ask my aunt. *Hmmm!* she hums
Hmmm! peering into the teacup, and watching the family
slurping coffee, deaf to the screams
They are drinking her into their body, the way they consume
our Blackness she says. *The way they consume us.*

As I begin the process of writing this letter to you, recurring dreams like these begin
to plague my nights. I ask myself – what is writing this letter unlocking in my
subconscious?

Dear White Female Friend,

This letter is about pure truth talk. I am writing to you to openly dialogue.
I am writing to express my true feelings. I write in an attempt to end
the continuous conditioned silence and suppression that I practise,
in the face of your daily micro-aggressions. The biases you perpetuate
and are wilfully ignorant about.

I write to radically eradicate a silence I have practised to protect my body
and sanity as a Black woman living in Britain.

Dear White Female Friend,

Let me tell you, hon, I will begin this letter several times attempting a dialogue. My
heart seeks to exhume a continuous practice of burying coffins deep into the pit of my
body pregnant with silences. Buried deep within my body, with no tombstones and
engravings.

I begin again – Dear White Female Friend,

I write this letter, black ink on white page, trying to speak my truth to you.
I write to be able to answer you back / to respond / to speak to you anonymously.
As I write I am aware that this anonymity seems a safe space to unpolemically speak to
you, my liberal white woman friend. To speak to you, the woman who inevitably places
me into uncomfortable spaces during some of our interactions. Spaces where I am an
open target for attacks. Spaces where any reaction on my part to your micro-aggressions
is perceived and reacted to as a threat.

I write to you praying that this letter will hopefully be a safe space where I am not
automatically regarded as the initiator or aggressor for speaking my truth to you.

Do you remember being with me on the bus the first time I was spat at?
When the old white man spat at me. It felt as if he had been storing up
that phlegm all day and he hurled it out of his mouth like a missile,
aimed at me, a child in school uniform, and fired. How no one spoke
up on that bus, not even you. All the white women there
and no one said a thing, just watched me, a Black child, wipe
the spit off my face and take the abuse.
And when I said – *you should be ashamed of yourself,*
a big man like you spitting on a little girl like me. How
he abused me – with N-words and *go back homes.*
When I was put off the bus for causing trouble by
you, white woman conductor. You, who stopped
the bus, saying you would not move till I stopped
making trouble. That was the first of many lessons
where I would be attacked verbally or physically
and penalized for it. You refusing to ring the bell,
letting the bus sit there until I got my angry attitude
off that bus. Evicting me instead of him. Although
as the bus stood stationary, he was pelting racist slurs
at me, a child in her school uniform, badge and blazer,
confirming her eleven-year-old status.
Me, this Black child penalized for being spat at
and speaking up. That is when the silencing began.
How many years would I be spat on, in everyday

places, the tube, buses, shops, and no one would
intervene against the white men, group of white
men, lone white man. And when I told you
one day, my white female friend, about
the avalanche of racial attacks, you, white
friend, said – *that seems too much – maybe*
you imagined it, it cannot be that much,
you said. *Britain has changed now,*
you said and I cannot defend myself,
having only the truth of my tongue
and burying this memory in the coffins
in my body. So, I lift my silence around
me like shields. And it is hard to lower
them now.

Dear White Female Friend,

This is not a dream. I write this letter to you as an African Caribbean Black British
woman living in Britain. As a dark-skin, natural-hair sister proud of her history, legacy,
and livity within this system.

After George Floyd's lynching, you requested books and references to enable you to
educate yourself about systemic racism and your own prejudices. But George Floyd
had just been lynched (a massive trigger for me and my Black kin) and there you were
making demands. Asking me/us to make your life easier.

I write this letter to say No! This letter will not be a translation of my experience for
your white body's comfort and convenience. My blood pouring out of scars you and
your country made, for you to suckle or reject. No, no bleeding will happen here. So,
this letter makes no attempt to educate, forgive, placate, or be silenced by you.

There are books out there, why can't you research for yourself? Why rest your burden
for knowledge on my racialized body? Do you realize you are asking me to haul my
hurts and trauma out of the buried coffins within my body, resurrect them and spread
them out on a mortuary table for you to feast yourself into enlightenment at my expense?
The ultimate desecration.

I write not as accusation, or to secure any apologies, as this means nothing and I am
tired of always being labelled victim. I am tired of being made to feel uncomfortable
when

I eloquently articulate my truth.

I write because I want you to know and somehow embody even an inch of the
uncomfortable awkwardness I feel when forced to react to a barrage of micro-
aggressions in order to negotiate every day of my livity in Britain. And each dart
is thrown while dishing out passive-aggressive English attitudes. I write because I am
fed up.

So, I will reiterate here that this letter is not an act of negotiation. No, it is an investment in this durational reading, involving a sustained uncomfortableness I usually endure, like this one:

> I remember the incident in the staff room,
> all the female lecturers in the English
> department sitting in a huge circle,
> talking and eating lunch. I had been
> working in the English department
> for over a year, and usually ate lunch
> in my office. Today as I walk into
> the kitchen to get my packed lunch
> out of the fridge, I see them all
> chatting and laughing. I see
> the white colleague who walked
> in before me, lunch in her hand,
> acknowledged and invited over.
> They all shift their chairs on that
> red carpet for her to join the group.
> I decide to join this lunch sisterhood,
> walk over to the circle, say hi,
> but no one responds. Twenty
> women's backs become hardened
> shields. Ears deaf to my sound.
> I was invisible there. The message
> was clear. And right in that moment,
> I have to decide: do I force my way
> into this circle, to sit and eat in
> awkwardness, or do I go back
> to my office and eat alone. I am
> the only Black woman in this English
> department. The only woman
> of colour in this red carpeted
> room. And as I walk out
> of that staff room, back to my office
> I realize that even though both decisions
> seem like a choice between the rock
> by the cliff and the rock in the sea,
> both decisions are still rocks.

Dear White Woman Friend,

This letter is not written for my redemption or to confess to any deed as I do not need your approval or useless conciliatory attitude. No, I write this letter to excavate my silences, my uncomfortableness, and my toeing the line.

I write this to articulate the many ways you ah bun down the Black skin woman inna Babylon.

I can knowingly tell you that our interactions and transactions are blood sacrifices, where I am constantly the slaughtered 'animal' spread out on the altar – yet no one ever admits to the bloodletting, and you, the perpetrator, arbitrarily deny responsibility.

This letter is me using the Black and white space to traverse a radicalized silence, a self-preservation silence, a violent and uncomfortable silence.

My friend's son had treated his mother
and I to a sauna for her birthday. We open
the door for the sauna. The steam
is blinding; there is one woman
sitting in there; we greet her and I enter
first, spread my towel and sit on it.
My friend, who enters behind me and pulls
the door shut, has locs down to her butt.
We sit a moment in silence, absorbing the heat,
and after a while you white women begin to
ask her about her hair. *Is it real?* you ask.
*Wow, it is long! Do you leave the jewels
in it? How long have you been growing it*?
We answer your questions then float back
into our own talk, before leaning
back into relaxation, steam and sweat.
After a long while you get up, say goodbye
and walk to the door, and only when
my friend's locs bounces back to hit her
thigh do we realize you have been holding
her loc in your hand, and playing with it
since we entered the sauna – our peace is
broken. We dress, shower and leave
immediately. And have not returned
to the sauna since.

Dear White Woman Friend,

You who claim to be liberal, yet remain blind to the inherited biases and racist assumptions used to slice the skin of Black women like me every day, in a competitive spirit that is offensive and subtle – you see skin before gender.

You easily advocate for animal, environmental and feminist rights, but never ally or advocate for and with us Black women. We are never allies and sisters.

There is countless evidence that throughout the history of the feminist movement, we have been trampled in the push for women's rights. We Black women have been made to see that women's rights are white women's rights and white women's concerns.

So interestingly, at intervals during any given day, my body, intellect, or sensibilities are assaulted in ordinary interactions and encounters with you. Or worse, I am rendered invisible.

I am in the post office, at the shop counter
in the queue at the airport, and the person
at the counter says next. The white person
behind me moves forward. *Wait, I am here.*
Can you not see me? No, I did not see you
there, the white person replies.
Once a white man said *Move out*
of my way Black bitch and because for
once I was not silent and refused to move,
he lifted me out of the way and went
to the counter. No one came to my defence.
No one said sorry. I was the only Black
woman in the bank. The server
served him, and when I objected
threatened to call security if I was
not quiet. At the counter, she said,
Sorry about that love; some people
can be so rude. He said he did not
see you there.
Why did you not refuse to serve him?
I asked. *Why did you not threaten*
to call – or actually call – security for him?
I ask. And she shrugs. *It was not worth*
making a scene. She replied.

I must say that one of the beautiful things about Covid was that this state-sanctioned, nationally-imposed retreat enabled my body to have a respite from having to deal with what the poet and author Claudia Rankine termed 'micro aggressions'. It enabled me to understand just how daily such incidences are perpetuated on my body.

Dear White Woman Friend,

Here I am beginning the letter again. I write to tell you how you ah bun down Blackness inna Babylon.

As I write this, I must tell you that my silence is so ingrained.
To talk back has never been my right,
To talk back is to make enemies.
To talk back is to render this body aggressive.
To talk back is to be labelled the angry Black woman.

To talk back is to render this body vulnerable.
To talk back is to threaten this body's job, artistry, ability
    to get more jobs as a freelancer.
To talk back is an act of self-sabotage.

And in another recurring dream the white little girl
in the playground approaches the Black
girl in her classroom / on the playground / at
the bus stop / in the cafeteria – calls her Samantha
then Yinka then Tamara – asks her - why her hair
is so funny, and doesn't care when in reply she flinches,
as if the question were a pitched heavy stone.

Dear White Female Friend,

There is that feeling of a fishbone being shoved down my throat –
how to react in a split decision.
It is as if I am eating several thick, unbuttered slices of hardo bread.
The dry bread pushes the bone down, doing its job slowly.
See, no matter how I react, there is always bruising in my throat,
and I am left with . . .
having swallowed that painful bone again.
So many bones gathering in the coffins within my body.
should haves / could haves / wish I had /
post-mortems dissected again and again.

Dear White Woman Friend,

I must say that I am shocked to find that the writing of this letter has not been as
cathartic as I felt it would be. It is triggering and bloody hard to write. My silence has
built up like limescale.

My Blackness is always a magnet for your fragile, fragile fragility.
There is a rhythm to these acts –
    you insult. I respond. you step back,
        ask – *why are you being so aggressive*?
Then you burst into tears.

I can respond with a soft, modulated voice and you will still cry
as if I have no right to speak back to you / have an opinion
about my body or my Blackness.
And then brap tap / plantation behaviour / you begin to cry /
reprimanding me / for my uppity behaviour.
Aggressive, you state,
I feel threatened, you state,
you are intimidating me, you cry,
you are bullying me, you sniffle into the Kleenex,

shoulders shaking.
All the while crying those white fragile tears.

I am unmoved by your Oscar-winning performance.
But your tears are not for my benefit – it is for the audience.
The spectators.   And boy, do they play their part!
Are you alright? they ask, rushing over / After all / after all / after all –
      you are being threatened   by the angry Black woman.
Or our colleagues rush over,
or the strangers at the bus stop rush over,
assess the scene: a Black woman versus a white woman.
They immediately crowd around you,
white woman – asking if you are alright –
      – patting your body –
      – hugging you –
      – offering tea –
      – offering you a seat –
      – a cup of water –
I try to speak up –   *shush / hush*   I am told
      – *Can't you see she is upset?*
      – *Don't upset her further,* they say,
      – *Can you not see that she is upset?*
      – *Leave it until she calms down –*   they say
and something about your tears ensures
that no one asks what has occurred –
just like that, I am both invisible and victim.

I have moved to the North and now wear earrings
with the slogan **Do touch my fro** on the bus,
in the sauna, on the pavement, in the supermarket,
in Leeds indoor market, on the train –
you white women hold, stroke, pat, grip and
compliment my hair.
When I get cross, you bawl tears and passers-by
rush up to you asking
Love, are you alright?
– what did she do to you?
Hands on my head like I am a pug.

Dear White Female Friend,

I have always wanted to write about the weaponized nature of your tears.
tears protect you / annihilate me.
tears uncomfortable / judging eyes.
tender flesh under my skin/ no chance to heal,
just another burial into the coffin of my body.
bruise scabs / another bruise.

Another dream –

Oh dear! A white woman legal clerk sits on the bus.
The magnificent afro on the woman
in the front seat compels the clerk's fingers
to pull and pat and say, *your hair is so so . . .*
until the Black woman swings her afro around, to glare,
then shouts, *Take your damn hand out of my hair . . .*

the tone slices the white clerk
into tears. Then she is a frog hopping onto
the Black woman's inky afro, all scented and bouncy,
hopping like this is a springy bed.

The aggressive tone slices the clerk,
leaving her a trodden autumn leaf soaked, heavy,
trampled on the ground. Feeling that it is unfair
as she has done nothing wrong.

Does she understand how weighted her rain of tears are?
Does she understand how many white women
have touched the Black women's hair that day alone,
and it is only noon:
the nurse, the elderly woman, the school girl
and this white woman, and that white . . . – all women.
Her rain is a puffed-up cloud of suppression.
Entitlement renders you, white clerk, obese
with those damn weaponized tears.

Dear White Female Friend,

Here everything is a wall
wall off and bruk down
wall up and bruk down,
one second, we coasting as friends
then the next minute scabs
one second, speaking to me pleasantly,
then the next you vex
one second you vex
then next is biblical floods,
then next is pleasant words again.
and I am always left burying more scabs /
second guessing myself /   asking – did I imagine this?
knowing this is white woman psychosis –   this   trapped performance
I am always unwillingly drawn into.

Dear White Woman Friend,

My skin and gender are your scrubbing board, a wooden board with splinters worn down by the knuckles of your palm clenching the untreated cotton, manhandling us both.

This is a letter stating my perception of reality in Britain where micro-aggressions come fast in personalities changeable like the British weather.

Dear White Woman Friend,

I want to let you know that sometimes your privilege is a plague on my soul, your tears and performance an Oscar-awarding act that I am forced to dissect like a social scientist.

You have always denied culpability in your own collusion and position of oppressor,
from plantocracy societies like the Caribbean colonies to present day.
You deny being an enabler, an accomplice, a slave owner, a perpetrator,
and when we view and place this all in the context of colonialism
– you shout *that it was in the past / the past is long dead / was so long ago*, / yet
I can tell you that your racialized thoughts were shaped on the plantation.

I am in the housing office to meet my housing officer.
She is convinced that I am cheating the system
and renting out my flat. Her evidence – *You do not*
have furniture, net curtains, you have clothes
on a clothes rail, she says, *and this is not*
how you people live. I know how you people
live, she tells me. I am doing a show
and with rehearsals cannot deal with this,
so my friend contacts every arts organization
that I work for – the British Council, national
theatres, schools, literature organizations –
and they all send letters stating that this
is the address that I live at. The British
Council verify that the occasions that
I have left the house with a suitcase
have been when I have been working –
travelling for them to work in schools,
universities, and arts organizations
abroad. The BBC verify that they have had
cabs pick me up from that address.
My friend has also gathered newspaper
articles about my plays, and
performances, and books published
both here in the UK and abroad. But
this woman is not convinced.
After the show finishes its season
and tours, I make an appointment.

The white female housing officer sits
in front of me, looking at the massive file
my friend compiled, but not believing. I
hear this, establish this from the tone
of the conversation. She speaks to me
like I am shit. I have never heard the term
'*you people*' sound so stink. Like shit
under her feet. Such scorn. *You liar*
and cheat – I will catch you and evict
you, she tells me.
And all I can reply is that I live there,
I cannot do anything else to prove that
I live there. *You people*, she continues,
like the lowliest swear word.
She leaves the office and I take out a poetry
book to read. When she comes back,
I calmly close the book, place it on the
table between us. *Poetry*, she mutters.
Poetry. Now I know you are trying to fool
me. You people can't do good
in the education system, much less
read, and you are pretending with
a poetry book. You are a liar and a cheat,
she tells me, *and I will prove that you*
don't live there. I will catch you out
and evict you, she tells me,
growing increasingly incensed.
Voice rising, spittle bursting out of her mouth
at my calm. I leave the office bereft.
A passer-by would see a Black woman
walking in the street, bawling into
her mobile phone to her friend.
Remembering the thick file
with her accomplishments
sitting between them on that table
and knowing. No matter what
accomplishments she has, she
will still be a *you people – Black woman.*
The housing officer's performance
was designed to make me angry,
and when I responded with anger
there would have been tears and
I would have been evicted for aggression
against the housing officer. But the bawling,
the emptiness – the toil it takes to stay
calm, to not react and play into her

stereotype. To accept her verbal abuse
in order to keep my house.
The shame and helplessness that I
will bury into the coffin in my body.
And these tears I cry on the street
into the phone are my anguish shared
with my friend alone.

Dear White Woman Friend,

The thing is, we can be friends for years then suddenly   one day I become like *'you people'* –   *'Oh, you are not like those other Black people!'*

Do you remember when I tell you about my experience
with black cabs in the 90s and during the 2000s,
when I would return from visiting my family,
take the Gatwick Express to Victoria Station,
then join the black cab rank, queue up. How
the cabs would not allow me to enter them.
Sometimes I would be there for over an hour,
as they rejected me for the white customer
in the queue. A Black woman saying Brixton
as her destination, rejected. How none
of the other white customers who saw
what was happening would object
or acknowledge. I told you a story,
trying to convince you. *It was late in the night,*
I tell you. *I had come in with my overweight*
suitcases from the Gatwick Express. And no cab
would take me. It was so cold – after Christmas,
it was so dark, and I just wanted to go home. Too
overweight to take the tube and having missed
the last one anyway. One driver returned; he had picked
up a couple before me in the queue, an hour before.
You still here love? he asked me. And when I stated
that none of the black cabs would take me,
he got angry, said he had daughters and would hate
for them to be left in the cold like that, late
at night in January. He apologised on behalf
of his fellow black cab drivers. I tell you the story
white friend and your response was that *Surely*
this could not have happened. Black cabs
would not do that, you said. *That has never*
happened to me, you said; *were you looking rough*?
You asked and once I challenged you – yep, it began
– the tears, the accusations, *you are being aggressive;*

I just stated my opinion. Yep, unexpectedly like that –
over a cup of herbal tea at my kitchen table,
you invalidated my experience, called me a liar
and then made it about you. Because surely,
Britain is not still racist and black cabs would
not behave like that unless something you said
warranted it. Unless something you were wearing
warranted it. I who began to justify myself
and my clothing and attitude. And just like that
our friendship flowed into the volcanic
performance of race.

Dear White Woman Friend,

I had assumed that this letter would be extremely easy to write. But I have found it quite triggering. I realize writing this that in order to deal with life, we as Black women have to push these daily micro-aggressive actions, alongside the corresponding feelings of hurt and betrayal perpetuated upon us by our white female friends, into the deepest recesses of our wombs and that being given permission to write a letter to you and tell you what I have wanted to say means painfully scraping the limestone back.

Wow, this has been a painful birthing – my writing room has become uncomfortable; I am sweating with this unearthing, my belly pains, as I attempt to excavate. As the memories dredge themselves up, I find myself asking – how do we stay sane when most of this racial war is fought within normal everyday settings and affects our psyche so much?

As I sit here writing this letter to you, my friend of over eleven years,
have begun to perform white fragility. You are locking me out of
a house that I asked you to look after. You have changed the locks
and refuse to give me access to my property and when I ask you for it –
you cry saying I am bullying you. You cry saying that this conversation
is causing you anxiety. You try to order me around with regards to
my own house. You damage my property and when asked about it
– you place yourself and your fragility at the centre of the drama
– stating that you are not being acknowledged for the services
you have performed for that house and showing no intention
of reconciling the situation. When I bring it up, your aggression,
the bullying charge is thrown at me, the tears are a waterfall.
And I cannot understand how it has come to this. How overnight
a white woman like you has entitled yourself with my property
and I have to fight you to reclaim it. It is incredulous, the audacity.
And when we speak, you bawl, saying *Can you not see how long
we have been friends and you are treating me like this?*
And I am an animal in her tone of voice, a pug to be patted
and put in my place. The coffin is overcrowded with this one.

Dear White Woman Friend,

There is no reconciling with this letter. It just shows how I continuously turn a corner onto your pot-holed roads. I carry on writing to you, trying to articulate a haunting that comes from living in Britain and our turbulent proximity, Black women to white women.

Sometimes I wonder – when do I get to be the delicate crystal perched on the shelf that can fall and shatter with a little breath? When do I reach the point where the coffins stop getting crammed with the bones of your entitlement? When can I exhume the coffins with ease?

Unreconcilable,

Your Black woman un-friend.

'In social interactions when micro-aggressions occur, the Black body becomes uncomfortable and silenced. Even as Artists we experience racism and are silenced. That silence is damaging to the body, mind, heart and soul. This project feels like an artistic intervention. It provides me as an artist and a Black Caribbean British woman with the opportunity to speak out in a safe way. To hopefully communicate, raise awareness and transform through a frank and open letter. I wanted a chance to speak the things I have never been able to articulate, find the language and hope this reading will be insightful and thought provoking as well as resonate and reflect other people's truths.'

Malika Booker is a poet and theatre maker, who currently lectures at Manchester Metropolitan University. She is a British poet of Guyanese and Grenadian Parentage and the founder of Malika's Poetry Kitchen.

Malika's pamphlet 'Breadfruit' (2007) received a Poetry Society recommendation, and her first poetry collection *Pepper Seed* (2013) was shortlisted for the OCM Bocas prize and the Seamus Heaney Centre 2014 prize for first full collection. She is published with the poets Sharon Olds and Warsan Shire in *The Penguin Modern Poet Series 3: Your Family: Your Body* (2017) and her poem 'Nine Nights', first published in *The Poetry Review* in autumn 2016, was shortlisted for Best Single Poem in the 2017 Forward Prize.

Malika hosts and curates *New Caribbean Voices*, Peepal Tree Press's literary podcast. A cave Canem Fellow, and inaugural Poet-in-Residence at The Royal Shakespeare Company, Malika was awarded the Cholmondeley Award for outstanding contribution to poetry (2019) and won the Forward Poetry Prize for Best Single Poem (2020).

I'm sitting alone on a bench in a busy courtyard. People rushing to and from a ███, wolfing down chips and pizza, wines and pints flowing. The bar is never not busy from the moment it opens in the morning, this is a great spot for people watching. I hold in a laugh when I notice someone apologising to someone who has just walked into them.

I like to find moments of quiet in the middle of crowds. Eavesdropping aside, I'm technically working right now. I've got loads of ███████ in front of me and I'm ████ and ██████, albeit rather leisurely. I assumed that looking busy would mean that nobody would try and speak to me. I can't be bothered with speaking out loud, just for now. A big chunk of my job is talking to people and smiling lots. I've never been here before and to be honest, it's a bit of a weird vibe. All these people, all this hubbub, excitement, tears, laughs, endless queues, flus running rampant, ████ ██████████ so much ████ flying all around us, piles and piles of it. This is no good for the environment.

I see you looking around. You smile in my direction and I act like I haven't noticed you.

Even though it's busy, there's still quite a few empty seats you could have chosen. But you plop yourself down on the one opposite me when you're done waiting for your pizza. I take note of the fact that you don't ask if the seat is empty, you just take it. I can feel you gazing at me while you stuff your food in your mouth. I don't want your eyes to look at me as much as they are. I do not want to catch your gaze in my own. I can't be bothered; I have a feeling that any interaction between us would leave an unsavoury taste in my mouth.

I think I've got one of those faces, it's too friendly. People love to come up to me and tell me whatever nonsense is on their minds. People who look like *you* often want to ask me questions about where I'm *really* from and then refer to the country as Rhodesia. To my face. You do look like . . . a generic colonial man. You look like someone who comes from inherited money.

And you're still looking at me. It feels voyeuristic now. The task I'm carrying out is not that interesting for you to be looking at me for so long. I don't think I could look at someone like this, someone who is clearly doing everything except looking back at me or acknowledging my glance in some way, without worrying that I was making the person uncomfortable. I don't want to know what you're thinking as you look at me. I'm really concerned that you might tell me.

Sometimes, I wish I had a perception filter that I could invoke at will so that certain white people can't see me. If they can't see me, then I don't have to suffer some of the fucking weird interactions I've had to smile through. White men in pubs who are old enough to be my dad, and sometimes even my grandad love love love to go out of their way to tell me that they think I'm beautiful. It makes my skin crawl, it's all in the way they look at you when they say it. Seedy. Creepy.

You finally say 'hello'. I smile and wave. Fuck, why didn't I bring my headphones with me? You ask my name and I notice something spark in your eyes when you hear a foreign word.

I ask you if you're here with a ▮▮▮▮ and you guffaw as if I've just said the most preposterous thing. I should have guessed by your hat; you are the one I was warned about. 'If he starts to speak to you, try and leave as soon as humanely possible,' they said on our training day. A part of it might be morbid curiosity, I'm a nosey fuck and they do say never to judge a book by its cover, right? I forgot for a moment that I'm here for a month, assuming we would only interact once and I'd know why I would want to leave a conversation with you as soon as possible.

I hoped you would eat your pizza and just go about your day when you were done.

I genuinely struggle with walking away from situations I feel uncomfortable in. I'll sit there, rage or fear bubbling away in my stomach but my face will look unperturbed.

'This city is very **white**, isn't it?'

For a split second, I thought you were asking me.

Opening a dialogue.

I thought, finally, someone said it – a bit weird that it's a white man saying it but white people love showing off how 'woke' they are these days.

It's always a bit weird listening to white people complain about white people. Was I about to hear another well-meaning white person go on and on about the racist things 'other' white people do? That's another one I have no idea what to do with. The strange phenomenon of white people telling me about their racist colleagues or grannies, going on and on about how much they can't stand racism. How much they love Black people and foreigners. Almost always unprompted, or maybe my Black face is the prompt and perhaps they want me to know they're not like *those other white people*.

I did kind of hope that maybe I'd get a chance to put into words the displacement I'd been feeling while wandering the pristine, litterless streets of this city. Since this particular bustling chunk of land is yours, I thought maybe you'd be able to explain to me why somewhere that advertises itself as 'intersectional' attracts a vast majority of white audiences from all around the world.

This city is very white. That's a fact. I can't deny that, I obviously have to agree with you. There are so many more people here than there usually are, the streets are heaving with bodies of people who love art and creativity and I don't understand why they're mostly all white.

It's a whiteness that I don't feel so often in Manchester. I do still feel it in Manchester: when I'm in a room full of people and I can count the non-white faces on my eight fingers and two thumbs. It's hard not to feel aware of my Blackness in moments where I'm the only one. It's hard not to wonder who will bring attention to it. How is someone going to point out that I am Other today?

Will it be touching my hair? A curiosity that I thought had died in the age of internet activism and infographics but still catches me out from time to time.

Will it be mistaking me for someone else? I've noticed this one happens a lot in gay clubs.

Will it be just one word? Words are my favourite thing in the world, I know how powerful they are. When they are weaponized, I feel it in my body.

'Yeah, it really is isn –'

'There still aren't many ████████ around. You know, when the ████████ first arrived here, they had to have **respectable** professions – **Doctors** and such, they weren't just letting **anyone** in.'

Of course, it wasn't a question.

This isn't a conversation.

That word. I have no idea how to respond to it. I have never heard anyone say it like that before. It sets off a chemical reaction, the kind you get when you feel like you're under attack.

Technically, it's just saying 'dark skin'.

But the 's' as the end.

And the 'the' at the beginning.

Coming out of *your* mouth.

It feels like the first time someone called me a ████ in primary school and I was the only person who didn't know what it meant.

It's weird having white people explain to you what racism is. How there are words that are created only to be used to express how much you don't like Black people or other people who aren't white. I asked them why.

That's just the way things are. 'Sometimes, people just won't like you and they'll call you names like that. They're racists. And there's nothing you can do about it. It's not your fault you're Black.' It felt unfair. I asked if I could somehow become white so that people won't hate me. They laughed; I think they thought I was joking.

I had just discovered **race**, and I didn't understand how it worked. I'd seen it, obviously I knew people all looked differently but **race** and the idea that not looking white is a bad thing and that people wouldn't like me because of it was a lot to get my head around as an eight-year-old.

I'd like to go back to the moments before that boy said that word, make sure I was somewhere else at that time, so I didn't have to hear it. That moment is just as real as right now, I can see exactly where on the playground we were, so I'd know where not to go.

I know that thinking like that is no use, because I know that someone else would have said it eventually. People still say it to me. I'd like to stop wondering who the next person to spout it will be. Sometimes people say it and it's not *that exact word* but it feels the same.

I sit there, my feet on your land,

Frozen   Black   skin.

There's a lump forming in my throat, it gets bigger and bigger as you keep talking. What am I supposed to say?

I get the impression you've said this before. The words just rolled off your tongue, I think that's just how you talk about Black people, or anyone who has dark skin.

I'm thinking of a million ways to respond, all I want is to get up and walk away. But I feel implored to say something. White men can't be running around saying '██ █████' at all, let alone at Black people. I don't understand how we got here. It's 2019 but surely we know that this is uncouth. Hasn't someone made him do some kind of anti racism training yet?

You haven't noticed that I am yet to say a single word since you said that word, you can't see on my face how many times my mind has flown away from this moment.

I want to get up and leave in the middle of your monologue about this city and its connections to slavery but my feet are stuck to the ground. Frozen.

You're not interested in what I have to say, you want an audience. You've talked about yourself a lot but you haven't asked me any questions. I know what your daughter does for a living, that you've spent a lot of time on 'the continent'.

I can tell you want me to be impressed by you. You happen to drop your 'friend ██████ ███████' into the conversation, you assume a proximity to royalty would make me want to keep talking to you.

I know you. You just want to be seen talking to one of the few Black faces in this very white crowd.

Now, you're telling me all about the house you've just bought in what you call

'Little Lagos'

'You bought a house in Lagos?'

I finally speak, confused and slightly lost. I must have missed a beat; how did we get to Lagos?

Your face lights up.

'No no, *Little* Lagos, can you guess where that is?'

I don't guess. I can feel it, somewhere in the place where my feelings sit that no good can come of this little game of yours, you are far too giddy and excited, I think you're about to say something racist.

'It's in Peckham, London. I call it Little Lagos though, that's what it feels like when you walk around there.' You tell me all about ███████████ of the neighbourhood.

I can tell you think that little quip is hilarious. I assume that it usually gets a laugh when you say it.

and I know I'm right when the next day you ambush a Black feminine friend of mine and she tells me you told her the same little quip while showing her your African masks that you proudly hang on display in your drinking den.

Symbols of spirituality and ritual have no place here. I wonder whose tribe you stole them from. I don't have to ask. You boast about your extensive travels on the continent. You say that 'it's a shame about your country because it's so beautiful, there's so much potential'.

A week later, you come to sit near me while I'm having my lunch. You don't acknowledge me right away. I don't want you to. I bite my lip as I overhear you bring up 'Little Lagos' yet again to another Black Femme. This one's American.

She laughs, she seems to find it funny, she agrees that that's what Peckham feels like. It takes all the power in my body not to throw my chips at both of you. You for being yourself and her for encouraging it and laughing at your racist 'joke'.

I notice your '███████████' phrase didn't find its way into your conversation with her. I wonder who you do and don't say it to. Why am I worthy of that having to hear that term over and over again and not her?

You make a point of finally acknowledging me as you get up to leave. You introduce me to the woman you've been talking to and leave us to chat

and when you've left, she tells me it's great that you know my name, because you are 'a really good person to know'.

You are the owner of land, after all. None of us would be here right now without your money. I Google you as I'm writing this and find that I was right to guess, you have millions. I can't help but laugh at the irony of finding you quoted saying **'We will be defined by what other people say about us.'** The article goes on to say that you generally 'don't reveal very much about yourself'. And I'm kind of stumped. This can't be the same guy but the space you are connected to is the same. You're repeatedly referred to as an 'eccentric millionaire'.

I've always hated those rich people areas where the parks are closed to the general public, and I find out that you are one of the people with a key to a garden I'll never be allowed to see and if I want to do my job, yours is the kind of place where I should want my work to be seen.

You tell me about your South African ex-wife, and how she was 'crazy' and a ██████ too. I don't care enough about you to ask for details that will encourage you to keep talking at me. And I don't want to encourage you to talk shit about someone who is a Black Woman. I want to ban you from talking to or about Black people.

I think at this point you must know I want to leave but you won't stop talking.

You're not finished being seen talking to the ██████

You tell me about your nephews and you call them ██████ too. I wonder if you say this to their face. Is this just the word you use to talk about Blackness? I still want to interject, to tell you that you can just say Black people. I worry that this would only encourage you to say 'Black' with an s at the end instead so I keep my mouth shut.

As the weeks pass, I notice that when you're not talking to white people, you target Black feminine people.

My observation is confirmed on one of my last nights here when you approach me,

Interrupting a conversation I'm having with a friend who is a Black man

You speak at me as usual and don't even look at him.

There's Black Men selling out ██████ on your land and you don't bother to acknowledge them.

They don't even know who you are but any Black feminine person who wanders in simply has to hear your 'joke' about 'Little Lagos'.

It feels personal. It feels like you want me to react in some way, like you want me to be the crazy ██████ screaming and shouting at you in the middle of the courtyard. Why else do you taunt me? I have to assume that these interactions are you trying to get some kind of reaction out of me. Maybe you see that the light is kind of missing from my eyes and you want me to say exactly what is on my mind and not what I think I should say as I wait for this all to be over.

There are some moments of joy. There are lots. If I put all the moments I had in that place together, it wasn't all bad. I didn't need you looming over me waiting to provoke me at any given moment. I made a habit of introducing myself to any Black person I found myself near.

Three Black Femmes sit at a table on your land.

Beautiful dark skin even darker after the sun's kiss,

We are braids and afros dazzling.

You, the landowner, come sauntering over with your beautiful little dog.

We ignore you and fuss over him.

I don't know why you say this, I think it's because we're not paying you any attention but I can't think of an explanation for why the following words leave your mouth:

'I'm sorry that my dog is white.'

The words float in the space between all of us.

Are you using the dog to apologise for your own whiteness? You've managed to piss off all three of us on our individual wanderings on your land. It seems you've come to bother us some more. Why are you obsessed with people who look like us?

Do you want us to comfort you? Laugh with you, tell you it's okay, that we all think you're great etc etc.

Before I even think about what to say in response, I stand and the question leaves my mouth.

'What the fuck does that mean, white man?'

You smile. I think it looks triumphant.

'What the fuck are you smiling for?'

You tell me that you're only joking.

'Well I'm not laughing. None of us are. ██████████ are you laughing?'

My friends shake their heads.

'Your joke isn't funny, none of them are – I hate to break it to you but you are not a funny man. Your dog is cute yeah but I hate you so why are you speaking to me?'

As if to add salt to the wide open wound, you tell me to calm down.

I didn't mean to scream 'DON'T TELL ME WHAT TO DO!' but it feels really good.

I keep talking, loudly. You try to interject but I am so overpowered with rage that I don't even hear the words you try to say.

I don't stand up, I float and fly around you and when my friends join me mid air.

'I hated the way you had us set up before, us looking up at you from our seats, you leering down at us. Why do you look at us the way you do?'

You don't say anything.

'I asked you a question, white man.'

Still you don't reply, but I can see you still smirking ever so slightly.

'If you're not going to explain yourself, you might as well fuck off.'

You mumble something about how you're proud of me and before I can cut you off you're waving your card in my direction. You've got three in your hand for each of us.

'Fuck off.'

You tell us to call you if we ever need anything,

In unison, we scream 'NEVER'.

You remind us that you're good at making things happen for people like us, beg us to look around at all that you've created on this piece of land.

A small-ish ball of fire forms in my mouth and I spit it out, aiming at you. It burns your hat clean off your head. The crowd goes wild. They think we are a pop-up performance.

'Leave,' I say, with venom in my mouth.

You try and explain how you can't leave your own land. My friends empty the fire in their throats, each of their fireballs turns your shoes to ash. I don't burn your hair and they don't burn your feet, but we have the power to do so if we want.

'WE BANISH YOU, WE BANISH YOU, WE BANISH YOU' all three of us chant in unison. We are in a powerful trance now, channelling the deepest powers of the Divine Black Feminine, we will use our powers to pick you up and drag you out again.

You try and laugh again, this time there's a genuine fear in your attempt.

'Leave, or we burn your piece of land to the ground.'

My friends and the crowd are still chanting your banishment.

You apologise for any offence caused, you pick up your dog and start to walk away.

'Leave the dog. We like him.'

You don't try and protest because the dog is already jumping out of your arms and walking towards us. You look back at us and sigh, an acknowledgement of your defeat. You leave.

No apology for a tender moment of bonding now soured by your memory. The crowd roars, a standing ovation for the three of us. We float and fly for the rest of the night.

I'm not even sure if you really exist now

You seem, almost a caricature.

You have the power.

I couldn't tell you how small you made me feel

Frozen, quiet.

The older I get, the more I've grown into myself; I am much quieter now than I used to be. Being the angry Black got tiresome very quickly.

A shell of my former screaming self, there's so many conversations I've decided not to have. I am too tired.

I can't fight every battle. I don't have that much power.

You have the power.

There was nothing my supervisor could do except apologise on your behalf when I told her about my interactions with you, and how they made me feel.

It was not her apology to make but I know the words will never leave your mouth.

You are still the owner of land.

mandla is a Zimbabwean-born, agender and queer writer and performer who uses names in place of pronouns. mandla's work draws on the artist's intersectional existence, with themes including race, migration, mental health, mythology, colonialism, gender and sexuality. Often using words as a medium, the artist is heavily concerned with communicating the many sensations associated with being a person. mandla's work exists in poetry, film, audio, playscripts and performance. 'as british as a watermelon' – the artist's first solo show – has toured across the UK, including venues such as Contact Theatre, Bristol Old Vic, Sheffield Crucible and Cambridge Junction. The show had its Scottish premier at the 75th Edinburgh International Festival as part of the Refuge programme in collaboration with the Scottish Refugee Council. mandla's work has been read, screened or performed at the Royal Exchange, the Royal Court's Jerwood Theatre Upstairs, HOME, Sydney Opera House and Summerhall.

Greetings,

So how is everything? Yes, I want to ask how life is but to some degree I already know. I know it's not easy and I want to say it will get easier but then I don't want to lie.

I would like to try and make it easier for you if I can, let you know that someone's got you, someone cares. I bet you're thinking I already know that, I've got my best friend. I know you do, I know you do. But there's something I need to tell you about that. Don't worry nothing bad has happened to him and he didn't turn up at a Halloween party in Blackface. You can breathe.

Exhales.

What is it then I hear you ask? I'll get to that.

I think the greatest gift I can give you right now is to tell you to be true to yourself. I keep thinking if only you'd known before that this is the only thing that really matters. Be true to yourself. Trust yourself. Go within. The answers will come. You will know. It's hard to think how much pain and angst you could have been saved. All that time and energy from trying to fit in and trying not to choke when your differences were rammed down your throat on a regular basis.

I get it. I really do. This stuff can make you ill. Louise Hay wrote a whole book about it, how navigating emotional trauma can manifest in physical illness. I wonder if that's why I have digestive problems.

I'm sorry for all you've had to swallow, all you've had to stomach. You can heal your life. That's the name of the book.

Sometimes the best medicine is simply getting things off your chest. That could mean bringing up what you've been holding on to, bringing up, throwing up, whatever works then so be it. But too often the moment is lost. You find yourself ambushed by some back-handed comment that can leave you flat-footed or worse, winded and by the time you recover the moment is lost. You know the ones. It's usually stuff about race.

'I'd never go out with a Black man' was thrown in as you and your friends raved about the brilliance of Michael Jackson's new *Thriller* video. It went by unchallenged. I'd be more worried about him being a werewolf, said no one. It was a bit like watching *Friday the 13th* or *A Nightmare on Elm Street* and concluding you would never go out with a white man.

I still have far too many occasions where I wish I could have the moment back, replaying it in an alternate reality where a little gentle education or even a sharp rebuke from me changes hearts and minds.

The hardest ones are from the people you think you know, you like and even care about. I know you've had these experiences.

I read a quote the other day, I think it was Abraham Lincoln, and he said, 'Most people are as happy as they choose to be.' What do you make of that?

If only it were true.

You were the leader of the pack. The only one in your group with any melanin or afro hair. It's been of interest to me that when there is a group of friends with one Black boy or girl that often they are the one the others follow. This was even before Black culture, clothing, language and music was so dominant. When not the leader, it could look odd and seem like an anomaly. Like the Black guy who became a skinhead in our area, running behind the rest of the thugs like a lapdog in his bovver boots with tattooed knuckles. Okay, an extreme example I know but for all his fronting, if you looked into his eyes as I did as a kid, he just looked lost. They nicknamed him Sooty, one of the original

Do air quotes for inverted commas.

'you're alright, it's the rest of um' crew. He was good for a laugh and great in a scrap. He was the one they pointed at to prove they weren't racist. If he ever made it out of the sunken place, he would realize he was the token Black friend and would give them the kicking they liked to give people who looked like him. They probably knew it too, which is why they always hunted in a pack. Rumour has it some of them joined the police but no idea what happened to him.

Conversely being the leader didn't necessarily mean you belonged. I could cry for the girl trying so hard to fit in that she had a gravity-defying fringe that she spent all day trying to pull down only for it to spring back up into its horizontal position. In your family, you had the good hair they would all say, so much of it was the envy of your sisters who blamed their own short afros on the incompetence of the white people in the children's home. Another story for another time. To you, your hair was a burden and like so many little Black girls in the eighties, the towel over your head was how you created your dream hair, flicking it from side to side in the dressing table mirror like you were in a L'Oréal commercial.

Worse still, there wasn't the skill or even the language in your home. I still can't believe you didn't have the language to request canerows – what is the plait in a plait thing you heard them talking about? Not canerows, that's for sure. And you rejected hair extensions, thinking they were only for those who wanted the appearance of longer hair. You had it but you didn't know what to do with it.

There was only one other Black girl in your year at school. She fitted in even less than you did, with her darker skin and long braids. When one false braid dropped out at school, it led to talk and laughter, kids laughing at the unusual, at what they didn't understand. I think you laughed too, privately feeling second-hand embarrassment, vowing never to have fake braids. That changed of course.

The other Black girl led you to the white boy. Another humiliation for her when she asked him to go out with her and everybody heard about it. It goes without saying he said no. It was obvious to everyone that a white boy wouldn't go out with a Black girl. It was unspoken but accepted knowledge that Black equalled ugly.

The mixed race among us fared better. The boys, two brothers, weren't short of female attention. They had long curls like MJ on his *Bad* album cover and were tall and thin.

There was one Black boy, excluded from his last school and the story went that every school refused to take him until our school said yes. He bullied every single person in your year group and you and your friends were a favoured target maybe because there was a Black face among you, reminding him of everything he disliked about himself.

He called you racial names – jingaboo and jungle bunny to name two – maybe names he had been on the receiving end of at his old school which still burned him, feeding his relentless anger. They say hurt people hurt people and you could see how much he enjoyed inflicting pain. He did underarm gestures, walking around like a chimp from the PG Tips adverts, popping his already bug-like eyes even further out of his head. You decided if they ever dropped out, you would play marbles with them. They'd be worth at least ten of the standard glass ones. His antics would make the white boys who followed him laugh and worse still it gave them permission to do the same. They tried in a low-key way, trying to walk the tight rope of joining in without offending the ring-leader who could turn on them if they went too far.

You stood up to him, hit him back when he attacked you and then he kicked you in the back and you fell over a fence. He snorted like a raging bull, rearing up ready to come again.

Somehow you and your friends escaped, running down a long dark road, seeing the figures of him and his crew as they re-grouped and then pursued you.

You arrived at the house of one of your classmates, the one who didn't go out with the Black girl (but who was kind about it). You begged for refuge and received it. They let you through their garage into their garden which backed on to a large open field that bridged their middle-class neighbourhood and your council estate. You all ran through the dark fields to safety.

It was no coincidence that you found yourselves at his house, a detour from a quicker route home but where there were no houses and no one to run to when the bully and his cronies caught up to you. You were only beginning to admit to yourself you liked this white boy and it wasn't long before you would admit it to your friends.

You had an acceptance that you were ugly or at least seen as ugly. It wasn't something that was open to opinions, it was just fact. You hated the way you looked to the point of not really looking at yourself in the mirror. You never really saw yourself, you only saw yourself through their eyes, the Black skin, the big nose they pointed out almost daily, the lips they called rubber. Would you believe people inject their lips now to look as full as yours? It's true.

Someone found you attractive but the attention you received was unwanted and inappropriate . . . Sorry, let's not go there now.

I hope you can look in the mirror now and see how wrong they all were. Black is beautiful.

There was something you perceived to be pure about this white boy who said no to the Black girl but who did it with kindness. It was the others who made a joke of it.

Accepting he wouldn't find you attractive meant you had to have another card to play. You would have to have a nice personality and you felt you could manage that. You were funny, or at least you seemed to make other people laugh unless they were just being kind. And he was kind, so that could work anyway. I know you hated how much doubt would creep in.

You tried not to think too much about it but you knew you could make him laugh and maybe if he laughed with you, rather than at you, he would like you.

The story was like a West End musical no one would pay to see, poor Black girl from the wrong side of the tracks, rich white boy from the posh neighbourhood. Through your council estate tainted glasses, anyone across the brook or beyond the perimeter of the multi-story flats was rich. Your school was made up of the haves and have-nots and everyone knew their place.

Except you.

Maybe because you knew he was the one white boy who wouldn't laugh at you, you asked him out. He said no but he didn't laugh. Then suddenly he was on the radar of your friends who had had lots of boyfriends already. One showed an interest in him and suddenly they were an item.

All your friends were white.

It was excruciating to hear the commentary on how he kissed and what he said and did but you didn't let it show. You were hard. A tough cookie and you didn't take any shit. Or that's what you wanted people to believe.

I know you're not as tough as you think you are or more importantly feel you need to be. This requirement for toughness, for strength, has been thrust upon you. Innocence torn away early, the need to be armoured up and guarded, an imposed necessity. One of the problems with this toughness is that people can forget you actually have feelings and there is no tensile test to find out how much pressure can be applied before you break. Remember you matter.

When the novelty wore off, that relationship soon ended and another friend made her move. You didn't know what the friend code was back then but if there was one, the rules did not apply here.

This friend saw you as her best friend but you had a new best friend now.

To the audience:

Show of hands if you agree you can you be best friends with someone who doesn't see you as their best friend?

Wait.

That's a no then.

Anyway, this friend didn't get to the kissing stage, she liked the older boys or rather the older boys liked her. A couple of weeks and she was bored. She was ahead in the puberty stakes.

So finally he was single and you were ready to go again. You let the dust settle a bit, we'd call it styling it out today but before someone else made their move, you made yours. I know you're not sure how you were able to be so bold, how you came back from rejection and the interloping of your friends but you did. You asked a second time and he said no.

So now it's personal. He didn't turn down your friends. Okay so you weren't attractive like them – or so you believed – but you were fun to be around and you would make him laugh. This time you asked why, dreading the inevitable answer about the colour of your skin. But no it wasn't that. You had a reputation. You were seen as one of the tough girls, a fighter although you had never had a fight at secondary school. There wasn't much you could do about that if that's what he thought.

You got on with life again.

Your hair had been getting you down for a while. You pulled it back into a bobble day in, day out, tried the fringe thing much to everyone's amusement and cried when your mum put in ugly plaits instead of canerows. You didn't know what to do with it. At the time jheri curl was a thing but it left stains on collars and furniture.

Your mum said no to dreadlocks, and although you feigned frustration, you were also afraid you would never be able to bear the pain required to comb them out. Relaxed hair at the time looked dry and stiff like burnt straw and didn't move like the hair in the shampoo adverts.

Yes, you wanted hair that would move, that would lay flat against your head, that you could run your fingers through and not scream every time Mum came at you with the red comb.

The red comb had the narrowest teeth and whenever it was time for that one, it was game over. The afro comb was bad enough but you had been known to run and hide when you were a bit younger when your mum would slap the red terror in the palm of her hand impatiently.

As a teen there were occasions when you actually left the house in a hat that you had to keep pulling down as your hair fought to get free. You would come back late as it was getting dark hoping for a reprieve but it was only agony delayed, not denied.

Your friends didn't get it. They only experienced the soft brush treatment, the type of brush you used on a Barbie doll. It was only one out of the myriad of things they didn't get or have to worry about.

They didn't have to worry about a brother who the police would always stop and question, even though it was obvious he had a learning disability.

They didn't have to worry that when anything bad happened at school that somehow your name was always called even if no Black person was involved.

They didn't have to worry about the NF graffiti where you played two ball telling Black people in derogatory terms to eff off back to their country or listen to chants about there being no Black in the Union Jack.

They didn't have to worry about parents calling them names like blackie, or saying their Black face frightened their babies or listen mortified as they used the threat of a Black man coming to get them to discipline their small children.

They didn't have to worry that the mother of the boys that they would like to go out with would have a problem with the colour of their skin.

They didn't have to worry when they were on the terraces at a football match about monkey chants each time a Black player touched the ball or about bananas being thrown on the pitch. You didn't even know what they thought about it, they didn't say anything, you didn't ask. You wanted to be one of them and that meant not pointing out the obvious.

You felt shame. Ashamed of your difference and all the connotations that went with that. There was no hiding place for you and there were so many times you wanted to hide, to be invisible or if you're completely honest to be like everyone else.

You hated that television gave fodder to the ignorant boys around you to make constant jokes, whether that was imitating Jim Davidson's Chalky, or pretending to be one of the Indian men from *Mind Your Language*. Bernard Manning made sure there was a stream of racist jokes which could be re-told and there was no one to ease the humiliation because it wasn't seen as controversial, it was mainstream.

What did that mean for you and how you felt about yourself? What did it mean for you and how others perceived you?

Do you remember the time in the headteacher's office in primary school, when she gave the 'We're all the same underneath' speech? After someone had called you some name and you had retaliated.

Apparently there was never an excuse to hit someone. If they called you a golliwog off the jam jar, you should just swallow it, I suppose. If you told a teacher, they would say stop telling tales. That's if they even listened because getting their attention was an art in itself.

If you needed them, they were busy but if someone told on *you* they had all the time in the world to tell you off and think of unique punishments just for you. It could be a strategy to hit someone, get told off and finally get your chance to explain why; and then they would say, 'You should have told a teacher.' Aaarghh. So frustrating. It wasn't like they cared anyway. Sticks and stones and all that.

Well names did hurt.

That time with the headteacher, when she said we were all the same underneath; well you said, 'Yes, I peeled back some skin once and I was white.' Yes, you did that; you said that. You couldn't scrub off the colour but maybe you could peel it like an onion. The headteacher looked at you, not sure of what to say. Was it pity in her eyes or amusement?

I wish she had said something reassuring, explained what she actually meant, but instead by her silence, her complicity, she normalized the idea that your Black body was wrong, a mistake and it was actually okay to be looking for white skin underneath. Another reality was possible.

Maybe the pain, the physical pain helped you to disregard the notion that you could simply peel off your own skin but it wasn't so easy to shed the idea that something was inherently wrong with being Black. In fact, the emotional pain of your difference was almost worse.

If only back then there was more representation, that you could see who you truly were and also what you could be. If only you had known about Queen Nefertiti or Harriet Tubman or Claudia Jones.

You were never taught by a Black teacher, never ever saw a Black member of staff in the classroom. You remember one Asian teacher in secondary who taught Chemistry, but unfortunately you were never taught by him. What would have happened if you had told him what you had told your headteacher. You would hope it would be more constructive, more empathetic, more life affirming.

That personal development class was another opportunity missed. A teacher talked about the groups least likely to do well in society. You never really liked her; she was strict, cold and gave off the vibe she didn't like you or anyone really. She had one or two favourites, as teachers always did, but this didn't amount to much as a smile from her looked more like a grimace or a sneer.

Out of the corner of her mouth, she listed women as the first group least likely to do well, half of us in the class; then poor, maybe about a third if poor equalled a particular council estate which to most of us it did; and then finally Black, which was just you.

Just you, the only Black face. Just you that fell into all three categories. Just you who was a poor, Black female in the room, equating to life chances of nil by the sound of things, if your sneering teacher was to be believed.

The worse part was everyone else knew it and you couldn't pretend otherwise.

It was like being branded, knowing your gender, your class and your race all diminished the opportunities you had in life, and that all of them together were so bad, the teacher didn't even attempt to quantify the consequences.

She could have taken you to one side once everyone had gone or found means to ensure you didn't leave that room feeling doomed, while the white, middle-class boys filed out with a spring in their step – with the cherry on the cake of a future already secured before they had sat a single exam or finished any of their education.

The disparities in education were obvious when you all met up in secondary school. Teachers would ask you things, test you and there were things the more well-off kids knew which your council estate crew did not.

When you asked them how they knew, they said they were taught it in primary school. You were a 100 per cent attendance kind of kid, never missed a day of school, were hardly ever unwell. Had to stand up in assembly to collect your attendance certificates feeling awkward and self-conscious with a handful of other kids.

You never liked the spotlight. You were an able student, did well in all your lessons, didn't really struggle – so you're thinking, how come you lot were taught that and we weren't?

These were the pre-OFSTED days.

There was tacit acceptance that life was unfair and the odds were not in your favour if you were poor and even more so if you were Black. Your older sisters would talk about the Ku Klux Klan and segregation in America. You learnt of lynchings and assassinations. You knew who Dr Martin Luther King Jr was and knew his 'I Have a Dream' speech. Mum was old enough to remember his assassination and that of JFK, and talked about civil rights as if they would never belong to you, no matter what Black people did or how many people died for the cause.

You watched scenes in Apartheid South Africa on the news, feeling angry and powerless. You sang 'Free Nelson Mandela' with an ache in your heart.

The images of crying babies with bloated bellies and flies buzzing around them filled you with sadness and shame. You wondered why people like you were suffering so much around the world, why you saw dead bodies with brown eyes but never blue. You struggled to separate who they were and who you were, feeling a kinship, but useless and confused.

Where were the building blocks of self and self-esteem?

You forget now, how much time passed between the second and third time of asking the nice boy to go out with you. It was a warm, dark June evening near to his house and you were stood under a street lamp, head down feeling shy. You had asked him to meet you, said you needed to talk to him.

You couldn't make eye contact. You learnt later that your struggles with eye contact weren't a lack of self-confidence but related to your neuro-diversity. But in this moment, you just felt shy, awkward, a little stupid but something was compelling you to ask him one last time to go out with you. Third time lucky and all that.

You were looking at the shadow he cast on the ground when you asked again and you were still looking down when he said yes. The elation you expected to feel didn't happen, more a grudging thought of 'well it's about time' and a relief that the ordeal was over and he had finally got with the programme.

There was no blood covenant, no contract, you didn't shake hands to seal the deal – it was a case of thanks, well that's that then, now we can get on with it.

You know now that there are no accidents and everything happens for a reason, and your compulsion as a damaged Black girl to keep pursuing this kind white boy was a divinely inspired act of survival. It came up often in the years that followed that you had to ask him out three times and also that he told you after three weeks that he loved you and meant it. Without that love you're not sure you would have made it.

During this time after leaving school, the boy who had bullied you at school came up to you in a nightclub, not quite believing what he saw. Your face hadn't changed but you felt different. He said your name to double check, complimented you and then apologised for 'all that stuff' at school. There was no punchline, you just said thanks but you learnt when you know your worth, sometimes others will see it too.

I digress. I have to break it to you. You already know your relationship wouldn't last forever. The challenges of being interracial never went away but you overcame them the best you could.

Once together at Carnival, he got a little glimpse of what life was like for you, feeling outnumbered, feeling unwelcome, feeling like he didn't fit in and this was only from vibes alone, no one explicitly said anything. In fact, people were welcoming enough, they were mainly indifferent if we're being honest, too busy eating jerk chicken or chewing sugar cane, and enjoying themselves.

You had similar taste in music, saw Whitney Houston and Tina Turner together, Bon Jovi, Gloria Estefan. Oh ey oh ey but these weren't the tunes you heard here. Nevertheless, the rhythm got you, it didn't get him but these differences weren't deal breakers. You were just grateful the experience gave him a small taste of what life was like for you, without any of the blatant hostility and prejudice which was part of everyday life. If anything, it brought you closer.

You know the relationship didn't last forever because you ended it, breaking hearts but not breaking ties. You had to find yourself outside of the comfort zone you created with him, unleash the parts of you that have felt suppressed trying to fit into his very white world that you believed would never truly accept you because of the colour of your skin. A hard lesson for any teenager. But you'll be forever thankful for him seeing you when no one else did and for helping you to believe there was nothing wrong with you.

Even with the relationship over, I know you rely on the enduring bond and the friendship to sustain you throughout your life. I know you sometimes ponder what you will do without him.

The good news is the friendship will continue but I hate to break it to you but be prepared to be replaced by another best friend. I know you won't find this easy and that's why I'm trying to soften the blow. This isn't a reflection on you or on him, it's just a part of life. You learn, you grow, you evolve and you will both love again.

You will still see him as your best friend and will find it hard to reconcile yourself with that. I'll ask again. Can you have a best friend who doesn't see you as their best friend . . .? Honestly, I don't really know the answer to that, I've asked the audience and now I'll have to phone a friend. I don't know the answer but what I do know is this.

White best friend?

Black best friend?

Any best friend.

Whatever happens, be your own best friend.

Know your worth and do you no matter how others see you.

You will encounter those whose friendship is conditional on you dancing to a particular tune.

Dance to your own tune sister, moonwalk if you want to moonwalk even if everyone else is voguing. Do the twist even if people expect you to Jive.

You'll keep encountering people who think Black people are inferior, who rail against Black History Month every October, who think they can say the 'n' word because some rapper said it in a song. Sometimes they are the people you least expect. Yes, challenge by all means but don't waste too much time and energy.

The great Toni Morrison said it best:

> The very serious function of racism is distraction. It keeps you from doing your work. It keeps you explaining over and over again your reason for being. Someone says you have no language you spend twenty years proving that you do. Somebody says your head isn't shaped properly so you have scientists working on that. Someone says you have no art so you dredge that up. Somebody says you have no kingdoms so you dredge that up. None of this is necessary. There will always be one more thing.

There is some other stuff I'd like to prepare you for. If you ever want to live in Spain, do it sooner rather than later. Also do you remember that moment in *Back to the Future* when Marty was trying to convince Doc Brown that he was really from the future and Doc Brown asked who is the President in 1985 and Marty said Ronald Reagan and Doc was incredulous because the idea was so ridiculous because Reagan was an Actor in 1955. Be prepared for something like that in the future.

I won't say too much more. I believe in you, you've got this.

Take good care of yourself until we meet again. God bless.

Love,

An old friend

It was a nice surprise to be invited to write for this exciting new project for Eclipse Theatre during what has been a difficult time for everyone and to have the opportunity to once again do what I love. It's great that

Rachel De-Lahay's powerful concept "My White Best Friend" has come to the North and I look forward to being part of it.'

Marcia Layne is an award-winning playwright whose plays include *Off Camera* (Alfred Fagon Award), *The Yellow Doctress* and *Legacy*, all for Leeds Playhouse. Other credits include: *Sister Esteem* (Paines Plough/tour); *Lost & Found* (Yorkshire Women Theatre); *Somebody's Son* (Hidden Gems Productions/tour); *Bag Lady* (West Yorkshire Playhouse/Tour for Hidden Gems Productions) and 'A Cut Above' for BBC Radio, an episode of the *Stone Detective* series.

Her afternoon play *The Barber and the Ark* (BBC Radio 4) was shortlisted for both the Sanford St Martin and Richard Imison awards. She was also commissioned to write one of the 20 Tiny Plays About Sheffield for Sheffield Theatres and was one of five writers to be commissioned by Coventry Cathedral to write a play for 'Meet Me in the Ruins', part of the celebration of 100 years of Coventry's Diocese and Cathedral.

Marcia has completed an MA in Writing and is currently working on her first novel, *Mango Season*, and a play, *By Any Means*, which received a bursary from the Peggy Ramsay Foundation.

Marcia has worked as a local government Arts Officer and is currently a Library Co-ordinator in Sheffield.

NOTE: The following should be read by a white British, middle-class, cisgender male or female in their mid to late thirties from the Northeast of England. In the envelope they receive containing the letter there should also be two pens and two blank pieces of paper and a small bar of chocolate – a Freddo is the perfect choice.

Hello, I'm Chris but today I'm going to be playing a group of Naomi's friends all mushed into one person. A white middle-class person who grew up in a rural area of Northeast England but managed to escape to a city for university and so broaden their horizons and life experiences. I think I am a good person.

I AM a good person, politically and socially aware. I give money to charity; I boycott Nestle; I do Veganuary and/or Movember. I go on protests about climate change, BLM, women's rights, the war in Afghanistan . . .

I understand that racism is structural and I have 'white privilege'. I have friends who are Black, South Asian, Middle Eastern, Chinese . . . One of these friends is Naomi, who out of the blue has sent me a letter. Which is weird, as she's never written me a letter before – not even a postcard.

But before we get into that, Naomi would like me to share the following facts and information with you.

- At the time of writing – In the UK there is only ONE female Chinese Member of Parliament, Labour MP Sarah Owen. She is joined by ONE other Chinese MP, Alan Mak of the Conservative Party. That's a total of TWO Chinese MPs out of 650. You may think this is evidence of progress and representation, but IF we wanted the House of Commons to accurately represent the number of East Asians living in the UK according to percentage of population, there should be **nine** times this number. That's eighteen for those of you who struggle with maths.
- In 2018 during a six-month period, East Asian actors accounted for just 1.7 per cent of cast appearances on primetime British TV. This figure drops to less than 0.5 per cent when ITV's *Strangers*, a rare 'one-off' series set in Hong Kong, is removed from the data set.
- East Asians are not only underrepresented in television, they are badly represented – usually cast in minor roles playing characters who speak with 'an Asian accent'.

Restaurant owners, triad members, victims of human trafficking, high school maths nerds, or wise Kung Fu masters. We blend into the background of the white protagonist's story – think Lilly in *Pitch Perfect*, who barely speaks above a whisper.

- On the flip side, East Asian faces were OVER represented in images related to the Covid-19 pandemic. An analysis of 14,000 images used by fifteen major news providers, between January and August 2020, showed that 33 per cent of these images (one third) featured East or Southeast Asian people, even though the stories were often unrelated to Asian people. Meanwhile, in the UK, hate crimes against Chinese people increased threefold during the Covid pandemic.

Naomi says,

*'In the media and on TV, people like me are either invisible or hyper-visible; now you see us, now you don't . . . and even if you **see** us, you will rarely hear us speak. So now I've got this chance to talk to you all, I hope you're listening.'*

Now on with the letter –

* * *

To all my white friends who at one time or another have turned around, looked me straight in the eye and said:

'Yeah, but I don't really see you as Chinese.'

This is for you.

Up until now I've bitten my tongue and swallowed the following words but . . .

I'M SORRY WHAT?

Who are you looking at? Cos it can't be me! Why are you acting like you've never seen my face? Because it's Chinese enough for a five-year-old in the playground to pull their eyes at me and sing,

'Ching Chong Chinaman . . .'

Chinese enough for a gang of teenagers to surround me chanting, 'CHINKY WINKY! CHINKY WINKY!'

Chinese enough for a white teacher on my first day in a new school to ask me, *'How's your English?'*

My face is SO Chinese it's noticeable from a distance, judging by the number of random men who shout 'NI HAO' at me from across the street. *SO* Chinese that, as a student walking down Curry Mile in Manchester wearing a backpack, people would call out 'DVD' at me as I passed by. To be fair, that hasn't happened for a good ten years – not with Netflix taking off. My face is SO Chinese, it made two police officers stop and think,

'She's not from here, better check she's legal,'

and ask me to produce ID.

On the plus side, this Chinese face meant I could get away with paying a half fare on the bus well into my twenties, cos hey, 'Asian don't raisin!' It's also helped me to avoid a number of fines on Manchester Metrolink.

Mock Chinese accent:

'Ah so sorry, my English no good. I buy ticket you now?'

Hmmmm . . . I wonder did you, a 'good' liberal, *Guardian* reading, white person, just read that last bit out loud in a Chinese accent, *in public*? I mean what you do in private is one thing but . . .

Awkward . . .

Pause.

What do you mean I'm not really Chinese?

Is it because I was adopted and raised by white parents in the whitest area of England? Does that somehow change who and what I am?

What makes someone Chinese?

Maybe what makes you '*really*' Chinese is being born in China, growing up in a Chinese family all speaking Chinese and only eating Chinese food?

And I, like some crude stereotype Brit, speak only English and schoolgirl French, and whenever you came round for tea my dad, depending on how special the occasion, would make either a roast dinner, shepherd's pie or sausage, egg, chips and beans. By the way, have you seen his Facebook profile photo? It's a tray of Yorkshire puddings he made that rose spectacularly! I know, it's *so* him.

I **was** born in Hong Kong though. If people had labels, mine would say, 'Made in Hong Kong'. But yeah, we all know what Hong Kong is like for knock-offs and fakes.

Maybe I'm one of them. At first glance I look like the real deal, but underneath . . .

Ben T, perhaps you were right when you said that in many ways, you're more Chinese than me, having lived in China for several years and being able to speak Mandarin. I totally accept you know more Chinese people than I do and your language skills ARE seriously impressive. Remember that time when we went to the noodle bar in Huddersfield and you not only ordered in Mandarin but went on to have a twenty-minute conversation with the owner? His face! He couldn't believe his eyes or his ears – this Prince William lookalike speaking his language completely fluently! Then he turns to me, who knows LITERALLY six words, and yeah . . .

I didn't feel Chinese then. Just a familiar shame; the one I always feel when I'm 'exposed' by a 'real' Chinese person.

You saw what happened in college, at Mandarin club, when the teacher decided to humiliate me because I said the wrong answer. He expected me to be better than all you white kids and laughed when I mispronounced my own Chinese name – having only ever heard it said by my white parents. Once he knew I was from Hong Kong, as a mainlander, he didn't think I was *really* Chinese either – telling me to go back to the takeaway I came from. So that ended my college phase of 'trying to reclaim my heritage'.

Oh, apart from the Asian hair streaks!

Do you remember? I think I tried every colour – pink, purple, red, blue, green . . . I probably would've had them even longer but then my great uncle died and my mum made me dye my hair back to black for the funeral. I was so pissed off cos it cost me 80 quid to get blue streaks put in and I didn't even have them for two weeks. The problem with being East Asian and living in Barnard Castle circa the year 2000 is that the only women you see who look like you are cartoon fantasy action figures or anime.

It still seems to be Hollywood's go-to style for the 'edgy' Asian woman. Think Yukio from *Deadpool 2* or Mako Mori from *Pacific Rim*, Knives Chau in *Scott Pilgrim* or even Tina from *Glee*. Tall Paul, please ignore what I said in 2009 about that show being progressive because it had more than one regular East Asian character. Though, as one of the most intelligent people I know, I'm sure it's obvious to you that despite *Glee*'s surface attempts at diversity and representation it was problematic as fuck.

Maybe what makes you '*really*' Chinese is knowing when you're turning yourself into a cultural stereotype and stopping – or at least being aware of what your actions look like from the outside.

Shona, do you remember what you said when I posted a photo from my wedding make-up trial on Instagram?

'Oh it makes you look more Chinese! If that makes sense.'

Honestly?

NO. What you said does not make sense.

'More Chinese.'

What does that mean? You think I can make myself look more or less Chinese on different days?

If only that was true! I'd have chosen to spend more time looking 'less' Chinese and avoiding a lot of hassle. Sophie, do you remember in Primary 1, when we were both angels in the nativity and I said I wished I had yellow hair like you? As the ONLY child of colour in Startforth Primary School, I just wanted to fit in. If I could, I would have spent the years between age three and eighteen, maybe longer, looking less Chinese.

What you really meant Shona was:

'You look more like what I think a Chinese woman should look like.'

Long black, poker straight hair;

red lipstick;

flawless, porcelain skin;

black eyeliner with the little upward flicks . . .

RELAX! It's cool. You're not racist, or at least *I'm* not calling you the R word.

What you said, what you thought about that make up, was EXACTLY what I wanted you to think. You and everyone else.

'*More Chinese*' is precisely the look I was going for, because my wedding involved a hidden agenda – nothing sinister, I promise. Neil is safe and our love is pure (puke – why did I just write that?).

The plan was to use my wedding day as an opportunity to gather all my nearest and dearest together in one place and remind them in a gentle but NOT AT ALL subtle way that I AM CHINESE. Wearing a red cheong sam, the lion dance blessing, serving food that YOU would recognize as Chinese like duck spring rolls.

Because after thirty something years of:

'*Yeah, but you're not really Chinese,*'

And:

'*Chinese people are. . .*' Insert lazy stereotype here and:

'*Oh, I don't mean you, obviously! When I said Chinese people, I meant people who are actually from China, not you; you're one of us.*'

Enough is enough.

The problem is, if you hear the same lie repeated over and over again, you start to think it's true.

I'm not really Chinese.

And so, for nearly thirty years of my life, I avoid other Chinese people, 'real' Chinese people, fearing their judgement and shame. As soon as they see me, they'll know I'm a fake and not one of them. I am a typical adoptee; my biggest fear is rejection. My university was LITERALLY across the road from Liverpool Chinatown but I never went there – not once in three years. I avoid groups and events for Chinese people because 'I am not one of them.'

But and it's a big **BUT**, with the best will in the world I'm not one of you either.

You can 'cover' me with your whiteness but I will never *be* white.

As a transracial adoptee, a white woman trapped in a Chinese body, I often feel lost between two worlds. And it can be pretty lonely, not belonging anywhere.

I am always 'other'.

You need to know, those words that you see as a statement of belonging, approval even, are isolating and harmful. For most of my life, the power of those words cut me off from the people I needed the most. They stopped me from connecting with the people who could show and help me understand the 'real' me.

Adoptees are often treated as blank slates, upon which adoptive parents write and project their dreams and desires. Our original identities are erased in order to make our parents' dreams come true – a child of their own – so they choose to forget that first I belonged to someone else, somewhere else.

Even now, in our supposedly progressive culture, transracial adoptees tend to be children of colour growing up in all-white families in mostly white communities. Unless their parents are particularly forward-thinking or self-aware, these children are denied racial mirrors growing up and never see themselves reflected in the faces of those around them. Do you know who else doesn't have a reflection? A vampire . . .

Monsters don't have reflections. The creature Victor Frankenstein created was the only one of his kind and his loneliness drove him to madness. I know you don't say those words to hurt me – you don't mean any harm – but hey, you've seen and shared those memes about intention vs impact. So, you do *know* better. Now DO better.

BE better.

Stop saying 'I don't see you as Chinese' like it's a compliment and I'm somehow exceptional. What's wrong with being Chinese? Thanks to Dr Fu Manchu and the CCP, the West has some very 'interesting' ideas about China and Chinese people. Your Sinophobia is legitimized thanks to media reports showing how China is a fascist state where people don't have human rights – just look at what's going on in Hong Kong and Xinjian. Chinese people can't be trusted; they're always plotting behind your back, cooking up Covid in a lab and spying on your internet searches. Who'd want to be a member of the cruellest race on earth? I mean look at what Chairman Mao did to his own people!

Okay, so the Chinese DID invent gunpowder and bombs and the handgun and lots of other things used to kill people – see also cannons.

BUT we're also responsible for making a lot of good stuff too, like paper and colour printing, fireworks, kites, matches, loo roll, clocks, alcohol! You even have us to thank for tomato ketchup. And let's not forget the good old compass, meaning you could find your way over the sea to sell us opium! Insert winky face/shocked face emoji here.

Stop whitewashing me so YOU feel more comfortable. How did you describe me once, Paul? Do you remember? I do.

'Just a hint of squint.'

Pause – let those words land with your audience.

Maybe what makes you '*really*' Chinese is believing that you are.

No, scratch that. What am I saying!

Obviously, it takes a bit more than that. You *do* need to have a Chinese ancestor hiding somewhere in your family tree. On that note, did you see online about that weird, TOTALLY white guy, who thinks he's Korean and got a whole load of plastic surgery to look like that guy from BTS? Oli London, that's his name.

If what makes you Chinese is simple biology, then actually I am VERY Chinese – over 88 per cent, with traces of Japanese, Korean and European. Yup! I spent nearly a hundred quid on a DNA test to tell me what I basically already knew. Cheers for making me so insecure, guys. You all owe me a tenner. PayPal is cool.

Don't you remember how I used to go bright red after half a bottle of Smirnoff Ice? It's called '*Asian Flush*'. No secret teenage drinking for me. A couple of sips of Smirnoff Ice and I was like a tomato. Becki, I appreciate your valiant attempts trying to cover it up with your foundation, as of course, in 1998, the Barnard Castle branch of Boots does NOT stock my shade (still doesn't) but what with you being the fairest of them all, my face just looked like a strawberry Cornetto. I used to be so jealous of you all, going out and getting pissed; sharing cocktail pitchers in *Flares* while I was on the J20 like a baby.

And as if the Asian flush wasn't embarrassing enough proof of my 'Chinese-ness', I'm also lactose intolerant – along with 70 per cent of all East Asians!

I know, I am SO much fun to have dinner with!

As much fun as these THREE smiley poo emojis here 💩💩💩.

Lucy, do you remember your mum calling my mum, saying she thought I was bulimic, cos every time I went to your house, we'd have ice cream for pudding and then I'd disappear into the toilet for a while?

I do still love a mint Viennetta though.

But . . .

Despite all this evidence of me being 'really Chinese', for a long time I was afraid to apply for opportunities targeting Chinese people, or East Asians, or the 'BAME' community (their words not mine). I thought they wouldn't want someone like me who's basically white. I'm not 'diverse', I can't bring 'authenticity' to your story about a Chinese family running a takeaway or talk about the hardships my ancestors endured during the Mao years. I don't really celebrate Chinese New Year and never have I ever eaten a mooncake. And while this disappoints some people, in the past few years I've discovered there are still plenty of people who think I'm Chinese enough to be paid for it.

YAY!!! for what you all call 'positive discrimination'.

If I'm Chinese enough for them, why not you?

What IS Chinese to you?

What makes someone Chinese in your eyes?

An accent? A passport?

Knowledge of Kung Fu?

Bound feet and a subservient manner? Should I put on a qi pao and kowtow to you, my white Western masters?

Do me a favour and close your eyes, and think of a Chinese person. What do they look like?

Whose face are you seeing right now? Jackie Chan, Jet Li, Gok Wan, Awkwafina, Gemma Chan, Sandra Oh?

Me?

Yeah, so Sandra is Korean, and so is the lead guy in *Shang Chi and the Ten Rings*, cos I know at least some of you were thinking of him – he's called Simu Liu.

If someone says the word 'China' to you, what do you think of?

Whatever you're thinking of right now I want you to say it out loud.

Go on – OUT LOUD NOW.

Actor says some things they associate with China.

Anything else?

Do me a favour. In the envelope, along with this letter, there are two blank pieces of paper and two pens. I want you to make a list of 'things that are Chinese' – not yet though; wait for it . . . we're going to make this fun.

I want you to choose a **WHITE** audience member who is also going to write a list at the same time as you. Each of you will have one minute to write down as many things that are Chinese as you can. When the minute is up, you will each read out your list. No editing, no censoring, no missing out 'embarrassing' answers. You need to pick someone to act as a judge who'll keep time but also look over your shoulder when the lists are read out to make sure there's no cheating. This person can be any ethnicity but in the UK today, only 7.4 per cent of court judges are people of colour, so you might want to even that out a bit here? Hint, hint . . .

Go ahead, pick your people.

Actor chooses a judge and a list maker.

Have you and the other white person both got pen and paper?

Yes?

A reminder, you have one minute to write a list of things that are Chinese.

Judge, do you have a timekeeping device?

Yes?

Judge – when you're ready count the players in with a '3. . .2. . .1. . .GO'.

Judge counts people in, players write their lists.

After one minute –

So now it's time to read out your lists. Decide between you who's going first. Judge, make sure each person reads out EVERYTHING on their list, even stuff they've crossed out.

Both lists are read. Maybe the person who has the longest list wins the chocolate bar or maybe the audience votes on who had the 'best list' and that person wins the chocolate?

Audience members, thank you very much for being good sports. You can now return to your seats.

So . . .

Did anything on your list embarrass you? It's okay; don't feel too bad. Unless all you wrote were items from the menu of your local takeaway.

Your ignorance isn't entirely your fault. I blame the media. You can only know what you know and work with the information available to you. Thanks to *Corrie* and *EastEnders*, even *Emmerdale*, even if you live in somewhere like Teesdale, you can still see Black and South Asian characters on your screens daily doing 'normal' everyday things just like you. Going to the pub, wearing jeans, getting a haircut, or taking their car to the garage. Meanwhile, East Asians don't even run the chippy or a nail bar – not since Mr Wong's THREE appearances on *Corrie* in 2005.

Maybe what makes you 'really Chinese' is not being allowed on British telly!

Or only on 'special' occasions.

To date, the only regular East Asian family to appear on a British soap are the Chois, who left *Brookside* in 1990 after only a year on screen. I hear rumours that a Chinese family is coming soon to one of the big British soaps, but what's taken them so long? I hope the answer to that question is extensive research to get things 'right'.

Cos when it comes to East Asian characters, British soap land does NOT have a good track record. We're going back a bit now – late 90s – but do any of you remember Dee, Eric Pollard's mail order wife? She was Filipina rather than Chinese, but my point is, the writers had her dressed in mini-skirts and high heels, catching ducks by the village pond and cooking them in a curry.

Then there's Xin Chiang from *Corrie* who married Graeme just to get a British passport and Orchid, Fred's Thai Bride who turned out to be a scammer.

Even when writers create an East Asian character who IS actually British, all kinds of weird stereotypes still appear. For example, Lilly from *Casualty*: an ambitious junior doctor who's also an emotionally repressed ice queen. So original right?

Television has often been used to normalize the unfamiliar. Think Hayley from *Coronation Street* and how she changed attitudes towards transgender people, or how *The Vicar of Dibley* made female clergy safe and acceptable. But East Asians, who make up over 20 per cent of the world's population, continue to be a rare sight on your screens. You're more likely to see a vampire than a Chinese face on British TV.

And when we *are* made visible, what's highlighted is always how we are NOT like you – with our unfamiliar food, strange customs and mystical beliefs. The powers that be want us to remain exotic and mysterious. Especially Chinese women who, at best, are portrayed as objects of sexual desire, simultaneously pure and submissive while also hypersexual and able to fulfil your wildest fantasies. At worst, we are pushy tiger-mums abusing our children, or scheming dragon-ladies with murderous intentions.

Even if TV producers manage to avoid Orientalist tropes, we are still a source of spectacle, a modern-day freak show. Think *Crazy Rich Asians* or *Bling Empire*.

How often do you see Chinese people being shown as British?

Because when you say I'm 'not really Chinese', what you're talking about is culture. While I have Chinese DNA, in your eyes, I am as British as a bulldog and white as a Mr Whippy ice cream; more cottage pie than congee; the Spice Girls rather than five spice. A banana – ughhhhh, I HATE THAT WORD! We ALL need to stop calling people after pieces of fruit: banana, coconut, mango . . .

Maybe what makes you 'really' Chinese is practising Buddhism and having a shrine in your front room where you pray to your ancestors. You celebrate Spring Festival by making dumplings with your Po Po, who gives you a red envelope full of money and tells you not to spend it all on White Rabbit sweets. At mid-Autumn festival the two of you make mooncakes full of sweet lotus paste and red beans.

And I get what you're saying, but it's a slippery slope, saying that to be Chinese you have to do or be X, Y and Z. That's basically the logic the CCP are applying to the Uyghurs in Xinjiang. In China today, there are fifty-six different **CHINESE** ethnicities, five major religions, and more dialects spoken than you can count. And still there is a desire in both East and West to present one and a half billion people as a cultural monolith.

Who, if anyone, should get to decide what being Chinese is?

Maybe what makes you 'really Chinese' is being part of a community of people who accept and recognize you as one of their own? It's more than meeting up to play mahjong or being invited to join in Sunday dim sum. Being Chinese is about who 'sees' you and how you are seen.

Being the age that we are, social media wasn't something we used until we were adults; and being honest, I think most of us are relieved photos from our teenage years aren't immortalized forever somewhere on the internet. But I do wonder what might have been different if, as a teenager, I was able to connect with other adoptees, other Chinese people living in white families, and compare notes – know that I wasn't alone.

I was thirty-two before I saw myself and my life reflected back at me via a Facebook post from another British Chinese adoptee who'd made a film about her experiences. By connecting with the filmmaker Lucy Sheen, who also turned out to be a playwright and actor, I was able to meet people from two different groups I hadn't been able to access before.

Firstly, she introduced me to other Chinese transracial adoptees – people like me who'd spent their whole lives having others tell them they weren't *really* Chinese too!

Secondly, Lucy also introduced me to other BESEA creatives. Hang on, do you all know that acronym? I think most of you do, but just in case it's 'British East and Southeast Asian' – BESEA. These people weren't adoptees but REAL East Asians and by working with them on various theatre projects, I learnt a few things about being 'really' Chinese. The number one point being that however Chinese you are, there is always someone who thinks they're more Chinese than you, and therefore superior.

The British Chinese community have created hierarchies and levels of 'Chinese-ness', according to if you're first, second or third generation, whether English is your first language or not, and how Western you are deemed to be. Parents and grandparents call their **own children** 'bananas' and despair at their lack of cultural knowledge or inability to speak their mother tongue. They fear they will forget their culture and who they 'really' are. People you and I would judge to be 'really Chinese' feel they are not

Chinese enough because they stutter and stumble when talking in Cantonese with their Po Po, or because they've never even been to China.

And this thinking isn't exclusive to the *British* Chinese. Back in the motherland, one group of Chinese are persecuting another and we see mainlanders calling Hong Kongers cockroaches and literally exterminating them.

Before I said that maybe being 'really Chinese' is about being part of a community who recognize and accept you as one of their own. It makes me uncomfortable, the idea that your identity depends on others' perceptions of you. But I think rightly or wrongly there's a lot of truth in that when it comes to how Chinese people view and treat each other.

This feeling of not being 'Chinese enough' isn't unique to being an adoptee, but something I share with many Chinese people of different ages and backgrounds. What's going on? Why this pre-occupation with 'cultural authenticity' and 'racial purity'? Where do these ideas come from? Why are so many of us judging our 'Chinese-ness' according to someone else's standards?

Maybe what makes you *really* Chinese is someone else telling you you're not!

'I was delighted to be invited to be one of the writers on this project as I loved the original version and the bold, imaginative and challenging work that was created. Rachel came up with such a great concept – giving people of colour space and a way to say stuff they never dated to before. It's fab this project has come up North and I can't wait to share my thoughts and feelings with you. They've been a long time coming.'

Naomi Sumner Chan is a Manchester-based playwright and dramaturg fuelled by salt and vinegar crisps and cups of tea. She leads new writing company Brush Stroke Order, working with artists to develop text-based work for live performance.

Her work has been performed at theatres across the North of England and in London including York Theatre Royal, CAST, Oldham Coliseum, Arcola Theatre and Theatre 503.

Her verbatim play about transracial adoption, *SAME SAME DIFFERENT*, was commissioned by Eclipse Theatre and toured to venues across the North of England in 2019.

Recent projects include *Wait I'm From Wuhan*, a digital commission for Chinese Arts Now and HOME and developing a TV drama spec script with BBC Writersroom. Current projects include writing an audio tour for Tamasha about Liverpool Chinatown and a commission for series 2 of Radio 4's United Kingdoms project.

NOTES ON THE TEXT/POSSIBLE PRONUNCIATION PITFALLS TO WATCH OUT FOR:

Segue ('seg-way' – always trips me up!)
Parisian (Par-iz-ee-an)
Gray Nicolls (a brand of cricket bat – GRAY not GARY Nicolls!)
Keighley (pronounced: keethlee)
Azaan ('uh-zahn' – Muslim call to prayer)
Ranatunga ('Ra-Na-Tung-a' – a Sri Lankan cricketer)
Petit Pois should be pronounced 'Pettee Pwa', until it's clear in the letter that it
    should be pronounced differently.

Dear Petits Pois Man,

You don't know that's your name. Surprise!

Actually, that 'surprise' is a little premature. I'll take it back for now. I will need it
again as we venture through this letter together. I'm not gonna lie, Petit Pois Man, there
will be a few surprises on this little journey. In fact I've even got a surprise ending, just
for you.

I wasn't sure whether to call you 'Petit Pois Man' or 'Mr Petit Pois'. In my head it's
always been 'Petit Pois Man', but I realize now I've written it down that it makes you
sound like a French pea-based superhero.

Mr Petit Pois on the other hand makes you sound like a bureaucrat working in a Parisian
civil service office, which I think I prefer.

It doesn't actually matter.

What matters is that you know, whatever iteration I choose for your name . . . it's an
insult. An insult that's designed to do one thing – strip you of your power and return it
to me. You took my power, see, and I want it back. I mean, you took a hell of a lot more
than that didn't you, but it all comes down to power in the end, doesn't it?

I've just realized that you might not even know that I'm talking to you! *You* don't know
you're called Petit Pois Man.

Actually, you know what, I'm going with Mr Petit Pois. 'Petit Pois Man' definitely does sound too much like a superhero now that I hear it out loud – plus I actually have a feeling Marvel might be developing a Petit Pois Man movie starring Ryan Reynolds.

Mr Petit Pois feels more . . . insulting, offensive, belittling. And boy do I want to belittle you.

So I think we'll go with Mr Petit Pois, like you're the Mr little 'pea man'. Yeah, Mr Petit Pois.

That's now your name. Boom! Shazam, just changed your name. Look at that power! Gosh, it's exhilarating isn't it, power? I can see why you enjoy it so much, why you've got no intention of letting it go. Shame you also have to abuse it, but hey, turtles are gonna turtle!

Is that a phrase? It should be. That's going in the Nick Ahad Aphorisms Notebook. Well, you know what they say, turtles are gonna turtle! I like that.

Anyway, yeah, Mr Petit Pois, you don't know that's your name, so how do you know I'm talking to you?

Well, as the politicians say, let me be clear. You're the guy who showed up at my cricket club one lovely summer in the early 1990s. I say 'showed up', I think it's more accurate to say you 'arrived', and didn't you bring the bells and the whistles with you. All of them. You were the definition of that phrase 'all the gear, no idea'.

You had literally never played the game in. Your. Life. And the minute you arrived at our Tuesday night practice session, you had the most expensive everything at the club.

Your pads – most expensive. Your gloves? Most expensive. And your bat! Oh, your bat. I'd got mine off Bilal at school for 15 quid. I didn't know the manufacturer, because the stickers had been worn off by time. I actually suspect now that Bilal just made it in his dad's garage. Your top of the range Gray Nicolls cost more than 200 quid. I knew because I used to look at the brochures of cricket gear I couldn't afford as bedtime reading. Probably why I failed English. Should have been reading Dickens.

A cricket bat that cost more than 200 quid! Funny thing – that beautiful, not a mark on it bat hadn't even been knocked in. You didn't even know a bat needed knocking in, but then you didn't know anything – anything at all – about this beautiful, sophisticated, complex, seductive, alluring game called cricket.

I'd been obsessed – Oh. Be. Sessed – by the game for a decade and my pads were second hand, my gloves had a massive hole in the palm and my bat was only mine because Bilal was a fat lad and needed money for extra chips at dinner time. And here you were, stepping on to a cricket field for the first time – EVER – with a brand new set of kit, in a brand new bag that cost . . . holy moly – I've just done the maths and realized your kit cost more than my first car. What a nobhead.

So that's who you are, Mr Petit Pois; you're the guy who turned up, post-divorce, looking for a new group of people to bray with (not play, bray) and who, like a turd in a swimming pool, contaminated my club, forever.

The night you became Mr Petit Pois didn't happen until a few years after you joined. It was a moment, The Moment, when all the damage you had done crystallized and was plonked in the middle of the table, made manifest. But the damage had been slowly happening for years.

My cricket club was so important to me. I was fourteen when I discovered it, the club where I belonged. I'd gone through two clubs over the space of three years trying to find the right fit. The first club was entirely white and I thought I belonged. Then we played against teams with Asian players and I'd hear all-too-familiar language and realize that I didn't 'belong' with this team at all. I was being temporarily accepted by the team by virtue of my half-whiteness.

I went back to that club for a second season, thinking I could cope or maybe the team had changed, but the language stayed the same whenever we came across a team with a brown-skinned player. Nothing changed. Although, not nothing – it was me who was changing. I was becoming bolder, starting to understand my place in the world, starting to understand that I was going to have to make some choices because people who look like me do.

So I chose to leave that team and found another club, closer to home in Keighley.

This team was entirely Asian.

I just realized something, Mr Petit Pois, you know this is true, but the people listening might think it's made up. It is a little bit too inconvenient. I mean, I can see it from the outside: an all-white team, then an all-Asian team – alright Ahad, easy with the metaphors. They're not gonna buy it are they?

Can we put a pin in your story for a moment and give the listener some background? Hang on, why am I asking your permission!!? Unbelievable, isn't it? This is a letter that **I'm** writing for you to read out and **I'm** asking **you** for permission to segue? Your white privilege is a hell of a drug isn't it! It's like I'm Neo before he met Morpheus, still plugged into the Matrix!

Let me try that again. Mr Petit Pois, I'm leaving your story for a minute for an important segue and I couldn't give a tiny rat's ass whether that's alright with you or not. In fact, I hope it isn't – it probably isn't, because solipsists like you need everything to be about them. Well this bit isn't.

So, Keighley. Keighley's a little Northern town near to Haworth, not far from Ilkley. Its closest big city is Bradford and the fact that you have to locate it by listing its proximity to other locations is an indication of what a shithole it is. And it is a shithole, there's no denying. Our town's only nightclub when I was growing up was called Room 101. We got an additional hotspot for a night out when I was teenager. That one was called the Rat Trap.

I like to think the town was being controlled by someone versed in Orwell and with a sense of humour, but, well, I know Keighley and that would be giving quite a lot of credit where I really doubt it's been earned. A town with nightclubs called Room 101 and The Rat Trap might raise an eyebrow to those who know Orwell's *1984*, but, yeah.

I don't think there's any irony or self-awareness in those names. I can say all this, by the way, because I am from Keighley. It's a shithole, but it's my shithole (and, brackets, I actually love it).

It's also where my mum and dad met when they were teenagers. My white nana and grandad (that's how I differentiate between the two when I talk about them – 'white nana and grandad' isn't what I called them) were pretty well known in the town as pub landlords. They famously ran a pub called The Vine, a magical place when I was a little boy. It was eye-opening when I went back a few years ago as an adult and realized that this back alley pub was the kind of place that someone who looks like me Should Not Go.

So my mum and dad met at school and started seeing each other and then when my mum was sixteen, her mum, my nana, tried to put her in a hot bath of bleach.

One of the pub's customers had warned my nana and grandad that their daughter had been seen kicking around town 'wi' some Paki'. So she needed bleaching. I know it sounds shocking, but . . . Actually, there is no but. The reason I can write it so casually is that it's one of those things that just passes into family lore. It's part of the story. It happened. I know it's shocking, but it happened.

After the attempted 'bleaching', my mum got on a train and went to Liverpool, where she and my dad lived in a caravan in Toxteth. They had 32 quid. He worked in his uncle's Indian restaurant and she sold cigarettes in a cinema.

At nineteen, they married. My mum wrote a letter to my nana and grandad, telling them the date and time they were going to get wed at Liverpool Town Hall. Amazingly, they turned up and my white grandad met my dad for the first time. Apparently, my grandad shook my dad's hand and said 'look after her'. Those were the first words my white grandad said to my dad.

Two years later, I was born, a little brown – brownish – baby. My dad got drunk. He's not much of a drinker, which is why he falls asleep on the drystone wall out the back of the pub. When I was two years old, my grandad stood me on the bar and I did impressions of Tommy Cooper and Frank Spencer for the regulars.

In Keighley, I went to Sunday School at my mum's Church of England Church. I got enrolled in and attended a Catholic School, so I went to Catholic Mass too – I was also circumcised and had the Azaan whispered in my ear because that's what happens to Muslim baby boys.

While all this religion might seem old fashioned, and the mixing of cultures seem quite of today, you have to remember that I was born in 1977. I think I might have been the only mixed-race baby in Keighley at the time. I was certainly the only one in my little world. I'll tell you how unusual I was: when I started writing for the *Yorkshire Post* in the early 2000s and my name entered the public sphere, the registrar who registered my birth wrote a letter to me at the newspaper, having seen my byline on a story. He'd remembered my name for all those years because he'd never registered one like it before in Keighley. Nicholas (chosen by my dad, I'll come back to that) Dennis (after my white grandad) Ahad (an Arabic name of Allah, meaning 'the one' or 'unique').

What I'm trying to say is that a very quick way to get a handle on Keighley and to understand something that is key to this whole story of how Mr Petit Pois got his name is that people in Keighley don't really mix. It's a former mill town, which means there is a not-insignificant population in the town from Pakistan, India and Bangladesh, but the communities stay within their own boundaries, keep to themselves. You know, like the British in Spain.

Do you know, Mr Petit Pois, that there used to be recruitment offices in those countries run by the British? Adverts were put in Indian newspapers, enticing people from the subcontinent to come to the 'motherland' to help fill all the vacancies (for which read do the dirty manual labour they couldn't pay people already here to do). You probably don't know that, Mr Petit Pois, probably haven't really thought about it, considered why the town looks the way it does.

My dad's name is Abdul. Not a lot of people know that. No, really, they don't. A lot of people know my dad – of course they do – he's one half of one of the only mixed marriages in town, married to a popular pub landlord's daughter and he became a bus driver before we moved into the cornershop because I guess we were a family that played stereotype bingo! So a lot of people know my dad, but they don't know his name. When he started on the buses, when I was a little boy – so we're talking mid-1980s – he told people his name, Abdul. But apparently in Keighley, in the 1980s, Abdul was far too complicated a name to pronounce. A bull? A ball? Double bubble? Oh no, Abdul was clearly too complicated. That's why most people think my dad's called Billy – that's what they changed it to on the buses. 'Abdul? Let's go with Billy shall we?'

And because most people think my dad's called Billy, is the reason I'm called Nicholas. I mean, look at me, Mr Petit Pois man! Do I look like a 'Nicholas'?! Nicholas is derived from the Greek and means 'victory of the people'. I'm derived from the Genghis Khan Mongol Empire and his armies that invaded the land known today as Bangladesh. That's why my eyes look like this – I'm clearly a bit Nepalese – which, incidentally, is why racist little white kids used to call me names they call Chinese people, leaving me way more confused than hurt.

My dad gave me a white name so I could pass in a white world. In fact, the reason that he gave me a white name, Mr Petit Pois, is actually linked to the reason you have the name Mr Petit Pois. I know you don't understand that yet, but I'll come to it.

Alright then, let's bring you back into this. The reason for explaining all of this is so that people who hear your story understand where I'm coming from – and hopefully believe me – when I tell them that while my first cricket team was all white, my second cricket team was all Asian.

Aaand . . . I didn't fit in there either.

As well as giving me a white name, another part of the pass my dad gave me was not teaching me his language. That way I wouldn't have an accent. I could 'talk English'. Man alive did that decision rob me of so much. I know it gave me a lot too, but I often think about the cost.

It meant that when I was with my second cricket team, with all the Asian lads, there was a literal language used that I didn't understand. My team mates would 'shabash' each other. I knew what it meant, I'd been around my Bangladeshi family enough to at least understand a few words, so when they shouted shabash after a particularly good ball or shot, I knew they were saying 'well done', but saying the word myself sounded strange in my ears and tasted funny in my mouth. It wasn't really mine. My dad decided he wouldn't give it to me; by not teaching me Bengali he didn't think he was depriving me of something, but giving me something. I understand why he did it – I don't think I'd be a radio presenter today were it not for his decision. But still. I'm not angry or anything, I'm actually just really sad at what I wasn't allowed to have because my dad, whose name was Abdul, not Billy, understood it was better in this world for me not to have certain things. Like the language that could have connected me to his homeland.

There were other differences too between me and my teammates. Ones that I can't name or define, but things that just separated me from the team. And that's really not the point of being part of a team, is it?

But I loved the game. Cricket's like that. If it gets you at the right age, it won't ever let you go; it's a lifelong affair. Even now, when my life's too busy for cricket, I can't walk past a field where a game's being played and not stop for at least a moment or two, like I've come across a photograph of an old lover.

I hadn't found my team, but I had found my game. Or the game had found me. Whatever, that's semantics. I needed a team where I could belong.

And then my all-Asian team played Airedale. Utterly chaotic, anarchic, frankly entirely batshit Airedale. The only team we played all year where the team was mixed. Asian lads and white lads playing together. Different languages being spoken and nobody batting an eyelid. Brown boys and white boys on the same team and everyone appearing to play their own style of game. Omar smashing sixes for fun with a stance that I had never seen in any of the coaching books I read. Coxy playing with a straight bat and calling properly using only the commands 'yes', 'no' or 'wait'. Kasim whooping like a lunatic behind the stumps, wearing a floppy hat that I'd only seen on the heads of the West Indies players on TV. Honestly, they were fucking mental.

I'd found my team.

I left the club I was with, went to Airedale's very next practice session, and they became my team, my home, my gang. It stayed my team right up until the moment you turned up, Mr Petit Pois, and took it away from me.

There's something about being mixed race that only other mixed-race people know. I don't mean the whole thing of not being brown enough for your brown community or white enough for your white community – everyone knows that, because us mixed-race people have been articulating that for some time now, ever since we decided that our voices and stories were worth telling.

No, there's another thing that happens to us that only we know about and it's something we don't talk about too much because, well, we're a bit ashamed of it.

You see, because we're not 'fully' or 'proper' or 'entirely' our ethnic selves, because we're a 'bit white', there's a phrase that gets said to us a lot.

'You're not like the rest of them.'

And in that phrase, Mr Petit Pois, the one I knew was pinballing around your head before you did what you did on the night you became Mr Petit Pois, lies one of the hardest truths we have to face as mixed-race people. Because we're 'not like the rest of them', we get told some real shit. I mean the kind of stuff white folk say to each other when they think there are no Black and brown folk around. You know? I know you know, because you did just that. You're far from the first to tell me 'I wouldn't normally say this in front of one of your lot, but you're alright; you're not like the rest.' I've been hearing it all my life.

Different versions of:

'You're not like the rest.'

'If only the rest of 'em were like you.'

And the one that really sticks with me.

'I don't normally like Pakis, but you're alright.'

You know what I said to that?

Thanks.

Fucking 'thanks'.

I was nine and he was a kid I used to play with on the streets outside our shop. He was thirteen, so I don't know what else I might have said – I was not a worldly-wise nine year old. But 'thanks'??!

I'm not nine now. I'm in my forties. And I honestly have a shiver down my spine recalling that memory. Every time I think of it.

'Thanks.'

The strange thing is I should have been prepared for that moment and had a comeback ready. I should have known it was coming.

You see, Mr Petit Pois, the likes of you have been doing what you do for a long time. The first time I remember it happening was perhaps the most painful racist experience of my life. It was when someone was racist to my dad.

It's a strange old beast is racism, for lots of reasons – like, you don't like me because I've got different pigmentation than you? That's a bit weird mate.

But it's also really strange in the way it impacts the victim. You see if someone calls you a cruel name, that's unpleasant: 'I'm a fat lad am I? Well bugger me, I didn't know that!' But when someone calls you something cruel and that thing has its roots in the colour of your skin – boy is that damaging and complex.

We all experience it.

Isn't that mad?

Every single person who is not white in Britain has, at some point, experienced racism. Amazing to think that you will never understand that, Mr Petit Pois; that you just don't have the empathy to get what I'm talking about. I'd beg you to read the words of Atticus Finch, but you almost certainly don't understand why it's weird that in our home town the nightclubs are called Room 101 and The Rat Trap, so I feel Harper Lee's prose would be wasted on you.

So when someone is racist to you there is this massive complexity of emotions and history of damage and pain that comes with it – and then you see someone say something racist to your dad, the man whose only reason for being on the planet is to protect you, love you, shield you from all the world's badness . . . and you realize that he's not even protected from this thing.

I'll tell you a story, that might help you understand.

I'm eight, and we go into a pub on a Sunday afternoon. My mum's family is proper white working class, so there's a lot of socializing in pubs on Sunday afternoons. I know my dad's different, but it's only looking back that I realize just how much he was doing, how hard he was working to try and fit in, to try and well, 'act white'. Thing is, my dad's really dark skinned, so it was never going to wash. He could act white as much as he liked, acceptance was always going to be a world away for my dark-skinned Bangladeshi dad. I'm standing at the bar and one of the other bus drivers that my dad knows is there. I like Coco. He's funny and he always seems to have people around him laughing. He's telling a joke to my dad now. I like listening to Coco and his jokes. I don't always understand them, but the musicality of a joke is easy to grasp, even for an eight year old. Coco's telling his joke and he starts saying words that are triggers to my young ears. They're only occasionally appearing, peppered carefully throughout the 'joke', but I've heard the words enough to know that this isn't nice. This isn't a funny joke. This joke, that Coco is telling my dad, is a racist joke. I want to throw my eight-year-old hands over my dad's ears and protect him from hearing this. I can tell from the rhythm that the joke is reaching its crescendo, there's been enough markers so far to tell me that this 'punchline' is going to hit my dad, hard, I need to protect him, I need to save him I need to . . .

Coco shares the punchline.

I look at my dad. We have a moment of painful, scarring, deep connection.

My dad laughs.

He's survived this far; got through all he's endured by being 'one of the ones that's alright'. In that moment I understand what it's like for my dad every time he goes to work and sits in the bus canteen, the place that I've gone to often that has a dartboard in the corner and smoke hanging in the air. I know that he has to laugh at these jokes and be 'not like the rest of them' if he is to survive.

He laughs now, at Coco and the racist punchline to his racist joke. I've just learnt a lesson about what life is going to be like.

It's a hard lesson to understand when you're eight.

Does that help you understand at least a little bit, Mr Petit Pois? I know you're a bit thick, but is that getting through at all? The image of an eight-year-old me, confused, watching my dad laugh at a racist joke his bus driver mate just told him in front of his mixed-race, brown-skinned child? Is it starting to have an impact?

There's a few more things I want you to know, that you need to be told about, before we can get to the reason for your name.

You know, I wish so much that you were a different kind of a person for oh so many reasons! But one of the reasons is one that will be a surprise. Ooh, here's one of the surprises I promised you at the beginning! Strap in.

If you were the type of person who, say, went to the theatre, I think it would be fascinating to sit and watch your reaction to one of my plays. See, you don't know this and I'm sure you never will, but you've appeared in three of my plays now! It's true! Mr Petit Pois, you're famous and you don't even know it!

I write plays for lots of reasons – to make sense of the world, to make a connection, to remind myself that I'm not alone in the universe – but one of the reasons is to reflect the world back at itself and who knows, maybe even effect a positive change. One of my plays, *The Chef Show*, is set in a curry house and you'll never guess what – you're a character in the play! I even use some of your actual, real-life dialogue! It's won awards has that play. Maybe I owe you a drink . . .

You appeared in a slightly more obscured character in another play, but I'm writing a new play, one that's going to be on at a big theatre – and you're in that too. Ah man, I wish you would see it. My dream is that you're flicking through a theatre brochure, see my name and decide to book tickets. You might even be trying to impress a date or something and come and sit and watch the play and see the scene where you appear and think about what you did and how it's stuck with me all these years and how damaging what you said was.

Unfortunately you don't spend your free time at the theatre. We all know that you spend your spare time, as you boasted at the cricket club during one game, travelling to Thailand to sleep with 'under-age girls working as prostitutes'.

Mr Petit Pois, do me a favour and apologise to the audience for that.

Oh, hang on, I have to write it for you don't I. Okay, in that case – hi audience, this is Nick, the writer of this letter. I'm really sorry you had to hear about that, the fact that Mr Petit Pois here really does do that. I was sorry and disgusted that he sat around during our cricket matches boasting about it to the team. My previously wonderful team, my little sanctuary from the world. Sorry you had to hear it, but, well, it's the truth. It's what he said to me. The world's a pretty horrible place sometimes because of people like that, isn't it?

Hey, Mr Petit Pois, leave a beat here would you. I think that needs a moment to sink in.

Count to five in your head.

Okay, good.

That needed a pause.

And by the way, 'under-age girls working as prostitutes' are not a thing – you meant 'children who are victims of sexual exploitation'.

I think we need something nice.

Bangladesh. It took thirty-two hours to get to Bangladesh the first time I went. I was thirty. Three decades of living as someone who was English **and** Bangladeshi before I stepped foot on the soil that half birthed me.

I remember watching Lenny Henry when I was a kid and he talked about going to Africa and feeling the soil and smelling the African air. I expected something similar to hit me when I arrived in my dad's village. I was heartbroken when I looked at the houses with their walls made of mud and roofs of corrugated iron and felt . . . nothing. I was meant to feel connected; half my soul is from this place. And yet . . . nothing.

It was about two weeks into my trip to Bangladesh, when life had slowed right down and when time is measured not by the watch or clock but by the moon and the sun, that it hit me. It came one afternoon when I was looking out from the front of my dad's house, considered the most impressive on the street because it had a toilet indoors. Across the 'street' I could see a jungle. Not trees, not a forest, A Jungle. I realized that a long time ago – all of my lifetime and most of my dad's lifetime ago, he stepped out of his house, into that jungle and emerged on the other side to a place that has tarmac roads, big red buses – and my future. He somehow did that when he was only a boy himself, and it was a journey he took that changed my story forever.

It's a story that's told over and over – the immigrant story, a tale of bravery and adventure, of the ability to see into a future that most can't fathom.

It's why, Mr Petit Pois, when you belittle us and do what you did, we should laugh in your face. We should laugh at your small life, working in the town where you were born; we should make fun of how tiny your ambition is and yet, because of history, circumstance and the arrogance of your forebears, for some reason you think it is you who has the power.

There's one more thing you need to know before I tell you how you got your name.

Immigrants, we get the job done. That's from *Hamilton*, another cultural gem I doubt you'll ever experience. When I saw it, I was virtually out of my seat when that line was sung: 'Immigrants, we get the job done.' It hit hard because boy don't I know it. From bus driver, to corner shop owner, to restaurant owner. My immigrant dad just kept ticking off the cliches as he went along.

I was about thirteen when my dad bought a part share in a curry house in Leeds, along with my uncle. You won't know this, Mr Petit Pois, but most of the 'Indian' restaurants in this country are Bangladeshi owned. That's a story for another time – one you'd get to hear if you saw my play *The Chef Show*.

I was really proud of my dad. A restaurant. An actual restaurant. Sure, it was over in Crossgates and you had to climb two flights of stairs because it was above a Woolworth's, but East India was a real restaurant. It's still there actually; my uncle still owns it. It's been a few years since I last did a shift.

I couldn't wait to work there. The owner's son? I wanted to work harder than anyone else, show them that I'd inherited the immigrant work ethic. Trouble is, Mr Petit Pois, I am to waitering as you are to a proper cricket stance. Entirely alien. I used to drop food, drinks, empty plates, full plates. As a waiter, I was a fucking disaster! My dad eventually fired me – although actually, that's technically not true. What happened was that I came downstairs one day – we were living above the shop – and I was in my waiter's waistcoat, ready to go – and my dad had already gone. 'Your dad decided he doesn't want you to work there anymore,' my mum told me.

Come to think of it, I'm not entirely sure I don't still work there. Maybe I was supposed to turn up for a shift last night?

Before my last shift at the restaurant I'd seen enough to understand something about the world that I wish I'd known sooner and paradoxically, something that I wish I'd never learned. My dad was the owner and I was proud of him for the position he had – but the rest of the world didn't care. The rest of the world saw a brown face and someone who was there to serve food – and that was it.

I saw my dad laugh and joke, and be livelier and more fun than I had ever seen him at home, and as the scales slowly fell, I realized I was watching my dad perform. Fuck me did that hurt. The hero who came from across the seas . . . performing for people like you, Mr Petit Pois.

I once heard someone 'doing an accent' at my dad. In his own restaurant! My dad told me that we listened to it, put up with it and at the end of the meal we take their money. I wanted him to have their money, but not to have to take all the rest. Why should he?

Well, he had a reason, I suppose. I don't fully grasp it. I think it's connected to the same reason that I am called Nicholas.

I think you know everything now. I think you're ready to hear the story of your name.

I might have shrugged it off once upon a time, the thing you did that made you Mr Petit Pois. My brother did. He was there that night. He's one of those mixed up mixed-race people, who's ended up with racist views of his own. Doesn't like Muslims, enjoys getting pissed with his white girlfriend, isn't attracted to 'dark skin'.

But I'm not like that. The rejection from the all-white cricket team, the refusing of acceptance into the all Asian team. The beatings I got at both schools I went to, especially from some nasty, violent little racist called Horsfall who I regularly pray is in prison somewhere. The jokes from Coco, the humiliations heaped upon my dad in **his** restaurant, in front of his eldest son – it's made me who I am; the person who my best friends jokingly say has a chip on his shoulder; the person, Mr Petit Pois, who was so affected by what you did that night that it's ended up in several of my plays.

You'd been with the team for two seasons. That first season you sponsored a matchball. I don't think an individual had done that before. You also got the company where you were some sort of middle manager to sponsor something else – I think you brought

500 quid into the club that first season from your company. A lot of money for a little cricket team on the outskirts of Keighley.

You're taller than me. Well, most adult males are, I'm only five foot five – and you have massive hands. I know because whenever you took a catch you'd stand in the field and say, 'Well, I have got massive hands.' Like a twat.

It's one of the most beautiful things about cricket: you can be a pot-bellied Sri Lankan and be one of the best captains to play the game, like Ranatunga. You can be a short-arse like Brian Lara and be the greatest batsman of several eras; you can be a chain-smoking gangly Englishman and be a genuine world class spinner like Phil Tufnell. It's mad that there's anything like it, really. Every other sport requires a level of fitness in order to excel – let's not pretend darts is a sport. I love darts and am mad about snooker, but they're games, not sports.

David Boon looked like the little beer-guzzling bugger he was and he was still a world class cricketer. It truly is one of the most idiosyncratic professional sports ever conceived. One of the reasons you can be a rotund little fella and play the game, or a skinny thing and excel, is that it requires so much technique and finesse. Simply being the biggest or strongest does not allow you to bludgeon your way into cricket.

Except you did, didn't you? At our level, which if I'm honest is only a little bit above village, technique finesse and class count for, you revealed, absolutely knack all. You had none of them and you scored a fifty before I ever did. You'd hit shots that looked – and there's no other word for it – disgusting – and they'd go for six. It was so upsetting to see something I cared about so deeply, something I considered such a thing of beauty, be slobbered over and mauled at by you and your big hands.

Then there was the wider effect of what you did to the team. The mixed nature of our team meant we bonded on the field. You started insisting on big drinking sessions after each match. I joined in – it was my team for god's sake – but the Muslim lads obviously didn't. If I thought you'd read *Julius Caesar*, I'd credit you with trying to use the tactic of 'divide and conquer'. I don't think you were that calculating about it though; you were just doing you. You know what they say, turtles are gonna turtle.

Then came the end-of-season meal. You suggested we go 'for an Indian' because who doesn't 'love a Bill Murray'. God, remembering all this reminds me – you really were a massive bell end.

We're in an Indian restaurant – actually, this one is Pakistani-owned, but the nuance couldn't be more lost on you – let's just call it a curry house, in Keighley. Actually, just opposite my Roman Catholic first school.

Things are getting boisterous. Well, your acolytes are getting boisterous. The Muslim lads of the team not so much – they're here because everyone always goes to the end of season meal.

We're ordering – you're making a show of asking the Asian lads what they fancy. And then you do it.

'Ere, mate, in my vindaloo' – of course you ordered a fucking vindaloo – 'in my vindaloo, can I have some petits pois.'

You wink at one of the team mates. **My** team mates.

The waiter doesn't understand.

'Petits Pois. Do you not know what petits pois are?' you say.

Hang on. You might have learnt how to say it since then. Let me write it phonetically, the way you said it that night, so you can share the full effect with the audience.

'Do you not know what pettee pwazz are? Pettee pwazz, I want my vindaloo to have pettee pwaz. Shall I come in the kitchen with you? I will bet you one hundred quid. I will bet you one hundred quid that if I come in your kitchen, I will find you have pettee pwazz. You're telling me you don't have any? I'm gonna bet you the price of this whole meal that if I come into the kitchen, I will find a bag of pettee pwaz. I'll come to the kitchen, come on, and if I find some pettee pwaz, our meal is free. Deal? Come on, deal, shake on it, I find pettee pwaz and our meal is free.'

Where the fuck to start?

First of all, the 'S' is silent in petit pois. I have no idea where you heard . . . hang on a minute. You heard it on *Only Fools and Horses*, didn't you? That's why you pronounced it like that.

That night, Mr Petit Pois, you took my team away. Some of my team mates laughed along with you – I don't blame them; it's always easier to laugh along. You made the Asian lads on the team, this one mixed team that I'd found after a three-year search, the 'others' at the table. You winked and nudged and expected me to join in and find you as hilarious as you found yourself because, as I'd heard several times in my life, 'I'm not like the others; I can take a joke.' You took the piss out of the waiters, made them feel uncomfortable just like the customers did to my dad in his restaurant. You reminded me that I would always have to pick a side because my side would never be assumed by the likes of you.

That night crystallized my whole lifetime – up until that point – of confusion and a sense of not having an anchor in the world. With your pathetic little performance you reminded me that this world is hostile and the acceptance I get in it is entirely dependent on the way I behave and the behaviours I'm willing to accept. If I laugh at people belittling waiters in the same way my dad laughed at Coco's joke, if I choose the 'right' side, then I get to pass; I get the badge of acceptance.

If I say 'stop being a fucking prick to this waiter who's doing his job, you oaf' – then I'm no longer one of the ones that's alright. I'm a chip-on-my-shoulder-having 'one of them lot'.

It was an important night, that night.

It was the night you got your new name, the one I've called you in my head ever since.

I hope you like it, Mark.

Or as I've known you ever since that night, Mr Petit Pois.

That's how you got your name and that's the Ending. Surprise.

'As a mixed-race person, my place in the world is forever in question. To be asked to work with Eclipse, a leader in the field of theatre working with creatives of colour is a huge honour, but also feels like it gives me a badge of acceptance I rarely get to wear.'

Nick Ahad is a multiple award-winning journalist, writer and broadcaster. Plays include: *Redcoats* (Mikron Theatre Company), *Glory* (Dukes Theatre, Red Ladder, Tamasha), *Partition* (Leeds Playhouse/BBC Radio Leeds), *The Chef Show* (Ragged Edge Productions, Stage Performance of the Year Rural Touring Awards 2018, Best Live Performance Cumbria Life Culture Awards), *Coming Home Together* (BBC Radio Leeds), *Muslamic Love Story* (DepArts) and *My Mum the Racist*; *Inner Voices* (JB Shorts). He is currently under commission with Leeds Playhouse, Rifco Theatre and Claybody Theatre.

TV writing includes *Emmerdale* and an original series developed by BBC Drama and Avatar Productions. He is currently writing on a primetime BBC drama and has series in development with Red Planet and Sister Pictures.

As a broadcaster, he presents the weekend mid-morning shows on BBC Radio Leeds and is a regular cover presenter of Radio 4's *Front Row*. He has also appeared on BBC Breakfast as a cultural commentator.

Former Arts Editor of the *Yorkshire Post*, he is North of England critic for Plays International and has written for the *Guardian* and *The Independent*.

NOTE: Words that are in italics are stage directions which should not be read.

Dear Callum,

When the opportunity to write this letter to you materialized in my inbox late last year, I'm not ashamed to say that my first response was to literally shit myself.

Well, not *literally*, to be fair. Metaphorically, not literally. If I'd literally shat myself, I probably *would* be ashamed of it and I probably *wouldn't* write about it in an open letter. Probably.

Basically, the opportunity to write to you had made me realize something quite significant, you see, which caused me to panic. It was a small panic, nothing major – one that I was sure I could deal with effectively if only I could remain calm.

But *then*, it made me realize something *else*, as well. And *this* thing, this *second* realization, caused me to actually, genuinely, properly, fully shit myself.

Beat.

(Again – not literally. I haven't shit myself in ages so it will never be *literal* when I say that.) (Most likely.)

But yeah, so, this *second* realization made me panic-shit myself *even more* than the first one. Now, I'm not bringing this up for no reason, because neither panic-shit was remotely fun to experience, Cal. I bring them up because, strangely enough, without these two panic-induced shits, you wouldn't exist.

So, if you'll indulge me, I wondered if I could share them with you here tonight – the two realizations and the two panic-shits they triggered. At worst, you might find them vaguely entertaining. And, at best, they might manage to get to the heart of what the hell, in fact, my problem is.

So: realization-and-panic-shit number one. I get the email offering the chance to write this letter to my White Best Friend, and mere moments after the riveting albeit fleeting jolt of joy at being offered work (and, more importantly, validation), my instinctive reaction was to think, quite naturally: who the FUCK am I going to address this thing to?

Now, don't get me wrong, Cal – this wasn't about a lack of options. I am *drowning* in options, to be honest – in truth, I have more White Best Friends than I know what to do with. I live with three white ones, there are three white ones from school, a *raft* of white ones from uni, my *ex* was white – *is* white! She *remains* white, yes. And *that* was. . . you know, there's a whole history there, her being white, which led to all sorts of – well, we'll get to all that later, so, yeah – basically, Cal, to recap, I cannot fucking well *move* for White Best Friends, at the minute. It's an infestation. Like rats in London, *rare* is the moment when I am more than six feet away from one. Like rats in London, or like. . . like *bumblebees* in Manchester – no, actually, that doesn't. . . that doesn't work, does it? Never mind.

So, yes, the panic-shit wasn't about *options*, Cal – it was about . . . *reactions*, really. I was panic-shitting over the potential *reaction* of my Unspecified White Best Friend, over the hurt it might cause them, over the damage it might do to our friendship, over the inevitable aggro that would follow my defending my choice when they inevitably confronted me, furious, *incandescent*, brandishing a . . . I don't know, four, let's say, *five*-star review from the . . . the *Guardian* . . . lauding the, for example, and I quote:

Air-quote.

'. . . *masterful* way in which Parmar deployed his *rancid* wit in order to – to – to callously decimate the *fragile* humanity, the – the – the delicate sense of *self*, the central *tenets* of the now – untethered *personhood* of his White Best Friend, who sat there, amidst the audience, ashen-faced, struck dumb, *drained* of what minimal colour he had to begin with, that pallid fuck, ruing the day he crossed his Devastatingly Loquacious and Gorgeous Brown Best Friend.'

Air-quote end.

Or words to that effect.

What's more, Cal, I immediately knew how that confrontation with the Unspecified White Best Friend would go. I'd tell them to chill; that it's irrelevant and meaningless. They'd say it was . . . 'treacherous and misleading'. I'd change tack and say that there was a . . . a 'core of emotional sincerity', or some such bullshit, which they'd begrudgingly accept. But they'd caveat said acceptance by saying I should have said something about it to them *first* – before, y'know, telling a theatre full of people about it.

Which *I'd* have to accept, with palpable begrudge, but also with the caveat that as a brown man living with the ancestral pain of the colonial legacy throbbing through my bones like early onset arthritis, surely I should be given a pass here, for excising my trauma the only way I know how – through my exactingly honed art.

Which they would of *course* accept, Cal, *un*begrudgingly – because while the Unspecified White Best Friend is *loath* to countenance criticism of their *own* past behaviour, like all good Woke Liberals they <u>*fucking love it*</u> when you bring up the sins of their *ancestors*. Yes, the Unspecified Woke Liberal White Best Friend that I'd have demolished in order to cynically fashion some racial trauma would chuck their great-grandfather under a fucking bus if it meant getting Brownie Points from their Brown Best Friend.

'No worries at all, my man,' the Unspecified Woke Liberal White Best Friend would say. 'No worries at all – I totally get why you had to exaggerate that miniscule incident that barely took place between us over a decade ago and write a letter about it – it's because my delightful cunt of a great-great-great-grandfather colonised the living fuck out of yours. *Which*, my Beautiful Strong Treacherous Brown Best Friend, is just *unconscionable*.'

So, long story short, I couldn't in good conscience pick a White Best Friend, knowing the fallout that would ensue. And no, before you ask, I couldn't just change their name, Cal, because they'd know. Deep down . . . they'd know. 'Cos although People of Colour are unrivalled in their prowess for detecting racism, when it comes to detecting *accusations* of racism, it is People of *No* Colour that have time and time again demonstrated the highest sensitivity – usually 'cos the accusation follows them having done something racist.

So, if I couldn't pick a White Best Friend because I feared the fallout, and if I couldn't just change their name 'cos they'd figure it out in a heartbeat . . . I hear our audience wondering who the fuck *you* are, then, Cal. Meaning we've reached the point where we should probably break the news to them. About how, you know . . .

Go on. Just say it. Don't be scared. Tell them. Tell the audience, Cal. Tell them you don't exist.

Loudly, looking out to the audience.

I don't exist.

Louder, please, Cal.

I don't exist!

Punctuated:

Louder. Please. Cal.

I don't exist!!!

LOUDER PLEASE, CAL.

I DON'T EXIST.

For the love of <u>FUCK</u>, Callum, as loud as you fucking well can!

I DON'T BASTARD EXIST!!!!

Alright, no need to swear, jeez. You sound so . . . *angry.* See what I did there? It was a joke 'cos that's what *white* people say to – never mind, we'll get to that later.

Anyway. Yes, you don't exist. This is correct, I'm afraid. You don't exist. You never have. And you never will.

And to be clear, I don't mean this in like a . . . spatially . . . empowering way – like '*I* exist in this space because I'm brown but <u>you</u> don't exist in this space because you're white and this is a safe space for <u>me</u> unlike out there which is a safe space for <u>you</u> yada yada yada' – although, maybe there's merit in that – but, my point is, *I'm* not making a statement about race. Well, I mean I *am* making a statement about race, that's precisely what I'm doing, but – you get the point.

I made you up. I made you up because I couldn't stomach writing to someone real. And, initially, I was *so* excited about you. Uncomfortable though the panic that led to your existence was, this was an opportunity to play God, Cal; to play Creator – to fashion out of nothing but the embers of my panic-frazzled mind a spick-and-span, tailor-made, purpose-built, brand-spanking-new White Best Friend, a White Best Friend of dreams to rival *all* other White Best Friends the world over – the Friendliest and Bestest and Whitest in the land, so white that you couldn't even look the fucker directly in the flesh lest its overwhelming fucking pallor did so inadvertently blind you! So scream it, Cal! Scream it to them – tell them, tell them just how white I made you!

I'm White!

Louder, Cal!

I'm White!!

LOUDER, CAL!

I'M WHITE!

Louder, my Beautiful White Best Avatar!!!!

I'M FUCKING WHITE!!!!!!

Beat.

Which is why I, above all people, was very surprised when, shortly after your joyful birth, Cal, around four days into this life-affirming creation process . . . I almost fucking killed you, man. And, being honest, I probably would have done – if it wasn't for the *second* panic-shit, which we'll get into in a sec.

But first: the reason I wanted to kill you was because, through no fault of your own, you'd really started to wind me up. You see, I'd decided to create you in my own image, Cal – I dunno why, maybe the playing God thing went to my head a bit and I became a bit narcissistic, or maybe it was just 'cos I wanted someone I'd really *know*, you know? So I made you an actor and a writer, like me. I made you twenty-seven, like me. I endowed you with *ever* so slightly above average aesthetics and an *ever* so massively above average economic privilege, complete with a private education and respectable degree from a reputable albeit not Oxbridge outfit – Russell Group, though, and definitely near the top end, Cal, so stop fretting. And I made it so that throughout your time at school, uni and professional life, you were loved by family, liked by friends and . . . *enjoyed* by most.

So I made us the same, more or less. Minus . . . you know . . .

But despite this similarity, this thematic overlap in our lives, or perhaps *because* of it – I started feeling this . . . *anger* . . . this . . . vicious, insidious, poisonous, overbearing *fucking anger* at you, bubbling up in me, and it took all my self-restraint not to abuse my divine privilege and control-alt-delete you back into the trash can of shit ideas from whence you came, right then and there, 'cos *fuck you,* I thought, fuck you for making me sad when I'm the reason you existed in the first fucking place.

And I was just coming to terms with the likely *reason* for that anger, which I'm sure you've already guessed, when the second realization and panic-shit hit. You know, the one where I actually fully shat myself. (Metaphorically.)

Put it this way, Cal: if you owe a debt of gratitude to the first panic-shit for leading to your creation, then it is to this *second* panic-shit that you owe a debt of gratitude for ensuring your survival. 'Cos this panic-shit made me realize I probably couldn't get rid of you, even if I wanted. You were here to stay.

The realization was as follows: that not only could I not handle the fallout from picking a White Best Friend, I also could not even think of a White Best Friend that actually *deserved* to be chosen for this.

Which was, honestly . . . *shocking* to me – almost twenty-seven years of life as a brown man with *multiple* White Best Friends and I couldn't think of a single one deserving of selection for theatrical destruction?

How could that be true? *Was* it even true? Or just another example of a person of colour being too full of self-loathing and a desire for white validation that they're tragically unable to recognize racism against themselves? Or maybe my White Best Friends are just better than all the other ones? Maybe I'm just real lucky?

Or! Maybe I'd just successfully weeded out all the Letterworthy White Best Friends long ago?! Maybe if I'd been asked to do this letter three years ago, it would have been a different story, Cal. Maybe three years ago I'd have had a fucking *legion* of White Best Friends to select from – a socially distanced *queue* round the corner of White Best Friends from whom to pluck my final candidate, all guilty of a whole plethora, a veritable *rainbow*, of racial infractions!

Maybe now, at this point in my life, aged twenty-seven, in the year 2021, I just didn't have any left. Maybe all of those who remained my White Best Friends who *used* to be Letterworthy White Best Friends, aeons ago, maybe they had been dealt with in satisfactory ways, the parties involved all having moved on or grown up or long since atoned. And yeah, maybe sometimes I'd been made to feel unheard or disrespected, Cal – but maybe we'd *figured it out*, in the end. *Processed* them.

And maybe as for the few tiny incidents that hadn't yet been fully processed, I realized that in order to write about them, in order to exploit them for our collective theatrical gain, I'd maybe have to engage in some form of . . . *exaggeration* – if not of the incident itself, then certainly of its *effect* on me. Which I obviously didn't want to do. But, equally, maybe I didn't want to *not* write a letter. It's a chance to work, a chance to write – and a chance to stick it to white people like you, Cal. Kidding. Ish.

So they were the two panic-shits. First, about the car-crash that would result in choosing a real White Best Friend; then, that I didn't even *have* an appropriate one to choose in the first place. So, instead, I created you.

And after a while, Cal, after I started writing, and thinking, and rewriting, and rethinking, I found those panics slowly starting to . . . subside. Somewhat.

'Cos ultimately, I think all these panics, all this constant prevarication and caveating and umming and ahhing and toing and froing, it was all just about me not feeling . . . as *qualified* to talk about race as many of the other writers for this event do. Because truth be told, Cal, my experiences of racism are genuinely not as bad as a lot of theirs. I don't get stopped and searched or racially profiled by police; I've rarely ever felt physically threatened on account of my race; people of my ethnicity are not overrepresented in the criminal justice system nor are they underrepresented in so-called aspirational jobs. I mean, don't get me wrong, Cal, I have experienced racism, and those experiences have been impactful, shit and traumatic – but they've also mostly been covert, not overt; occasional, not incessant; upsetting – but rarely dangerous.

So I figured that that was really what I was panicking about – that anything I would come up with, any incident I would dredge up, would just feel . . . *small*. To the audience. 'So fucking what?', I feared they'd think. That was why the early stages of writing this letter were so difficult – I didn't think I had any real right to write one, really.

But then these panics started to go away, as I started to write, because I realized it didn't really matter that I didn't have a specific incident to write about or a specific friend that had injured me or a specific event I needed to process . . . I realized that none of that matters, because the truth is, Cal, I still think about my race more than I think about *almost anything else in the entire fucking world*.

I still spend hours upon hours wondering if a seemingly harmless look was intended as it was received; hours upon hours fretting about whether my brownness will hold me back professionally, socially, romantically; hours upon hours indulging in a mental chaos weighing up words and looks and gestures and fucking *tones*, Cal – trying to ascertain intent, malice, annoyance, indifference, bigotry, hatred.

And I spend yet *more* hours wondering where the fuck I'd be if I *hadn't* spent those hours worrying about that stuff. If every hour I'd spent fretting about the colour of my skin had been spent on other things, important things, the kinds of things that you, Cal, get to think about instead, what could I have figured out or accomplished? Or fucking . . . *invented*, I don't know. And I mourn for those hours, sometimes, Cal.

And I knew there must be a *reason* for this obsession, right? A reason why, despite my relative privilege when it comes to racist experiences, race obsesses me more than anything else in the world. And I knew that *that* reason might be worth writing to you about, Cal – and so the panic started to go away, because now I had something to say; because now I had something to write; because now I had a story.

Which is all I ever wanted for this letter. A story. To tell our audience – not because my life is so important or interesting or fucking . . . *worthy*. But because I've got one. A story. And once I'd figured out what it was, it started to explain things. Things I'd been confused about my entire life, things I'd beaten myself up over repeatedly, things I still felt deep shame about.

And that shame is why I felt so angry at you in the aftermath of your creation, Cal. 'Cos, you see, for as long as I can remember, I've been surrounded by something *else*, some . . . *thing* that isn't me, and been told both implicitly and explicitly that that *thing* is preferable to *my* thing – it's cooler and funnier and sexier and more beautiful and way better at acting and comedy and writing and everything else.

And then you came along, Cal, and you could do all the things I could do, 'cos I played God and I created you to be like that, to be exactly like me. But for the purposes of this letter I also *had* to give you that one thing that I could never have, that I'd always wanted – not because it's objectively better ('cos it's not), but because everyone had always *told* me it was better.

And if the things you obsess over as a child never fully leave you then I realized I'd essentially wanted to be you my entire life, Cal – which is a thought that made me cry as I wrote it. It wasn't that I *didn't* want to be *me*, necessarily – it was just that I *also* wanted to be white. I wanted to be me *and* I wanted to be white. I wanted Me to be Me but Me to also be White. And who are you, Cal, if not the White Me?

And it hurt me so so much, genuinely, because I had honestly thought I was past all this. I knew that I'd felt that way my entire childhood, all throughout school, uni . . . but until that anger spiked up in me after creating you, I wasn't aware that that hunger for whiteness was still there, lurking around, not all that far from the non-white surface. And I was so ashamed for not being truly past it. And that shame made me sad, which made me angry, which made me *need* to find a target to direct my rage at, and you were right there on the page, so even though I knew it wasn't your fault, you became that target. And I do know it's not your fault, just like it's not the fault of any individual white person that I feel things like this, but I do.

Like, I know it's *not* your fault that the very first thing that occurs to me if someone ignores me or is rude to me or takes an immediate and *inexplicable* dislike to me is that they don't like me 'cos I'm brown. That they'd prefer me if I were white. And I know that it's not your fault that part of me *gets* it; part of me *gets* why they'd prefer if I were white, part of me thinks 'fair enough', 'cos maybe I'd prefer if I were white too, 'cos maybe I've spent longer loathing brownness than liking it.

And I also know it's not your fault that there's something inside me that makes me want to blurt out I'm an actor in any conversation as quickly as is humanly possible, so that the person I'm speaking to knows *immediately* that I'm not like *other* brown people – because I know I might *look* like one but they shouldn't confuse me for *those* brown people because I'm *different*, I'm loud and confident and funny and attractive and sexy and *artistic* – and that's not what brown people are like, is it, so they should know straight away that *I'm* different – so different that they're better off conceiving of me as not-brown, actually.

And I know it's not your fault that the whole acting thing in the first place, the whole me wanting to act and write and be funny and all of that crap, that that probably originated from a desire to get away from brownness in the first place. At least, 'brownness' as I perceived it back then. Because I pretty much never saw brown faces doing funny or cool things on TV or in films so I thought maybe I'll do funny or cool things on TV or in films and then, by definition, I won't be brown anymore.

And I also know it's not your fault that when I was fourteen, a mate said to me as we were coming out of a party, a party in which I'd yet again failed to kiss a girl, he said that it wasn't my fault I hadn't kissed a girl, that it was just 'cos I'm Asian, that's why I've never kissed a girl. And I know it isn't your fault, Cal, that I agreed with him so vociferously that *even* as the other guy we were with laughed and shook his head and said 'so harsh', I interrupted him to say that our mate was right, no doubt about it, that that *is* the reason, it *must* be – and I meant it too, I wasn't being polite, I did genuinely rate his diagnosis.

Spot fucking on, I thought. And even now, thirteen years later, it's hardly your fault that I still do think there was logic to what he was saying, even though it was obviously a pretty unkind thing to say aloud, to my face, with a smug little cunty smile plastered on his smug little cunty face – in the sense that my Asianness *did* make me feel supremely ugly which *did* make me supremely unconfident around those girls that of *course* they didn't want to kiss me; those girls, who probably never thought twice about the colour of my skin, or maybe they did, who fucking knows, this is my point – I have no idea how much of this is in just *my* head or is it in my head precisely because it's in everyone else's head as well? It's such a headfuck, Cal, to not know if the biggest problems in your life are to do with the power of the colonial legacy or simply the prominence of your cheekbones; centuries of white supremacy or the strength of your jawline? The media's constant characterization of South Asians as weird, unfashionable and uncool – or am I just genuinely a fucking loser?

And it's not your fault if you don't know the answer, Cal, 'cos I don't either. And while we're absolving you of blame for this, we may as well exculpate of you any responsibility from what happened when I was nineteen, too – so a whole five years after that incident, ten GCSEs and four A-Levels and half a year of a History degree later, having incidentally at this point in my life already read Malcolm X's autobiography and been moved to tears by his description of the excruciating agony of what Black men in Harlem would do to their scalps to make their hair look more like white people's hair, how they would literally burn their flesh with lye, cooking their natural hair until it was limp – it isn't your fault that, despite me having read that passage, I'm in my first year of uni, aged nineteen, that a mate of mine comes up to me when we're a bit pissed and says he thinks I'm pretty good-looking, that I've got great bone structure, that I've got the *bone structure of a white man*. It's neither your fault that he said that nor that my response was to genuinely swell with happiness, so deeply and unreservedly proud that someone thought I was so attractive that I was actually closing in on whiteness. And it's not your fault that when it became our little private joke after that where he'd randomly say 'great bone structure', I'd every single time feel that little buzz, unmistakably, because it was a reminder of how close I was to that thing I'd always wanted. That thing that you have, Cal; the thing I gave you.

And it's not your fault I gave it to you, just like it's not your fault that throughout the entirety of my three-year relationship with my ex, I'd feel a little jolt of joy if we were ever out and I saw a brown man with a brown girl, because I'd think the fact that my girlfriend was white meant I was doing better, which is so unbelievably fucked up that I'll be surprised if this paragraph even stays in the letter. And when I told her about it, after we'd broken up, she obviously had no fucking idea, because why would you think that your boyfriend's good mood at dinner is because he's the only person of colour in the restaurant with a white partner? And it's not your fault, Cal, that this toxic fixation contributed to (along with a load of other reasons that have nothing to do with my race, of course), but it probably contributed to me not being a good boyfriend, sometimes, because that fixation hinged on an insecurity, which was rooted in an inferiority complex, which could manifest in anger, and that anger made me say nasty things sometimes. 'Cos the intensity of the feeling of validation that her whiteness gave me was directly proportionate to the intensity of the fear that I'd lose her, and it.

So yeah, these things aren't your fault, Cal. They're not mine either. They're just facts, memories – and signposts on the road to answering some big questions. Questions like: 'Why am I preoccupied with race?'; 'Why did I hate being brown?'; 'Why have I always been so obsessed with whiteness?'

And it helped me answer a final question, too, Cal.

'Has any of this changed?'

And I realized it has. It has changed. And the reason I know it's changed, is because of you, Cal. You see, in the end, which is the part we're arriving at now, I realized I actually *needed* to write this letter to you, Cal. I didn't know it until it was almost done – but I *needed* to write a letter to the White Me. To tell him about some of the things that have happened over the course of my life that have made me want to be white, so that I could forgive myself for that fact.

But it *has* changed now, Cal. Because I don't want to be the White Me anymore. Writing – and writing this letter, in particular – changed that.

Because before writing existed in my life, I truly saw no tangible benefit in being brown. Growing up, it was never remotely cool to be brown. I despised it, problematized it, held it accountable for every bad thing that ever happened to me.

And then I started writing, and I started writing about race, and I started conceptualizing my pain and my fixation on whiteness, and I started making stories about it during those hours upon hours of fretting, and I started realizing that I had a perspective, that I had things to say, and that other people were interested in those things, so interested they'd pay me money to write a letter about them, a letter which might hurt to write, yes, but which might eventually teach me something that the teenaged me would simply never have believed – that being brown is the best fucking thing that's ever happened to me.

So fuck no, I don't want to be the White Me anymore; I don't want to be *you* anymore, Cal. I feel brown and I feel me and for the first time, I feel so so happy about that. So in your last few moments of existence, which ends, of course, with this letter, you should too, Cal – feel happy, that is.

Please, Cal, please feel happy. Please feel happy and feel good and feel warmed by the knowledge that wherever you go, which, granted, is only as far as this stage ends, and for as long as you live, which, granted, is only a few seconds longer, that you will always, forever, have a Brown Best Friend who loves himself just as much as you love

Yours
Nikhil x

Nikhil Parmar is a Mancunian playwright, screenwriter and actor. His debut play, a one-man show called *invisible*, premiered at the Bush Theatre in June 2022. He is currently developing several originals and adaptations for film and TV. His acting credits include *Trollied* (Sky), *Foundation* (Apple), *This Way Up* (C4/Hulu), *Brassic* (Sky), *Gran Turismo* (Sony), *The Rig* (Amazon) and *On the Edge: Mincemeat* (C4).

NOTE: Directions are in italics, so you shouldn't read them, but do them. The dots on separate lines indicate pauses. Excluding the section titles (Section 1, Section 2, etc.), everything else should be read out loud.

For this piece the following props will be needed: a chair, a bright orange bucket hat and a Snickers bar. Before the performance begins, the chair should be placed in the middle of the stage, and the bucket hat and Snickers bar on top of it.

SECTION 1

Hello!

This is a greeting from God.

No, sorry, no, Samuel Rossiter.

This is a greeting from Samuel Rossiter.

Hello!

I'm the writer of this piece.

I am VERY excited because I'm from a screenwriting background, and this is one of my first theatre commissions. And we're literally in the Royal Exchange. My words are literally being said in the depths of the Royal Exchange.

Holy. Mama.

And writing for theatre is very different from writing for the screen. In theatre, the writer is God. The writer is literally God. God with a capital G. God with a capital G O D.

God god god Samuel Rossiter god god god Samuel Rossiter god.

I think you get it.

Anyway, it's super exciting and I'm super excited to be here in the room with you. Even though you probably don't know what I look like, so you can't congratulate me on this

185

amazing piece because it's going to blow your mind hahaha is that the nerves talking I don't know I hope you'll like it lol okay we're getting off track let's get back on track –

.

.

.

Hello!

This is Samuel Rossiter speaking through the actor who's currently performing this piece.

As the writer-god of this piece, there are a few rules that you have to follow. Because writer-god aka Samuel Rossiter says so.

Understand?

Indicate for the audience to say yes. If they don't:

You can say yes.

Indicate and wait for the audience to say yes.

Okay good!

> Rule number 1. You, as members of this audience, cannot get out of your seat at any point during this performance.

and

> Rule number 2. One person in this audience, who is sat in one of the front rows, must wear this orange bucket hat on their head for the rest of the performance. The reward will be this delicious Snickers bar, which you get after the performance. Any volunteers?

Take the orange bucket hat and the Snickers bar and hold them up to the audience. If there are any volunteers, give the bucket hat to them. If there are no volunteers, pick a member of the audience and hand the bucket hat to them. Put the Snickers bar next to the chair on the floor and wait until the performance is over before giving it to them.

Do not continue until the bucket hat is on someone's head.

Good!

Okay, so, this letter is addressed to everyone Sam has met when he was aged eighteen to twenty-five.

— — —

Move to a different part of the stage. Point to the person who is wearing the bucket hat and stare directly at them, and do not stop staring or pointing until you finish saying these names. Take your time:

Tyianna Alexander

Samuel Edmund Damian Valentin

Bianca Bankz

Dominique Jackson

Fifty Bandz

Alexus Braxton

Chyna Carrillo

Stop pointing and staring, and move back to the same part of the stage you were on before.

— — —

Sorry! Sorry, that was weird. Writer-god Samuel Rossiter making me do weird things.

So, Sam has changed throughout the ages of eighteen to twenty-five, as most people do. So the way he's introduced himself has changed too. But for simplicity's sake, this is how he would introduce himself a year ago, aged twenty-four.

Let me describe him a little bit to you for some context:

- Six foot tall
- Broad shoulders
- Dark features
- Can actually grow some facial hair
- Looks a little bit Chinese (he's mixed race)
- Probably wearing a vest
- Repeatedly snubbed for *GQ*'s 'Sexiest Man Alive' 1996–2021

You'll meet him wherever, and he'll say:

Clear your throat and do your best impression of Samuel Rossiter.

'Hello, I am dashingly handsome Samuel Rossiter and I can grow a respectable amount of facial hair, how are you?'

— — —

Move to a different part of the stage. Point to the person who is wearing the bucket hat and stare directly at them, and do not stop staring or pointing until you finish saying this section:

'After 3.5 years, it's become an extremely difficult climate to work in amidst a tsunami of bucket hat phobia. The hatred directed at us has taken an immense personal toll on me. While it's nothing compared to what bucket hat people experience, I'm burnt out and tired of the abuse.'

'Right now in this country, bucket hat people are facing an unprecedented, coordinated campaign of vitriol and misinformation driven by large swathes of the UK media. If you are in the media, please do more to stand up for bucket hat people in the newsroom and publicly. This is an emergency.'

Stop pointing and staring, and move back to the same part of the stage you were on before.

— — —

No, not really. It'd be more like this:

Clear your throat and do your best impression of Samuel Rossiter.

'Hi, my name's Sam! I'm a mixed-race English/Chinese writer and actor from Hong Kong, and am now based in Manchester. How are you?'

Well, that's the short version at least. And, as Sam says, that's the version from a year ago. Because moving forwards, he's going to change it a little bit. So it'll be more like this:

Clear your throat and do your best impression of Samuel Rossiter.

'Hi, my name's Sam! I'm a mixed-race English/Chinese writer and actor from Hong Kong, and am now based in Manchester. I'm also a bucket hat man. How are you?'

.

.

.

Yes.

You heard that right.

Sam is a bucket hat man!!!

Save the surprised gasps please, he knows, shocking revelation, end of times, four horseman coming in about five minutes, etcetera etcetera.

So, Sam's going to give you some background information on his childhood and teens now, as that time in his life is definitely not the focus of this piece. You see, bucket hat narratives are still very much stuck on the realizing-in-your-teens-and-trying-to-tell-people-and-sometimes-it-goes-well-but-most-of-the-time-it's-super-depressing narrative, and it's very boring. So:

- Sam realizes he's a bucket hat person when he's thirteen
- He tells everyone else in his school year about it and it goes surprisingly well
- There is some very shitty authority at his school who won't allow him to wear his bucket hat fully in school, which is a very painful and horrible 0/10 experience
- But Sam gets through high school generally alright

Sam also realizes something.

A few years into wearing his bucket hat, he discovers that he can put his hand on the hat, grip it tightly between his fingers, and lift it up and away from his head.

It's not something that all bucket hat people can do. Some must wear their hat at all times. Glued to their head, unable to take it off, there for the whole world to see.

But Sam realizes that he is not confined by this particular law of physics. Sam can move his bucket hat around. Put it in his pocket, behind his back, hide it from people. So when they meet him for the first time, they'd never know that he was a bucket hat man at all.

So, when Sam graduates high school and starts university, he has a plan.

He just wants a fresh start, you see.

So, he'll put his bucket hat in his pocket, just initially, and meet new people in his life. Make sure they get to know him as a person first. Then, after a few months, he'll take that bucket hat out of his pocket, and he'll tell them about it.

He just wants to be treated like everyone else.

He doesn't want to be looked at differently because of something he can't control.

And you know what? He can do whatever the hell he wants.

It's his own damn life.

— — —

Move to a different part of the stage. Point to the person who is wearing the bucket hat and stare directly at them, and do not stop staring or pointing until you finish saying this section:

'People think that bucket hat kids are lunatics who have no idea what's going on in the world. People think bucket hat kids are just handed their bucket hats without any questions asked, but that's not true at all.

'We have to read a lot, we have to ask questions, we have to fight. We're forced to be a lot more mature than most kids I know. This ruling is honestly terrifying,' he tells the BBC.

.

'The young bucket hat people I'm talking to now are experiencing deeply distressing mental health problems,' she says.

'To be a young bucket hat person nowadays requires a bigger fight than ever, but most of the bucket hat people I see do not have any fight left in them.'

Stop pointing and staring, and move back to the same part of the stage you were on before.

— — —

So.

Sam is a bucket hat man.

But, take the bucket hat away, and you just have . . .

Sam is a man.

Sam loves being a man.

Being a man is so easy.

He hopes everyone here knows about all the privilege that men have. He's not going to bother listing them out because he feels like that might come dangerously close to mansplaining.

.

Well.

He's going to do it anyway. Because, you know . . .

So, a few benefits of being a man include:

- Walking home at night without the fear of sexual assault
- No confusion over what to wear to formal work functions
- The ability to get ready in a concise twenty mins because of differing beauty standards
- Pockets in all, and I mean ALL, of your trousers.

Sam is happy.

His theory is right – without the bucket hat, people treat him based off his personality and not a bright piece of clothing he's now hidden away.

He meets new people at university, he gets a girlfriend when he moves to the UK, he manages to find a day job, he starts to make progress on his acting and writing.

It's all going very well.

Sometimes, he hears conversations about bucket hat people.

You know the scene – it's most probably a middle-aged white person who starts off the conversation like:

In your best RP accent:

'What has the world COME TO? People think they can be anything these days! What, if I put on a gold chain, does that suddenly make me a celebrity? It's just gone too far!'

Day jobs, friends of friends, a certain ex-girlfriend's parents . . .

Sam has heard it all. And most importantly, with no visible bucket hat people in the room, Sam has heard people chiming in and agreeing. Asking what the deal is, a lot of debate around, you know . . . why bucket hat people exist in the first place. Should they even exist?

And Sam always tries to defend bucket hat people, but sometimes he just lets it go. Because it's not worth arguing, yes, but also because it would look weird if he defended bucket hat people that passionately.

It would put him in jeopardy.

People would ask why he's so invested.

And he's tired. And he's drained. And he just wants no trouble.

So a lot of the time, he doesn't fight back as hard as he should.

Sam sees bucket hat people on the news.

They're always in the news these days, especially in this country.

This country loves loves loves to shit on bucket hat people.

Put 'em on telly so we can look at 'em. Put 'em on telly so we can laugh at 'em. Put 'em on telly so we can thank fuck we don't know anyone like that in our own little lives. And the experts, too. The ones who know how wrong it is. Get 'em on and we'll listen carefully. We must know what to believe. We're dying for it.

It all makes Sam very very angry.

But again, Sam does not share this news as much as he should. He does not comment on it, he does not go on long rants on Facebook like he wants to, he does not scream and shout and rage publicly.

It would put him in jeopardy.

People would ask why he's so invested.

And he's tired. And he's drained. And he just wants no trouble. He just wants to live his life.

So Sam keeps his mouth shut. He rages silently, and he lives his life.

There's just so much to care about these days.

Care about this, care about that, sign this, post that.

If you don't care, the world will burn.

Well . . .

Have you looked around you?

The world burns whether we care or not.

So what's the cost of a little silence?

— — —

Move to a different part of the stage. Stare at the person who is wearing the bucket hat for a good while. Enough to make them uncomfortable.

Clear your throat.

Hi.

Hello.

Um.

I know what you are.

So.

Please could you just leave?

Just leave.

Stop staring, and move back to the same part of the stage you were on before.

— — —

But . . . Sam goes back on his plan.

He waits a few months after he meets new people, and he wants to take his bucket hat out of his pocket and show them.

But . . .

Well . . .

He . . .

Can't.

He just can't.

He's been out there, you see. He knows what the general public think of bucket hat people now. It scares him.

It's the conversations. It's the news. It's the fear. It's the rage.

And besides, why is it relevant at this point? The new people he's met in his life know who he is as a person, so why do they need to know about this particular part of him? It doesn't change who he is.

It's just an extra label other people will put on him. An extra box they'll painfully squeeze him into.

So . . .

He doesn't tell them.

He shuts his mouth.

And he lives his life.

Pain and danger free.

— — —

Move to a different part of the stage. Stare at the person who is wearing the bucket hat for a good while. Enough to make them uncomfortable.

Excuse me.

You're making me really uncomfortable.

I have nothing against you kind of people, okay? I've seen you on the telly, I know what you're like.

Just stay away from me, yeah?

You can't be in here with me.

So go.

Now.

Get out of here.

And we won't have any trouble.

Stop staring, and move back to the same part of the stage you were on before.

– – –

Question:

If a tree falls in a forest and no one is around to hear it, does it make a sound?

.

.

Or

If a person does not tell you about a part of themselves for seven years, does that part of them cease existing?

.

.

Or

How long can you keep telling yourself that the only reason you don't tell people about said part of yourself is because you don't want to be defined by it, before you realize you're lying?

SECTION 2

Dear Actor,

Take a seat on the chair, and read these instructions to yourself carefully.

Take a good few moments for yourself on this chair.

Because for this next section, you will need to channel all of your hate, your fear, your rage, your disgust, your ugliness, your anger, into it.

You really need to commit in order for this to work.

But I trust you, you beautiful actor. I trust you to really give this your all. You're here for a reason, and I know you will give this everything you have.

That bucket hat person, sitting there in the front row, is the person you hate most in your life. This person has taken things from you. This person has lied to you. This person has hurt you. They have hurt your family, your parents, your friends. This person hates you. They actively hate you, they want to hurt you for nothing at all. They have done horrible things to you. Think of all the horrible things that people have done to you in your life. This person is responsible for all of it. Every, single little horrible and awful thing, they have done to you. This person is the fucking devil. And now is your chance to really hurt them.

Visualize whoever you need to under that bucket hat. You must hate them with every ounce of your being.

Take as long as you need on this chair to prepare yourself.

And when you're ready – get off the chair, and give it to them.

Get out.

.

.

.

I told you before, get out. You're making me uncomfortable. Get out.

.

.

Look around you. It's not just me. Look at these people. You're making everyone uncomfortable. Get out.

.

GET OUT.

I asked you nicely. Get out.

I know what you are. I know what you're 'trying to be'. It's not working. It's delusional.

And this is what happens, when people think they can be anything these days.

Like I can be a tree if I want to. Or a chair. Or a penguin.

It's ridiculous.

And you can do it out there, out in fucking fairyland, but not here. Not with me. So get out.

Get out. Now.

.

GET OUT.

You think you're fooling anyone?

Everyone in this building knows what you are.

Spotted you a mile away, walking in here with everyone else.

Thought to myself – I'd have a nice night at the theatre, nice little treat, then I saw you.

Think you're hard to spot?

You must be joking.

You're not fooling a fucking soul.

These people are too nice. They're thinking the same as me, you know. They're looking at you. They know it's wrong. They think it's sick too.

So do us all a favour, yeah?

Get out, and we won't have any trouble.

.

Why are you doing this?

Do you want the attention, is that it?

You want everyone looking at you? Gawking at you?

Your mummy never give you enough play time? Your daddy on the liquor, was he?

So you dress up like this, and you come out, and you walk right into this theatre thinking you're going to be the belle of the ball?

No.

You make me so uncomfortable.

You make me sick.

And you're not staying here with me.

So get out.

.

GET. OUT.

You're so stupid.

You had it all. You were born with it.

So much fucking privilege. Anything you wanted to do, you could've done it.

But instead you choose this? You choose to become this?

What's wrong with you?

Do you have any idea what's going on in the world? Any idea how many problems this country has?

And in all of that, you choose to become this. Walking out here in public, putting it on display. Showing yourself to children. Like it's normal, like they should think it's normal.

You're disgusting.

You don't belong here.

You don't belong anywhere in public. Anywhere people can see you.

You're just wrong.

So get out.

.

I'll get my husband. I'll do it. I'll bring him in here, he'll beat you black and blue.

Do you want that?

Is that what you need?

He'll drag you out by your fake fucking wig.

He'll rip those clothes right off you, expose you for what you really are.

Let's see it all, hmm? Everything you're hiding. All of your 'bits' and 'pieces'.

Get out, you sick fuck.

GET OUT.

.

I hope you don't have children. Can you imagine? Raising more perverts. More sick freaks.

Is that what happened to you? Was your daddy like this too?

This is your last warning.

Get out.

GET. THE. FUCK. OUT.

.

Right.

I'm getting my husband. He'll have you, he will.

Given you enough chance.

Think you might just need a good beating.

.

GET OUT.

GET OUT GET OUT GET OUT.

GET THE FUCK OUT OF HERE.

YOU FUCKING SICK FUCK.

GET OUT.

GET OUT.

GET. OUT.

Go back to the chair and sit down.

Take a moment for yourself. Breathe.

Do whatever you need to do to come out of it – close your eyes, breathe deeply, count to ten. Take good care of yourself to bring yourself out of it, to calm down.

Take as long as you need.

When you're ready, go on to read Section 3.

SECTION 3

I gave you two rules at the start of this piece.

Do you remember?

Rule number 1 – you cannot get out of your seat at any point during this performance.

Rule number 2 – someone in the audience sitting in the front row must wear a bucket hat.

What did I not say?

I did not say:

You cannot speak up.

You cannot defend them.

You cannot shout back.

You. Just. Assumed.

So why? So what?

So many things to care about these days. What's this one little thing? I don't stand up for someone at the Royal Exchange, they'll be fine at the end of it. It's just a performance. We'll all go home at the end of the day.

What's the cost of a little silence?

— — —

Eight weeks into 2021, seven trans and gender non-conforming individuals have been tragically murdered.

Last year, a total of forty-four fatalities were recorded by the Human Rights Campaign [HRC]. The majority of these people were Black and Latinx transgender women.

2020 upheld a devastating record as the most violent year towards gender non-conforming people since HRC documentation began in 2013.

Tyianna Alexander . . . was the first known death of a transgender or gender non-conforming person in 2021. The twenty-eight-year-old Black trans woman was shot to death ▓▓▓▓▓ on January 6.

Samuel Edmund Damián Valentín, a transgender man, was killed on January 9 ▓ ▓▓▓▓▓▓▓▓▓▓▓.

Bianca 'Muffin' Bankz, a Black transgender woman, was shot to death in her apartment on January 17 ▓▓▓▓▓

Dominique Jackson . . . was shot to death on January 25.

Twenty-one-year-old Fifty Bandz . . . was murdered ▓▓▓▓▓▓ on January 28.

Forty-five-year-old Alexus Braxton . . . was killed in her apartment on February 4 ▓ ▓▓▓▓.

Chyna Carrillo was tragically murdered outside her home in ████████████ ████████.[1]

– – –

22 December 2020.

Earlier this month, three High Court judges ruled that children under sixteen with gender dysphoria are 'unlikely to be able to give informed consent to undergo treatment with puberty-blocking drugs'.

Dame Victoria Sharp, sitting with Lord Justice Lewis and Mrs Justice Lieven, said: 'It is highly unlikely that a child aged thirteen or under would be competent to give consent to the administration of puberty blockers.'

Theo, a fourteen-year-old trans boy who suffers from extreme gender dysphoria, came out as trans when he was eleven. He is still waiting to see a gender specialist, and last year he tried to take his own life.

Theo's mum, Loreto, says that even when Theo was lying in intensive care 'connected to pumps and with tubes through his nose', she could not secure him any gender identity help.

'People think that trans kids are lunatics who have no idea what's going on in the world. People think trans kids are just handed medication without any questions asked, but that's not true at all.

'We have to read a lot, we have to ask questions, we have to fight. We're forced to be a lot more mature than most kids I know. This ruling is honestly terrifying,' he tells the BBC.

A clinician who currently works within the NHS GIDS [Gender Identity Development Service], told the BBC her patients are now being left alone to deal with distress.

'The young trans people I'm talking to now are experiencing deeply distressing mental health problems,' she says.

'To be a young trans person nowadays requires a bigger fight than ever, but most of the trans people I see do not have any fight left in them.'[2]

– – –

17 May 2021

Hi, some ~personal~ news: I'm taking a yearlong sabbatical from @stonewalluk starting 24 May

Being the Head of Media for Europe's largest LGBT+ charity has been a dream come true. I'm so proud to have led such an incredible team (@jo_estrin & @therealjun0369) 🫶[3]

But after 3.5 years, it's become an extremely difficult climate to work in amidst a tsunami of transphobia. The hatred directed at Stonewall has taken an immense personal toll on me. While it's nothing compared to what trans people experience, I'm burnt out and tired of the abuse.[4]

Right now in this country, trans people are facing an unprecedented, coordinated campaign of vitriol & misinformation driven by large swathes of the UK media.

If you are in the media, please do more to stand up for trans people in the newsroom and publicly. This is an emergency.[5]

Jeffrey Ingold, Head of Media at Stonewall UK. Twitter.

.

.

.

.

So . . .

Tell me honestly.

If you had a choice

Would you wear that bucket hat, or not?

.

.

.

.

I break up with her ten days after my twenty-fourth birthday.

She cries and screams and walks out of my flat, and I've not seen her since.

Three months later I ask for a phone call. For some closure, some peace.

It lasts three hours. Lots of sobbing on both ends.

I say thank you for everything that you did for me.

I say thank you for loving me, even though I'm trans.

She says it was never about that.

I say yeah . . . but I don't believe myself.

Four months later, I realize something.

The reason I don't tell people I'm trans when I first meet them.

Not because they should get to know my personality first.

But because I don't think they would want to be friends, acquaintances, lovers with me, if they knew.

.

I get some Talking Therapy on the Indigo trans health service.

I tell my therapist:

I am very comfortable being a man.

I've known it in my bones, in my soul, since I was thirteen

But I think I am not so comfortable being a trans man.

She says:

You've put it in the cupboard for such a long time, but it seems like you need to bring it out now. Hold it up to the light, embrace it.

Make yourself whole again.

.

.

.

Make. Yourself. Whole. Again.

—   —   —

So . . .

Here's to all the people I've met, aged eighteen to twenty-five.

And to all those I will meet, aged twenty-five and onwards.

A little revision, if you will:

.

.

Hi, my name's Sam!

I'm a mixed-race English/Chinese writer and actor from Hong Kong, and am now based in Manchester.

I'm also a trans man.

.

.

.

How are you?

Give the bucket hat person the Snickers bar and thank them.

REFERENCES

1 Raza-Sheikh, Zoya. 'Remembering the Seven Trans Individuals Who Have Been Killed in 2021'. *Gay Times*, 22 February 2021, www.gaytimes.co.uk/life/remembering-the-trans-individuals-who-have-been-killed-in-2021/
2 Hunte, Ben. 'Puberty Blockers: Parents' Warning as Ruling Challenged'. *BBC News*, 22 December 2020, www.bbc.co.uk/news/education-55369784
3 Ingold, Jeffrey. (Jefflez). 'Hi, some ~personal~ news: I'm taking a yearlong sabbatical from @stonewalluk starting 24 May Being the Head of Media for Europe's largest LGBT+ charity has been a dream come true. I'm so proud to have led such an incredible team (@ jo_estrin & @therealjun0369) 🖤' 17 May 2021, 3.11 pm [Tweet].
4 Ingold, Jeffrey. (Jefflez). 'But after 3.5 years, it's become an extremely difficult climate to work in amidst a tsunami of transphobia. The hatred directed at Stonewall has taken an immense personal toll on me. While it's nothing compared to what trans people experience, I'm burnt out and tired of the abuse' 17 May 2021, 3.11 pm [Tweet].
5 Ingold, Jeffrey. (Jefflez). 'Right now in this country, trans people are facing an unprecedented, coordinated campaign of vitriol & misinformation driven by large swathes of the UK media. If you are in the media, please do more to stand up for trans people in the newsroom and publicly. This is an emergency' 17 May 2021, 3.11 pm [Tweet].

Samuel Rossiter (he/him) is a trans man and mixed-race writer and actor of English/Chinese heritage. Born and raised in Hong Kong, Samuel is now based in Manchester. He is an alumni of the New Earth Writer's Academy 2020 and was a recipient of the Greater Manchester Artist Hub Reboot Fund. Samuel was selected to have new work performed at The Lowry's Shoots Scratch Night, and was also selected to be a part of the Royal Exchange & Warner Bros Discovery Writers Exchange Scheme and is currently on attachment to the Royal Exchange Theatre.

NOTE: Directions in italics are not to be read aloud, please just follow them.

There is a box on the table. Please can you unpack the things from it and place them on the table. Feel free to arrange the dabqaad (the incense burner) and dhiisha uunsiga (woven container) into a composition.

Hi Miss

I don't think you remember me. It's been over ten years since I last saw you. It feels weird to be addressing you like this. But, here I am. I'm sure that reading this letter in this setting will be a bit of a surprise for you, but don't get shy now.

I've been thinking about you a lot recently. When I finished school I thought, 'that's it, time to move on'. But actually, you left a lasting impression on me.

When I signed up for your class, I had visions of what it would be like, two hours a week of pure creativity, a contrast to the heavy load of my other subjects. Boy, I did not know what I signed up for!

From the first class, I felt that your tone was off with me. I dismissed it and thought you were just a normal teacher who had her favourites. I was my English teacher's favourite so I couldn't take all the spotlight for myself.

But then, I noticed that things weren't normal.

I recall you telling me to look at the other girls' work when we were drawing an apple. We were all looking at the same object and I didn't see a real difference between my drawing and theirs. You said my shading needed work. Fair enough.

But then this comment became a broken record – 'look at how she's done it', 'see where she has made it darker', 'ask your table for help'. It was embarrassing and I'm pretty sure you knew that.

In fact, I remember that I was having a particularly rough day and I couldn't be bothered with you. My friend took my sketchbook and quickly drew the leaves we were studying for me before you could notice. She laughed it off but I don't think she knew how much that meant to me.

Anyway, you came over and you looked at the drawing. You studied it for a second and came up with some critique about composition. Was this not the work of the girl you were telling me to copy all term?

You never found out about this. How do you feel now?

Sitting in that class, I would think 'what is her problem?'

Of course, I'd never dare say anything. I thought that maybe you had stuff going on. I strongly believe that hurt people hurt people. So I just left it alone.

Each week I'd come in with a fresh outlook 'new week, just do your best and hopefully it'll be okay'. I'd roll up my sleeves, put on my apron and get stuck in.

During one term, I remember learning about successful artists and you tasked us with recreating some of their works. Sorry, let me rephrase. You tasked us with copying some of their works. Like literally, we'd look at a photo and copy it into our sketchbooks. I never saw the point of that.

In one class we were studying Patrick Caulfield. You were talking about his use of bold colours and lines. When it came to copying 'Wine Glasses', you said my lines were too thick. When I did Roy Lichtenstein's 'Whaam!' you complained about the scale and told me to start again.

When it finally came to creating my own work, I was weary of experimenting – sticking to what I knew I could do best. This portfolio would be assessed, there was no room for me to mess it up.

I would spend hours after school and on weekends working on my portfolio. I put in so much effort and I'm not sure why, when it felt like an uphill battle every time I walked through your door. Was it to prove myself to you . . . or to myself? Either way, I knew that I was so much more than you gave me credit for.

You gave us some broad categories to choose from for our portfolios – music, culture, sport etc. I was sick of doing the same stuff in our classroom and hearing about the same English and American artists so I chose culture. I wanted to celebrate my Somali heritage and showcase something different.

Remember I did that pencil drawing of a *dabqaad* and *dhiisha uunsiga*? Did you trip up reading that?

When I told you what they were called, you laughed at how hard it was to say and proceeded to refer to them as 'the pot and the basket'. You didn't put any effort into getting to know how to pronounce the words.

I doubt you've learned since then so let me spell it out phonetically for you – 'deesha oonsiga' and 'dab-qaad'.

Look at them. These items are not just a pot and a basket.

Please pick up dhiisha uunsiga and hold it high.

This was woven by hand. Purple, blue and green carefully interlaced for hours. This weaving process is one of the oldest traditional Somali art forms. It is an important part of womanhood and is more than just a container or a 'basket'.

Please put it down and pick up the dabqaad.

This *dabqaad* is not just a 'pot'. It translates loosely to 'fire raiser'. 'Dab' – fire and 'qaad' – to raise or to carry.

It carries *uunsi*, the most powerful scent in the world. My sweetest childhood memories are highlighted by the smell of *uunsi*. I remember sitting at my mum's feet as she brushed and braided my hair, the fragrance filling the whole house. I remember Eid mornings where me and my siblings would bicker to be the one to carry the *dabqaad* around the house, making sure the smoke got to every corner. When *uunsi* was burned it was a sign of joy, we had guests coming, we were celebrating something or food was ready. It lifts spirits like nothing else. This *dabqaad* represents that feeling for me.

I want you to take a moment to experience that feeling but let's come back to that at the end. I don't want you to set the place on fire before the end of this letter!

So, I drew the *dabqaad* and *dhiisha uunsiga* in my sketchbook. I also drew a collection of my mum's *atar* and painted a picture of the Masjid-Al-Haram from a photograph I took when I visited Mecca.

You scribbled notes all over my sketchbook. Almost every page was branded with your disapproval. These pieces of work that I spent hours on, just disgraced in a matter of seconds. At the back of the sketchbook you stapled in the marking criteria with justifications for your comments and 'ways to improve'.

What you didn't realize was that you were not only marking my work, you were marking my life. This is when I realized that the art world wasn't built for someone like me.

You'd always make sure to sprinkle in the idea that you wanted to see my 'style', my 'voice', my 'identity'. Was this a way of protecting yourself? To show that you called for something different? Was this to show that you welcomed 'diversity'? Whatever that means.

Please enlighten me, what exactly does that even mean?

When I did express my identity, you limited my creativity to fit into a restrictive tick box exercise.

This idea of marking art is so bizarre to me. Art should not be graded. After all, isn't it supposed to be subjective?

And subjectivity is based on personal opinions and feelings, right? Do you see where we're going with this?

How would you feel if your art was graded, scribbled all over?

Let's find out. You've got a pencil and piece of paper there. Pick an item, any item and do your best line drawing. I'll give you one minute, stop when you hear the bell.

There is a kitchen timer in the box. Please set it for 1 minute.

Please pick a random object and sketch it using the materials on the table. When the timer goes off, please return to reading the letter.

Done? Now I want you to give it to the audience and they'll be the judge. Please pass it around and have them mark it, they can write their thoughts directly on the drawing.

Audience, I'm speaking to you now. I know some of you will have dressed up for tonight, just wanted a nice evening out at the theatre. You don't want to tread on toes or feel uncomfortable but then this whole concept is uncomfortable, so be honest in your critique. If you like something, say it. If you don't like something, say it. When you're done give it back.

If you've got a pencil under your chair, raise your hands.

Please set the kitchen timer for two minutes.

Please pass the drawing to the audience whose hands are raised for them to mark. This may feel uncomfortable, just wait whilst they do so and take it back when the timer goes off.

Time's up, take a look and read what they've written.

Please read any comments on the drawing.

It's not nice is it, Miss? Did you feel vulnerable? Exposed? Uncomfortable?

I was raised to be respectful and kind to my elders. I was always polite to you, I showed up ready to go, no matter how much you tried to beat me down or devalue my work.

As I got a bit older and I tried to process my school years, I found myself making excuses for you. I realized you were young, still in your first few years of teaching. Maybe you felt some pressure and it was taken out the wrong way. Maybe you'd never come across people like me before. Maybe you had preconceived notions. The media narrative didn't help at the time. Now I realize, whatever it was, there really is no excuse. I was a child.

When I finished your class, I was so relieved. But I was also hurt. I couldn't look through my sketchbook and be proud of my work. All I saw was stress and anxiety.

So at the end of the school year, I ripped up the whole thing. Recycled what I could and binned the rest. I stopped drawing and painting for years after that. You made me lose the love for it and it would take a while for me to find it again.

You can turn around and say 'that's just how it is, it's just school'. Let's just get one thing clear, this letter is not a personal attack on you. It's more to do with what you represent.

It's not just school. See I have dealt with versions of you ever since I left school. A guy in my group for my Collaborative Arts Practice module at university. My manager at my first job in the arts. People who act as if they want you there and value your differences but really do everything to make you feel as uncomfortable as possible. And they do it so you don't even know it or so that you question yourself.

If you gave me a penny for every time I've said 'maybe I'm just overthinking it', let's just say I'd probably be in Bora Bora right now.

I was the only Black girl in your class. I was the only Muslim girl in your class. Little did I know that your art class was a microcosm of the world that I would experience every day as an adult working in the creative industries.

It's strange but I want to say thank you for showing me what I'd have to deal with from such a young age. Despite all the challenges, I know that my voice is needed here. I'm lucky that the world is different from ten years ago. We still have a long way to go but I'm lucky to be surrounded by people that value my art, cheer me on when I want to try something new and never, ever, judge or grade my work.

I know I am right where I am meant to be. And for a kid who you made feel less than, I've done alright for myself. You can catch me at my solo shows or writing for TATE or making TV shows and films or curating exhibitions. I'm a multi-hyphenate. I get to be creative and make art every day for a living. How cool is that? Bet you never expected it, did you?

In the last couple of years I've taken on the role of mentor, helping young people from different backgrounds join the creative industries and the arts. I've visited schools and delivered talks about my journey and have seen kids as young as eleven get excited at the possibility that they too can do this. I've recognized that they've been told 'no', or made to feel othered. I've shown them it's possible and I can't wait to see what they do in the future.

I hate listing things off like that because I don't mean to brag.

Actually – I do. Because I don't brag enough. I did that. I'm doing that.

Now it's time for you to take several seats and have a slice of humble pie.

But before you go, this *uunsi* is my gift to you to say thank you and goodbye.

Please follow the instructions carefully.

- There is a lighter there. Put a charcoal tab into the *dabqaad* and set it alight, wait until it glows red.
- The *uunsi* is in a little silver container inside the *dhiisha uunsiga*. Take some out and put it on top of the charcoal.
- Leave it alone and let it burn.

Good luck. I hope the smoke alarm doesn't go off.

Please follow the instructions and then resume reading.

Do you smell that? If you've done it correctly you will smell the sweet scent of frankincense, sourced from the Boswellia tree in Somalia.

If you've done it wrong it'll just smell like burnt charcoal and we'll all have to evacuate. I won't apologize, I gave you the instructions so this one's on you.

Yours truthfully,

Your worst student ever.

Yasmin Ali is a writer, artist and producer from Liverpool. Her work often explores her identity as a Black, Scouse, Muslim woman as well as shining a light on other underrepresented voices and experiences.

Yasmin has been working in the UK television industry for the last five years, most recently as a Storyliner for a long-running BBC TV drama. As well as this, Yasmin has exhibited her solo work with Tetley Gallery, Output Gallery, Liverpool Arab Arts Festival and Writing On The Wall. She has written for a range of publications and websites including gal-dem, Tate, BBC, *Ethos*, *ROOT-ed* and *The Double Negative*, and took part in the BFI's 2020 Script Lab.

Yasmin started writing on the Liverpool Everyman and Playhouse Young Writers' programme as a teen and she was delighted to have had her work shown on stage as part of the Everyman's chapter of *My White Best Friend – North*. The letter feels like a full-circle moment and a celebration of how far she has come since then.

'IF ONLY WE KNEW HOW SIMULTANEOUSLY ASTONISHING AND INSIGNIFICANT WE ARE'

Dear Friend,

'You're a dickhead', and I hope that sounds Northern in your head as you read this,

You. Are. A. Dickhead full stop . . . it feels really freeing to write that down.

Let your eyes absorb these words into your brain.

I wanted to write you this letter . . . and free myself from the idea it would hurt you, because I can't keep swallowing sentences in fear that I might suffocate from all the letters in the alphabet that I've not allowed to form into words,

I've started this letter many times with apologies, with ideas of not letting myself down, telling myself to be kind – to live out slogans you now see knitted on park benches, and stoic ideals to make it clear I'm not a bitch.
But now I realised, that's where you've always had me – the minute I would say anything that might question or offer a difference of opinion you would shut me down; even worse you would tell me that it's in my head or you would cry . . . you would even fucking cry sometimes . . .
And I would feel . . .

Do you remember the cheese plants we bought? . . . Well the one I have needs watering . . . all the plants do really . . . the 'die hards' are still with me since the first lock down . . .

Those plants hold on with a tenacity and love for their existence.

Dear Friend,
The fiction of this world serves you, that's why you don't question it . . .

Dear Friend,
You take up space and you're allowed to,
You forget you are given space, I'm always made to question and think every inch of air my body occupies, forever made to feel like a guest in this country of your ancestors,

Dear Friend,
Why do you try to make decisions for me?

Do you remember the time I told you that the hospital decided I was an illegal immigrant not entitled to NHS care and they sent me a bill for about £4,000 and you said, 'leave it, be grateful', I explained further to you that I have a Manc accent and Manc ways, that I know the streets of Rusholme and Moss Side like the back of my hand, the only thing that made me 'foreign' to the one nurse was my face and head wrap, I told you I was going to email the people in charge . . . and you just laughed some more in your witch vibe ('cos you have a witch vibe); you told me to be grateful, not to make a fuss and to stop stressing, you said some stuff about it being a full moon and something being in retrograde

I wasn't stressing I was telling you facts but somehow that's never enough . . . it makes me think that immigrant girls are never enough in our home cities no matter how many years and memories are formed in these places we call home. . . .

Dear Friend,

But . . . Let's go back.

I went through some difficult things and you were there . . . you came in the guise of love and peace

How you were there for me, at times.

I have an image of you on all fours cleaning my floor when my baby bump wouldn't allow me to fold over and complete simple tasks and I was grateful for that

But then you decided to tell people my business, when you know I'm more private than the Queen's knicker drawer

And you took liberties of answering my phone and opening my mail . . .

After the baby bump situation became a baby and hormones settled, I decided to contact you less but you create drama to keep me occupied to keep us connected; whenever you sensed I was not in need of you, a new drama would happen, you create an issue for us to work through.

You're creeping ivy, poisoned ivy around an oak, you mimic the image of the host and grow limbs from the structure of the tree.

As if you're moulding yourself to my life

Have you ever watched that film *Single White Female*?

I think you're reenacting a version we should title 'Single Head-wrapped Female'

I would feel myself draining as you would thrive off hearing of any woes.

And beneath the talk of new age energy and light your words are blades that cut sharp, dare I say anything wrong or offer my opinion you are quick to correct me and tell me what to do . . . being your friend has been like a near death caused by a thousand paper cuts . . .

You stood on my doorstep one night, it was late autumn, you stood on my doorstep to deliver the new drama, the new issue, to keep us connected

You knocked on my door in haste

The streetlight placed an orange halo around your head, you were slightly stooped, with a furrow in your brow, looking like an unambitious sunflower . . . and I'm looking at you through my eyes, I ask you if you're okay . . .

You tell me about the danger you think a cousin of mine is in, at first I think I mishear you, but no . . . there you stand telling me that you fear for my cousin and she is in a dangerous situation with her partner . . . but at this point it's been two years of you and I've clocked your energy . . . I tell you my cousin is fine, that their partner is a sweetheart from what I've noticed, I ask you what's the evidence? Have you spoken with her? . . . This is the best bit . . . you tell me it's something you 'sense' . . . and we both know you don't understand people of African heritage . . . you misread situations with Black people all the time, you always suggest that there is something they are doing wrong, you tell me often how you think Black men are abusive partners, you never listen to people's truths but decide for them what the issue is . . . I know you do that because you do it to me all the time,

You're like that nurse in *Misery* – hobbling people into co-dependant relationships for days . . .

Part of your problem is you underestimated me; you underestimate Black women in general since you assume we'll be as dim-witted as you

It's like your brain can't compute dark faces with regional accents knowing what's good for their own lives, **without** your input

Why do you feel a need to get on a white horse and save the day, offering solutions to situations when you could just choose to hear someone's words?

Your crystals and moon water are not everyone's go-to pain relief

Dear Friend,

If I'm bodying you, don't fret . . . I will give you your burial rights. . . .

There was a night . . . do you remember when Black Lives Matter was becoming global news and we were in lockdown, we decided to 'face it together', to isolate together for a month or so . . . just to add in hindsight I must have been out of my mind

The heat of one particular day gave Manchester that tropical evening smell

We went to an event that night which was hosted by a friend of yours, we parked up and we walked through a leafy part of town and the summer night was thick with greenery and thick with love and thick with lies,
The trees were beautiful – this is something my soul loves but you trouble me – somewhere in my body I can feel the dis-ease . . . because before we set off to your friend's party you made a comment after we watched the news, you said, 'the Black Lives Matter campaigners really need to think about all the other groups who suffer, all lives matter' . . . I mean come on . . . so now each step walking with you feels like a confused lie

Now in that moment whilst we were navigating the beautiful streets of Manchester in street light heading to your friend's party – I felt as if I had no skin, I felt I would have to ready myself to watch my own thoughts and therefore my words

We arrive at our destination, there are a group of people outside that belong to your friend's party, they are looking at something across the street, a few women in glitter dresses, most of the guys looking like they are personal PAs to Chairman Mao in those jackets and dark rimmed glasses, most of them caring about not caring – giving themselves an edgy vibe but their accents and public school ways give them away – why do posh kids desperately seek to come across as hard?
We all find ourselves stood outside like a wild meadow in between two dual carriageways,
They were all looking across the road
They were watching a police car and another vertical,
Do you remember what they were witnessing, we joined in the viewing too. . . .
The police were stopping a Black family with children in their car, it makes my eyeballs sting,
And we watched,
While we were all stood there watching, you hugged a few people and I mumbled a few 'nice to meet yous', but we stood staring, the police didn't even bat an eyelid our way, all the whiteness of the group we were in must have given us a pass in this lockdown gathering,
Someone said, 'don't worry they won't say anything to us, if they do we'll tell them we're all isolating together', we laughed,
My stomach hurts,
I felt like I was stood in safety by being with you, that my presence was explained by the white people in my company stood outside this fancy home, but this family . . . well . . . and those children . . . well. Those children had to watch their parents explain themselves, 'Just dropping a family friend and heading home', they said,
My stomach was doing flip flops, 'cos no one ever stops me when I'm with you or people who look like you,
My stomach hurts and I want to intervene in some way but the parents I see have got this just fine,
It's not their first time being stopped by the police I bet 'cos this is England,
My stomach hurts, 'cos it reminds me of the police beating up my eleven-year-old brother and bringing him home shook with tears,

It reminds of the time a police man dragged me across Piccadilly Gardens when I was seventeen for protesting and under his breath just for my ears called me a 'little bitch' as his fingers pressed deeper into my skin,

It reminds me of all the times the police have stopped me to ask where I was going . . .
It reminds of being in youth theatre and running outside the theatre building in a game and security calling the police and telling them I was a young Black lad trying to break in and that I had a weapon,

It reminds me of the police officer who was yelling and sneering at my older sister that our home is disgusting, my sister was twelve and I was witnessing this aged nine, this vision shattered all the positive ideas of story books found in school, the books that showed me a smiling police officer and that they were there to 'protect us'

As we stood outside, some smoking, some laughing but all watching,
I turn to you and say, 'this is wrong', that the police need to not harass families . . .you come back with the line you love to say . . .'the police. . . they're just doing their job'

Your friend's venue/home type building was beautiful, many plants were in plant pots outside in bloom, the clematis withering elegantly around the porch framing us. As the family drive off we make our way inside

Before we go in you tell me that the host is very fancy and to not act too excited or be overwhelmed by how fancy it is . . . This is another reason why you're a dickhead, in case you forgot

The living room space is one of those massive living rooms out in Wilmslow that look like an Arts Council-funded art gallery

By happenstance I know a few people there and we separated off into different company other than each other

The whole place is busy, people are stood in small groups or couples in the corridors, stairs and corners, they look like pieces of art against the white minimalist style, and the tall green plants of this large home

I stand in the open-plan kitchen leaning against the counter listening to the people around me talk, you're on one of the sofas in conversation but looking at me, even when your lips were moving you were looking at me across the space

This makes me feel uncomfortable, you're always obsessed with being the one who introduces me to people, I suppose this is vexing you

You're looking at me so intensely it makes me feel like I'm doing something wrong, I think about your warning before we came in . . . You don't own me though, I'm not currency for you to show off in front of your friends

You wander around the space, smiling at people but keeping your eyes focused on me . . . I see you out the corner of my eye

Why were you looking at me so intensely?

Your eyes are piercing at me across the gallery-like room, it made my skin burn I wanted to run far away

I don't love you like that and you don't love me in that lover's way, so . . . ?

Your eyes pierced like pincers pinching my skin,

You were dancing in stillness,

You were like a form caught in a convection wave undulating,

Hovering you were, hovering in my periphery constantly looking my way, as if you were scared . . . your darting eyes glaring as I walked around, you watched my interactions with friends

You watched When I poured myself some water,
You watched When I moved my bag,
You watched When I blew my nose,

When I leant forward away from the kitchen surface,

When I placed my elbow down,

You watched as I smoked a cigarette and in my head wondered if I was pregnant again,

You watched me

Someone beside me says, 'Is that your friend? She's been looking at you solid for the last twenty mins', I ignore them

What was all that about then?

Finally you came over and said, 'You look really lovely, I was just saying to . . .' (You waved your hand in the direction of a mutual friend) '. . . that you're like a model, and he said "of course she is!" Oh it made me laugh' – you said all this for my ears, but made sure that everyone in the room could hear and see your act if they so wished

You know I don't like attention like that in new spaces, but you are a witch who feeds off me being uncomfortable

You laughed really hard then, it was weird, I knew and saw the dynamic between us, could still feel the residual heat of your stares pricking my skin, and I laughed right along . . . uncomfortable . . . uncomfortable in my own self, inhaling and exhaling . . . does laughing without any need shrivel your internal organs and give you wrinkles?

Somewhere in-between my brain and eyes I knew the truth, that we were being disingenuous but I laughed anyway . . .

That's why I have to tell you these things

Just as you were watching me that night . . . I am watching you in this letter

You laughing in that room with all these people around reminds me of all the other times you laughed

You laughed when I told you about the time the midwives said if I refuse to be induced that I would have a dead baby; I'm seven months pregnant and this person says, 'You wouldn't want a dead baby', she was trying to coerce me into something my mind and body knows there is no need for, as well as several doctors,
I told you that and you just laugh, told me to, 'Let people do their jobs', that they are 'under a lot of pressure',
So next check-up I find myself smaller, hunched shouldered and apologetic . . . bullshit . . . somehow my body felt like a sacrifice . . . you laugh at most things I tell you in confidence . . .

At this party you are confirming what you are . . . a definite knobhead . . . You finally left me to listen to the people talking around me in the kitchen area

There's music playing out of a sound system somewhere by the large windows framed in green heavy velvet material, there's a mixture of stuff playing. 'Juicy' starts blaring out . . . don't you think it's funny, twenty-five to thirty years ago this type of crowd would have openly sneered at Biggy . . . now they can't get enough, all cultures that can be sold have now become mainstream and now belong to everyone who can download it or buy it . . . but I digress, back to you being a witch

You dance to the music, with an inner energy, without a care to the flows played from the sound system,
You sing in your power, and I think, 'this is someone who loves herself' . . . I'll give you that . . . you have taught through your actions at times the power of putting yourself first . . .

Part of me must ache for that, to feel safe in the swinging of hair from shoulder blade to shoulder blade to music, like life is a fucking advert

And I'm watching and knowing that not enough of this world has deeply articulated immigrant girl ways . . . yes I think part of me must ache for that free and selfless way you're moving right now

You are beautiful, in the physical sense, in that moment as another track begins to play you switch on your energy and walk across the room leaving a wave of broken necks in your wake

I think a small inside part of the broken-necked people in that room hoped they would some how also magically become aesthetically beautiful by a weird sort of osmosis through the eyeballs . . . but we know . . . for magic to happen – they would have to be petals and you the sun . . . And you are no *raatid* sun, more of a self-serving vacuum

'Hey!'

You shouted over to me in your dance, I look over, as does most of the room, about seventy bodies are in this space . . .

You say, 'Look at you, look. at. You. Aren't you lucky . . .' You point at me and everyone looks in the direction of your pointing finger, more eyes pinch my skin

'You're Black but you have European features!' you yell over the music

'Come dance with me', you yell some more

You get on with more dancing

Some of people around agree and then conversation carries on with whatever banality we were discussing

If this was a movie it would be the point where the protagonist would dash holy water and a religious symbol at your head, unfortunately I have neither of these things to hand

I can hear the blood roaring inside me, it sounds like the ocean; did I consume the ocean for a moment to soothe the fire that wants to erupt . . .

You've spread your spores like a fungus yearning to grow, populate

Sometimes lyrics of songs pop into my head,
Like Marley's '*who feels knows it lord*' – that Rasta lament beats in me now and then . . . I didn't understand it before but now I do

I pulled you up the other day on what you said at the party and you told me to 'stop being sensitive', that 'anger should not be your first go-to emotion'; you told me to 'stop being dramatic' . . . do you see how you're a witch? You choose to not listen and put it all back on me, as if my truth is a figment of my imagination. To you the burning and pinching of skin . . . these sensations, the embarrassment, the humiliation I felt, does not even warrant a conversation between friends? Can you not see I'm entitled to express how I feel?

When I pushed further, you asked, 'Why are you attacking me?' You looked like you were going to cry, I'm so sick of it, just go on and cry, go on, your tears are like acid rain that destroys fertile soil, killing the roots of anything that lives before it can even begin to imagine how it might grow

You make me feel like a foreigner . . . but back to the bloody party

Later that night everyone is slightly more merry, that boy I told you about is there

He comes over to me to say 'Hi'

We converse for a bit, he takes up room like an old movie star leaning against the kitchen surface beside me.

'I think you're hot', he says closely, the air feels warm and thick with the vibe of secret lovers,
At some point I tell him, 'I fancy you',
We kiss but that vibe, that wanting, that beauty quickly fades,
I don't even want to really kiss him in that particular moment . . . but I had a thought that maybe I misspent my youth being too good reading books when everyone else was out dancing

I think this is probably just fucking capitalism brainwashing me to hold onto some sort of state, that relies on my dis-empowerment like all women – for us to buy shit, to make us 'feel better', but like a Maccy D's meal it never satisfies and is far from nutritious,
This is the lie we fight on many levels

'I fancy you', I say to him again like a liar,
'I think we're just friends', he says,
He doesn't know that I've never asked a boy for a kiss so brazenly so boldly – I retreat into familiar lands

You come over at this point, singing to a Fleetwood Mac song, the boy and I are silent, he takes the opportunity to move away rather than stand in silence with me

'I saw you with him', you shout . . . 'if he just gave you a cold shoulder you should let him know you're angry', you say

MY WHITE BEST FRIEND

— NORTH